FOOD
SAFETY
FOR PROFESSIONALS

Second Edition

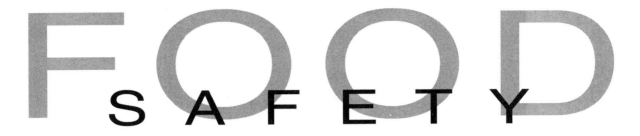

FOOD SAFETY

FOR PROFESSIONALS

Second Edition

Mildred M. Cody, PhD, RD
M. Elizabeth Kunkel, PhD, RD, FADA

American Dietetic Association
Chicago, Illinois

Library of Congress Cataloging-in-Publication Data

Cody, Mildred McInnis, 1950–
Food safety for professionals / Mildred M. Cody—2nd ed.
    p. cm.
  Includes bibliographical references and index.
  ISBN 0-88091-194-8
  1. Food. 2. Food poisoning—Prevention. 3. Public health. I. Title.

RA601.C58 2001
363.19'2–dc21

2001046223

The views expressed in this publication are those of the authors and do not necessarily reflect policies and/or official positions of the American Dietetic Association. Mention of product names in this publication does not constitute endorsement by the authors or the American Dietetic Association. The American Dietetic Association disclaims responsibility for the application of the information contained herein.

10 9 8 7 6 5 4 3 2 1

CONTENTS

PREFACE

There are many books written about aspects of food safety. Some focus on pathogens or on chemicals; others are how-to's for improving food service systems; some focus on food law and its application. Because there are so many public and personal issues surrounding food safety, one book cannot answer every question for every audience.

This book, in its second edition, responds to the needs of the dietetics professional, the practitioner most likely to work with individuals who require food safety guidance. Dietetics professionals may work in public health, in clinical settings, in education, in food service, or in other settings. Their common ground is their goal: linking food and food behaviors to health. The content of *Food Safety for Professionals* focuses on the aspects of food safety that are important to their practices. They include

- knowledge of toxic agents;
- information on foods and their associated food safety issues;
- reviews of applicable food safety surveillance programs, laws, and regulations;
- consumer needs and their food safety behaviors; and
- basic food safety programs in food service settings.

Because food safety is evolving, this book is completely revised from its 1991 edition. While many of the basic concepts and vocabulary of food safety remain the same, some of the field's immediate concerns have changed. This book addresses many new initiatives—surveillance programs and consumer education programs—that deal with these concerns. In addition to updating information, *Food Safety for Professionals*, second edition, includes several new components that are important to practicing dietetics professionals:

- **On-line references for journal articles, governmental and non-governmental agency recommendations, and educational materials.** Where possible, these materials are noted so that busy professionals who might not have a convenient research library will have access to the current materials they need to review alternatives, make recommendations, and communicate their recommendations to their various audiences.

- **Suggestions for Continuing Professional Education.** Food safety can be a part of every dietetics professional's continuing professional development, since it is an important part of food guidance for each individual and for every group served by dietetics practitioners.

Appendix B, Continuing Professional Education, invites dietetics professionals to include food safety in their lifelong learning through using the ADA Professional Development Portfolio model. It offers alternatives for developing individualized strategies to implement what has been learned through application in professional practice.

The Commission on Dietetic Registration has approved ten Category II hours of Continuing Professional Education credit for professionals who demonstrate a mastery of the book's content and successfully answer the Self-Assessment Questions in Appendix B.

- **A strong focus on vocabulary to provide dietetics professionals with a useful tool for reading current literature.** The glossary is extensive and context-specific to dietetic practice. The first time that a glossary term appears in this book, it is bold-faced to make a review of important terms easier. Also, many abbreviations and acronyms in current use are explained in the glossary.

- **Extensive resource listings.** Appendix A contains resource listings for dietetics professionals, including many agencies that have food safety foci. The listings are annotated to show what the agencies have to offer and how to access those offerings

We would like to acknowledge the patience and expertise of the ADA publications staff, especially Gill Robertson, Diana Faulhaber, and Judith Clayton. We would also like to acknowledge the students and colleagues who reviewed much of the text and made very constructive suggestions. We would name them individually, but, through the blind review process, we do not have all of their names. We also recognize the continued support of our families and colleagues. Thank you.

Missy Cody
Beth Kunkel

CHAPTER 1

INTRODUCTION

Food safety is a core component of public health and of personal health. It is an integral component of *Healthy People 2010* (1) and *Dietary Guidelines for Americans 2000* (2). As illustrated in the ADA position statement on food and water safety (3), food safety is a national dialogue that is important to dietetics practitioners in all practice settings.

Successful public health initiatives such as **pasteurization** of dairy products and juices, water purification, and **inspection** programs have reduced the incidence and severity of foodborne and waterborne illnesses in the United States over the past several generations. Diseases such as scarlet fever, **typhoid** fever, and polio, which were significant foodborne and waterborne diseases two generations ago, are infrequent in the United States today. The virtual elimination of these diseases from foodborne sources reflects a true public success.

Our current food safety **laws** have roots in history, literature, and science. Passage of the Pure Food and Drug Act of 1906 followed consumer movements spurred by Upton Sinclair's novel *The Jungle,* which described squalor associated with the meat-packing plants of Chicago, and by Harvey W. Wiley's "pure food crusade" against food **adulteration**. The Pure Food and Drug Act expanded and other laws developed to direct food production and marketing in the United States. Similarly, through public hearings, popular culture, and scientific research, we are discussing food **irradiation**, the application of biotechnology to foods, and interrelationships between the environment and the food supply. These discussions may also lead to laws that define our public food safety goals and actions on a national scale.

With expansion of the food supply beyond national boundaries and with more U.S. citizens traveling abroad, U.S. food safety discussions have expanded, too, and are continuing through *Codex Alimentarius,* an international food safety policy-making body. International discussions are perhaps more difficult, as we examine trade and health issues through language and cultural barriers. Today, problems of food safety in our sister countries may affect us, too. The current **cholera** pandemic reached the United States through illegal personal food imports, for example (4). Concerns about illegal **pesticide** residues in imported foods, *Listeria* in imported cheeses, and mad cow disease in European beef fuel U.S. consumers' concerns about global food products, even as we select imported items from market shelves. Additionally, these concerns, and many others, are important for dietetics professionals working in countries outside the United States, especially in developing countries.

Through various **surveillance** programs, we are learning more about the safety of our food supply and developing the baseline data to further public

1

health and research initiatives aimed at decreasing the incidence of **foodborne illness.** These surveillance programs are a major part of the food safety infrastructure in the United States. They illustrate the food safety picture in the United States for domestic and imported foods. Through their pictures we see the changes in food safety problems. For example, the Total Diet Survey illustrates that food is no longer a primary exposure route for lead (5). The **FoodNet** surveys show the brief history of *Cyclospora* **outbreaks** in the United States (6). While these programs are invisible to most citizens, they provide the information needed for policy decisions that affect each of us.

Even as we improve the safety of food offered to the public, we are learning that food is personal. Consumers make choices when they select the foods they eat, and consumer behaviors affect the safety of food. Is personal choice always informed choice? Are consumer food behaviors contributing to a **safe** food supply? **Risks** of foodborne illness are not the same for everyone. This can make choice (especially informed choice) difficult.

Many free-living individuals in the United States are more at risk of foodborne illness than their friends or family members. Indeed, life changes, such as pregnancy, onset of some diseases, treatments for some conditions, and simply aging, can make individuals more susceptible than before. Some persons may react individually to food ingredients; being severely allergic to an ingredient can be difficult in today's ready-to-eat, mixed-food world. "Free-living" means being responsible for food selection choices and safety behaviors for food marketing, storage, preparation, and service, whether eating out or eating in.

Institutionalized populations are frequently among the most vulnerable. Institutionalized vulnerable populations may enjoy some controls in food production that improve the safety of their food supplies. However, they may also face additional problems, such as cross-contamination from caregivers who feed several individuals at the same mealtime or direct exposure to **pathogens** from foods brought in from outside. Programs in these facilities call for special recommendations to meet the nutritional needs of clients and for stringent controls to meet their food safety needs.

Recognition of the personal responsibilities for food safety helped launch two major consumer-focused programs—"Fight BAC!" (7) and "Home Food Safety . . . It's in Your Hands" (8). These programs focus on food safety behaviors that can make a difference at the point of food use: clean, cook, chill, and separate. Having four simple directions does not make food safety easy, though. These messages require interpretation to be used correctly. The "Home Food Safety" program is part of the American Dietetic Association's commitment to food safety for the public. This program emphasizes the position of the ADA on food and water safety: "The public has a right to a safe food and water supply" (3). Its messages are delivered by dietetics professionals through many delivery systems and are tailored to clientele based on surveys of actual consumer behaviors. Its information pieces give the whys and how-to's for cleaning, cooking, chilling, and separating to avoid cross-contamination. The whys are important because research is showing that more-educated consumers are taking greater risks than less-educated consumers (9). The how-to's are important because fewer Americans are learning about food safety by cooking with their families or by taking academic courses (10).

While food safety is an area of dietetic practice that overlaps other professional practice areas, dietitians are the only healthcare practitioners who include food safety as a core competency. While new physician education materials focus on diagnosis and management of foodborne illness (11), physicians themselves report that food safety is not an area they discuss with their clients because it is not as closely aligned with medical treatment as other areas, such as heart health and smoking cessation (12). Nurses and physician assistants may review some general eating recommendations with clients, but they seldom have the training to operationalize food guidance recommendations. Environmental health specialists inspect public food retail establishments, but they seldom counsel individuals. Dietetics professionals are the healthcare practitioners who are expected to apply knowledge of food, **toxic** agents, and clinical conditions to deliver appropriate food safety guidance to individuals and to vulnerable groups.

Dietetics professionals serve a wide audience—from individuals who are highly susceptible to foodborne illness to individuals who simply need basic food safety guidance to individuals who need specialized information, such as information on food allergies or food safety during international travel. Further, in many practice settings, such as hospitals, child-care facilities, and long-term-care facilities, dietetics practitioners supervise preparation of food and training for foodservice workers. Also, in their personal lives dietetics professionals serve themselves, their families, and their communities through their food safety choices and behaviors. To serve such varied audiences, dietetics professionals must be able to interpret food safety recommendations in many settings.

Food safety is a complex puzzle. It is complicated by **emerging pathogens,** issues associated with applications of new technologies, individualistic responses to food components, and populations with special needs stemming from weakened immune systems or lifestyle pressures. To complete the portrait of an individual, the dietitian must have the correct pieces and link them together. The four simple pieces in public awareness and education campaigns—cook, chill, clean, and separate—are documented by surveillance programs to be keys to consumer food safety behaviors. They are simple reminders of the basics. However, each of those four puzzle pieces becomes many puzzle pieces when applied to different foods, to environmental situations, and to the vulnerable populations often served by dietitians. For example, "cook" means different temperatures for different foods. It may also mean different temperatures for different populations; for example, current recommendations are that deli meats be cooked until "steaming hot" for pregnant women (13). Dietetics professionals can interpret each of these terms for individuals or for groups. The number of puzzle pieces (recommendations) changes as the portrait of the individual changes or the setting changes.

Sometimes the background of the portrait changes. When a new pathogen emerges or a chemical emerges at **hazardous** levels in the food supply, we may add another puzzle piece—selection. Selection is a personal choice. Selection is also a critical food safety behavior for some individuals. For example, eating raw oysters is riskier for adults with liver disease than for healthy adults (14). Eating soft cheeses is riskier for pregnant women than for other women (15). Eating a brownie at a school party is much riskier for a child with tree-nut allergies than for other children (16). Selection is an important puzzle piece for the background of many portraits. Dietetics professionals are the healthcare practitioners best able to help their clients make informed choices about food selection. To do this, professionals must know where to find the information they need and how to apply it.

Food Safety for Professionals, 2nd edition, offers information to help dietetics practitioners find and link the food safety puzzle pieces together. It is a reference to answer questions. It offers resources for personal and client education (many available on-line, if you do not have access to a research library). It offers opportunity for reflection in the practice role. It poses questions for research. While food safety is an evolving puzzle requiring frequent information updates, the puzzle outline as we view it today is a four-sided frame—clean, cook, chill, and separate. The information inside the frame forms slightly different pictures for different audiences, which is the excitement of putting the puzzle together.

CHAPTER DESCRIPTIONS

Chapter 2, Potential Toxic Agents

"Toxic agent" is the term used to describe either harmful chemicals or pathogens. This chapter focuses on toxic agents, the types of foodborne illness they cause, and their associated symptoms. The chapter includes extensive information on bacterial, parasitic, and viral pathogens and resources for dietetic practice.

Chapter 3, The Food in Food Safety

Food is the **vehicle** for toxic agents that cause foodborne illness. This chapter defines **potentially hazardous food** and discusses safety issues within Food Guide Pyramid groups. It also describes barriers to foodborne disease, including technologies currently in use to extend the safe shelf life of foods.

Chapter 4, Food and Water Safety Surveillance Systems in the United States

Surveillance systems monitor indicators of food and water safety. This chapter discusses the following surveillance systems in the United States: CDC's Surveillance for Foodborne-Disease Outbreaks, the Foodborne Disease Active Surveillance Network (FoodNet), the National Molecular Subtyping Network for Foodborne-Disease Surveillance **(PulseNet)**, the FDA Pesticide Program, the Total Diet Study, the USDA Pesticide Data Program (PDP), and the EPA Cumulative Exposure Project (CEP). The chapter includes current data for all programs.

Chapter 5, Laws, Regulations, and Regulatory Bodies

This chapter offers a brief overview of the major food safety laws and regulators in the United States. It also gives information on food recalls.

Chapter 6, People and Their Food Safety Behaviors

This examination of people's food safety behaviors describes populations most susceptible to foodborne illness, how consumers' demands affect the food supply, and consumers' food safety knowledge and behaviors. It provides information on factors that contribute to foodborne illness and related resources for dietetic practice. It also describes consumer programs focused on food safety behaviors.

Chapter 7 Foodservice Programs That Reduce Foodborne Illness

This chapter offers a brief overview of the systems required to develop an integrated food safety plan in an institution, including standard operating procedures, standard sanitation operating procedures, and Hazard Analysis Critical Control Point systems.

Appendix A, Farm/Ship to Fork: Resources for Dietetics Professionals

This appendix includes an annotated directory of governmental and non-governmental resource agencies for dietetics professionals. Annotation includes URLs for resource materials.

Appendix B, Continuing Professional Education

This appendix contains a self-test of 83 multiple-choice questions for continuing professional education credit. This self-study program has been approved for ten CPE hours for registered dietitians. The appendix also includes examples of objectives that can be used in a professional development portfolio.

REFERENCES

1. US Department of Health and Human Services. Food safety. In: *Healthy People 2010.* 2nd ed. With Understanding and Improving Health and Objectives for Improving Health. 2 vols. Washington, DC: US Government Printing Office, November 2000:10.3–10.19. Available at: http://www.health.gov/healthypeople/Document/pdf/Volume1/10Food.pdf. Accessed May 12, 2001.
2. US Departments of Agriculture and Health and Human Services. *The Dietary Guidelines for Americans 2000.* 5th ed. Washington, DC: US Departments of Agriculture and Health and Human Services; 2000. Home and Garden Bulletin No. 232. Available at: http://www.usda.gov/cnpp/DietGd.pdf. Accessed May 25, 2001.
3. Ingham S, Thies ML. Food and water safety—position of ADA. *J Am Diet Assoc.* 1997;97:184–189. Available at: http://www.eatright.com/adap0297.html. Accessed May 27, 2001.
4. Cooper G, Hadler JL, Barth S, et al. Cholera associated with international travel. *MMWR.* 1992;41(36):664–667.

5. Lofgren JP, Macias M, Russakow S, et al. Blood lead levels in young children—United States and selected states, 1996-1999. *MMWR.* 2000;49(50):1133–1137. Available at: http://www.cdc.gov/mmwr/PDF/wk/mm4950.pdf. Accessed May 27, 2001.

6. Shallow S, Samuel M, McNees A, et al. Preliminary FoodNet data on the incidence of foodborne illnesses—selected sites, United States, 2000. *MMWR.* 2001;50(13):241–246. Available at: http://www.cdc.gov/mmwr/PDF/wk/mm5013.pdf. Accessed May 24, 2001.

7. Partnership for Food Safety Education Web site. Available at: http://www.fightbac. org. Accessed May 26, 2001.

8. The American Dietetic Association Foundation–ConAgra Foundation. Home Food Safety . . . It's in Your Hands Web site. Available at: http://www.homefoodsafety.org. Accessed May 26, 2001.

9. Yang S, Leff MG, McTague D, et al. Multistate surveillance for food-handling, preparation, and consumption behaviors associated with foodborne diseases: 1995 and 1996 BRFSS food-safety questions [CDC surveillance summaries, September 11, 1998]. *MMWR.* 1998;47(SS-4):33–57. Accessed May 25, 2001.

10. Food Marketing Institute. Food safety: a qualitative analysis. Washington DC: Food Marketing Institute; 1996.

11. Centers for Disease Control and Prevention. Diagnosis and management of foodborne illnesses: a primer for physicians. *MMWR.* 2001;50(RR-2):1-67. Available at: http://www.cdc.gov/mmwr/PDF/RR/RR5002.pdf. Accessed May 26, 2001.

12. International Food Information Council (IFIC) Foundation. Physicians' attitudes toward food safety education [IFIC Web site]. September 2000. Available at: http://www.ific.org/proactive/newsroom/release.vtml?id=18121&PROACTIVE_I D=cecfcfcdc8cdc6cec8c5cecfcfcfc5cecfcacacbcecac8cfcfc5cf. Accessed June 9, 2001.

13. Centers for Disease Control and Prevention. Listeriosis: frequently asked questions [CDC Web site]. January 1999. Available at: http://www.cdc.gov/ncidod/dbmd/ diseaseinfo/listeriosis_g.htm. Accessed June 7, 2001.

14. US Food and Drug Administration. If you eat raw oysters, you need to know . . . [FDA Web site]. July 1995; updated January 28, 1999. Available at: http://vm.cfsan. fda.gov/~lrd/oyster.html. Accessed May 27, 2001.

15. US Food and Drug Administration. Keep your baby safe: eat hard cheeses instead of soft cheeses during pregnancy [FDA Web site]. July 1997. Available at: http://vm.cfsan.fda.gov/~dms/listeren.html. Accessed May 27, 2001.

16. American Academy of Allergy, Asthma, and Immunology (AAAAI). Position statement: anaphylaxis in schools and other child care settings [AAAAI Web site]. Available at: http://www.aaaai.org/professional/physicianreference/ positionstatements/ps34.stm. Accessed May 27, 2001.

CHAPTER 2

POTENTIAL TOXIC AGENTS

Foodborne illnesses result from exposure to toxic agents that are carried into the body through food or water. Foodborne toxic agents can be biological or chemical. Foodborne biological agents that can cause disease are called pathogens. Pathogens may be **bacteria, parasites, viruses, prions,** or **fungi**. Toxic chemicals in food include chemicals produced by pathogens growing on food, agricultural residues, industrial wastes, toxicants formed during cooking or processing, and naturally occurring toxicants.

Foodborne illnesses are either **infections** or **intoxications.** Toxic agents that cause foodborne infections and intoxications elicit the same general symptoms in everyone, although some people may be more susceptible (or have more natural resistance) than others. This uniform response makes infections and intoxications different from individualistic responses to food, such as **allergies, intolerances,** and sensitivities. Some general principles of foodborne illness and individualistic responses to food are outlined below, followed by descriptions of specific toxic agents. For more detailed discussions of these principles and toxic agents, more expanded references are available (1–8).

TYPES OF FOODBORNE ILLNESSES

Foodborne Intoxications

Chemical toxicants preformed in food cause intoxications. Scientists describe these toxicants by source, action, or chemical nature. For example, **saxitoxin** is a toxicant found in shellfish that can cause respiratory failure. It is a naturally occurring, shellfish (source) alkaloid (chemical nature) that is a neurotoxin (action). Another example is aflatoxin B, produced by specific molds growing on grain. Aflatoxin B is a **mycotoxin** (source) bifuranocoumarin (chemical nature) that is a liver toxin (action) and a probable **carcinogen** (action). Complete **toxicity** statements include the agent (purified chemical), dosage, route of administration, symptom(s), and species affected. Oral routes of exposure compare better to dietary exposures than other routes, such as inoculation or inhalation. Mammalian species, especially primates, provide data most closely resembling human responses.

Most chemicals in food do not have toxic effects when consumed at normally occurring or expected dietary levels. To cause toxic effects, they must be resistant to digestion processes or be converted to a toxic form during digestion. For these reasons, it is important to identify the **dose** and the circumstances of exposure when describing foodborne toxicants. For example, chemicals that are toxic when inhaled may not exhibit the same toxicity when they are consumed; asbestos can cause lung cancer when inhaled, but it will not cause lung cancer if consumed.

The stabilities of toxic chemicals to cooking and to digestive processes also affect their potentials to cause foodborne illness. Botulinum toxin is considered heat-labile, but thorough cooking is required to ensure its destruction (9–10). Toxins produced by *Bacillus cereus* and *Staphylococcus aureus* are heat-stable; normal cooking or reheating will not destroy them (9).

Foodborne Infections

Foodborne infections occur when pathogens in food survive digestive processes and overcome the **host**'s natural defenses. There are two types of foodborne infections—**invasive** infections and **noninvasive** infections. Microorganisms that penetrate the gastrointestinal mucosa and multiply intracellularly cause invasive infections. Noninvasive infections result when microorganisms grow in the intestine without actually penetrating tissue.

The normal environment of the gastrointestinal tract reduces survival of many organisms. Acid conditions in the stomach and bile acids secreted into the small intestine inhibit many microorganisms. The intestinal mucosa also serves as a physical barrier. Gastric motility reduces the time microorganisms have to establish an infection. Alterations in the gastrointestinal tract, including ulceration, reduction in stomach acidity, changes in the gut epithelium, and reduction in peristalsis, increase a person's susceptibility to foodborne infections.

Additionally, the intestine has two defenses specifically designed to combat infectious organisms. Intestinal phagocytes located along the gastrointestinal tract engulf and destroy infectious organisms. Also, the gut is one of the body's major lymphatic organs, and it is readily sensitized to infectious organisms. Antibodies along the gut control bacteria and viruses, although they are less effective against parasites. **Immunocompromised** individuals are more susceptible to infections because they do not produce sufficient antibodies required to protect the gut. Also, diseases such as Crohn's disease can produce "leaky guts," allowing pathogens and allergens to cross the gut wall and enter the bloodstream.

GENERAL SYMPTOMS OF FOODBORNE ILLNESS

The most common symptoms associated with foodborne illness are gastrointestinal, because the gastrointestinal tract is the first, and usually the only, tissue exposed to toxic foodborne agents. For infectious microorganisms to cause symptoms other than gastrointestinal distress, they must invade the host. Toxic chemicals must be absorbed into the circulatory system to travel to other tissues. For examples, *Trichinella spiralis* can invade smooth muscle **(trichinosis),** and **hepatitis** A virus can cause liver disease. Botulinum toxin and some mushroom toxins can cause paralysis, respiratory failure, and death when they are ingested and absorbed. Symptoms associated with some specific toxic agents are described in Tables 2.1 through 2.3. *(continued on page 32)*

TABLE 2.1   Descriptions of Specific Foodborne Bacterial Pathogens

Bacillus cereus	
General Characteristics	*B. cereus* is an **aerobic,** toxin-producing, spore-forming bacterium. *B. cereus* spores are frequently dustborne and airborne. In the latest foodborne-disease outbreak summaries (1993 to 1997), *B. cereus* was responsible for 14 confirmed outbreaks, representing 691 cases and no deaths (Table 2.4). There is no active surveillance for *B. cereus* food poisoning.
Disease	*B. cereus* produces two types of toxins. One toxin is a large molecular weight protein that causes diarrheal illness similar to that caused by *Clostridium perfringens*. For this illness, onset of watery diarrhea and cramps occurs within 6 to15 hours of consuming contaminated food. The other toxin is a heat-stable peptide that causes nausea and vomiting within 0.5 to 6 hours of consuming contaminated food. These symptoms are similar to those produced by staphylococcal intoxication. The death-to-case ratio for *B. cereus* food poisoning is 0, and there are no known sequelae to *B. cereus* food poisoning.
Implicated Foods	A wide variety of foods have been implicated in *B. cereus* food poisoning. Because *B. cereus* is in soils and dust, it frequently contaminates cooked product that is left uncovered, such as rice or fried rice in restaurants or barbecue served at large outdoor functions. Also, *B. cereus* spores survive pasteurization in milk. Other implicated foods include vegetables and fish. Meats, milk, vegetables, and fish are usually implicated for the diarrheal-type outbreaks, and rice and other starchy foods are usually implicated for the emetic-type outbreaks. *B. cereus* does not grow at recommended refrigerator temperatures (below 41°F/5°C), but it can grow at slightly higher temperatures (50°F/10°C).
Susceptible Populations	All persons are believed to be susceptible to *B. cereus* intoxication. However, milk drinkers may acquire some immunity from continuous exposure to small amounts of *B. cereus*.
Human Transmission	*B. cereus* is not transmitted person-to-person, and there is no evidence for contamination by food handlers.
Controls	COOK food thoroughly to destroy growing *B. cereus* bacteria. COOL refrigerated foods rapidly to reduce growth of *B. cereus* bacteria. SEPARATE cooked foods from the environment by covering them to reduce their contamination by airborne *B. cereus* spores.

Sources: References 9, 13–14, 95–98

Campylobacter jejuni	
General Characteristics	*C. jejuni* is a **microaerophilic** organism, which means it requires only small amounts of oxygen. *C. jejuni* bacteria are commonly found in the intestinal tracts of cats, dogs, poultry, cattle, swine, rodents, monkeys, wild birds, and some humans. It is also carried by flies. The bacteria pass through feces to cycle through the environment; for that reason they are also found in untreated water such as streams and ponds. In the latest foodborne-disease outbreak summaries (1993 to 1997), *C. jejuni* was responsible for 25 confirmed outbreaks, representing 539 cases and 1 death (Table 2.4). Current reports from the Foodborne Diseases Active Surveillance Network (FoodNet) show 15.7 laboratory-confirmed cases of campylobacteriosis per 100,000, one of the highest rates of foodborne illness caused by a single toxic agent in the United States.
Disease	Campylobacteriosis is the most common cause of bacterial diarrhea in the United States. The disease is not well characterized. It may be an invasive infection or a non-invasive infection. The organism produces a heat-stable toxin that can cause diarrhea. The primary symptom of campylobacteriosis is diarrhea, which may be watery or sticky and can contain blood (usually **occult**) and fecal leukocytes (white cells). Other common symptoms are fever, abdominal pain, nausea, headache, and muscle pain. The illness usually occurs 2 to 5 days after ingestion of the contaminated food or water and generally lasts 7 to 10 days. Relapses are not uncommon (about 25% of cases). Complications are relatively rare. Infections have been associated with a short-term, reactive arthritis [strongly associated with people who have the human lymphocyte antigen B27 (HLA-B27)]. Other reported complications (sequelae) include hemolytic uremic syndrome, meningitis, recurrent colitis, acute cholecystitis and urinary tract infections, and Guillain-Barre syndrome.

TABLE 2.1   Descriptions of Specific Foodborne Bacterial Pathogens *(continued)*

Disease *(cont.)*	One death from campylobacteriosis was reported in the latest five-year outbreak summary from CDC. The estimated case/fatality ratio for all *C. jejuni* infections is 0.1, one death per 1,000 cases. Fatalities are rare in healthy individuals and usually occur in cancer patients or others who are immunocompromised. Twenty cases of septic abortion induced by *C. jejuni* have been recorded in the literature.
Implicated Foods	*C. jejuni* frequently contaminates raw chicken (20% to 100% of retail chickens). Improper handling or cooking of chicken are the most common causes of foodborne campylobacteriosis. While undercooked chicken is the most recognized cause of campylobacteriosis, lettuce and fruits cross-contaminated by raw chicken have caused two recent outbreaks, demonstrating the potential for **cross-contamination** of other foods. Raw (unpasteurized) milk and water from untreated sources such as streams and ponds have caused other current outbreaks. *C. jejuni* does not grow at refrigerator temperatures.
Susceptible Populations	Anyone may become ill from a *Campylobacter* infection. Host susceptibility determines the infective dose, which may be as small as 400 to 500 bacteria for some individuals. This illness occurs about 35 times more frequently in persons with AIDS than in otherwise healthy persons.
	Although anyone can have a *C. jejuni* infection, children under 5 years of age and young male adults (ages 15 to 29) are more frequently afflicted than other age groups. Individuals whose immune systems are weakened by **chronic** illness, such as AIDS, or by medical treatment, such as immunosuppressive therapy, are most susceptible to health complications from *Campylobacter*.
Human Transmission	*C. jejuni* is a fecal organism found in many species, and individuals who carry *C. jejuni* in their gastrointestinal tracts may be asymptomatic. It can contaminate hands of food preparers through petting animals or failure to wash hands properly after bathroom use. While infected food handlers are not considered a major cause of food contamination, cross-contamination of food by food handlers with poor hygiene is possible.
Controls	COOK • Cook all poultry products thoroughly. See Chapter 6 for information on cooking. • Use a thermometer to measure internal temperatures of cooked foods. • If you are served undercooked poultry in a restaurant, send it back. CLEAN • Wash hands with soap before and after handling raw foods of animal origin. • Wash hands thoroughly after toileting, changing a diaper, or touching pets or pet products. • If you have diarrhea, do not prepare foods for others. SEPARATE • Separate raw foods from cooked foods. • Prevent cross-contamination in the kitchen. Use separate cutting boards for foods of animal origin and other foods. Carefully clean all cutting boards, countertops, and utensils with soap and hot water after preparing raw food of animal origin. • Prevent drips while thawing foods in the refrigerator by thawing foods on the bottom shelf in a container large enough to hold the liquid released as food thaws. SELECT only pasteurized milk and treated water. Do not consume unpasteurized dairy products or untreated water from ponds, streams, and the like. PUBLIC HEALTH • Pasteurization of milk reduces public exposure to *C. jejuni*. • Sewage control and water treatment have reduced campylobacteriosis outbreaks.
Selected Educational Materials	• *Campylobacter* Questions and Answers (99) • Foodborne Illness: What Consumers Need to Know (100) • Food Safety for Persons with AIDS (101) • *Campylobacter* Infections: Frequently Asked Questions (102)

Sources: References 9, 11, 13–14, 99–106

TABLE 2.1   Descriptions of Specific Foodborne Bacterial Pathogens *(continued)*

	Clostridium botulinum
General Characteristics	*Clostridium botulinum* is an **anaerobic,** toxin-producing, spore-forming bacterium. Of the seven types of *C. botulinum* recognized (A, B, C, D, E, F, and G), types A, B, E, and F cause human botulism. Typing is based on the antigenic specificity of the toxin produced by strain. *C. botulinum* spores are widely distributed in nature; they are found in soils, water, and intestinal tracts of humans and other animals. The spores are dustborne, waterborne, and airborne. In the latest foodborne-disease outbreak summaries (1993 to 1997), *C. botulinum* was responsible for 13 confirmed outbreaks, representing 56 cases and 1 death (Table 2.4). There is no active surveillance for botulism.
Disease	Foodborne botulism is an intoxication caused by ingestion of preformed neurotoxin in food. Botulinum toxin is heat labile and can be destroyed if heated at 176°F (80°C) for 10 minutes or longer. This requires thorough cooking of dense food products. A very small amount (a few nanograms) of toxin can cause illness. Onset of symptoms in foodborne botulism is usually 18 to 36 hours after ingestion of the food containing the toxin, although cases have varied from 4 hours to 8 days. Early signs of intoxication include marked tiredness, weakness, and dizziness. These symptoms are usually followed by double vision and progressive difficulty in speaking, swallowing, and breathing. Botulinum toxin causes paralysis by blocking motor nerve terminals at the myoneural junction. The paralysis progresses symmetrically downward. When the diaphragm and chest muscles become fully involved, respiration is inhibited and death from asphyxia results. CDC outbreak data report 1 death in 56 cases from foodborne botulism in the 1993 to 1997 reporting period, a death-to-case ratio of about 18 per 1,000 cases. Additionally, a patient with severe botulism may require a breathing machine as well as intensive medical and nursing care for several months. Patients who survive an episode of botulism poisoning may have fatigue and shortness of breath for years, and long-term therapy may be needed to aid recovery. Infant botulism is a different form of the disease. It is a noninvasive infection in which ingested spores colonize and produce toxin in the gastrointestinal tracts of infants (persons under 12 months of age), which are less acidic than those of healthy children and adults. Clinical symptoms of infant botulism consist of constipation that occurs after a period of normal development, followed by poor feeding, lethargy, weakness, pooled oral secretions, an altered cry, and striking loss of head control. In the United States there are around 80 cases of infant botulism each year. Another, as yet poorly described form of botulism involves adult cases that may also be noninvasive infections. In the reported cases, the patients had surgical alterations of the gastrointestinal tract and/or antibiotic therapy. Those procedures may have altered the normal gut flora and allowed *C. botulinum* to colonize the intestinal tract, as in infant botulism.
Implicated Foods	Most of the ten or so outbreaks that are reported annually in the United States are associated with inadequately processed, home-canned foods, but commercially produced foods have been involved in some outbreaks. Sausages, meat products, canned vegetables, and seafood products have been the most frequent vehicles for human botulism. Two separate outbreaks of botulism have occurred involving commercially canned salmon. Restaurant foods such as sautéed onions, chopped bottled garlic, potato salad made from baked potatoes, and baked potatoes themselves have been responsible for a number of outbreaks. Also, ethnic fish dishes have been responsible for several recent outbreaks of botulism in the United States— kapchunka, a traditional Native Alaskan smoked fish (both hot- and cold-smoked), and molona, a traditional Egyptian uneviscerated salt-cured fish. Honey is the one dietary vehicle of *C. botulinum* spores definitively linked to infant botulism by both laboratory and **epidemiologic** studies. *C. botulinum*, types nonproteolytic-B, E, and F, can grow at refrigerator temperatures. Since *C. botulinum* is also anaerobic, it can grow in MAP/CAP refrigerated foods.
Susceptible Populations	All people are believed to be susceptible to the foodborne intoxication. As described above, infants under 12 months of age are susceptible to infant botulism, and persons who have undergone treatments that might alter the normal gut microflora are susceptible to noninvasive infection by *C. botulinum*.

TABLE 2.1   Descriptions of Specific Foodborne Bacterial Pathogens *(continued)*

Human Transmission	*C. botulinum* is not transmitted person-to-person, and there is no evidence for contamination by food handlers.
Controls	CLEAN produce thoroughly before cooking or preserving food to reduce potential levels of contamination. CHILL • Chill cooked foods for later service. Do not store cooked foods at room temperatures. • Purchase only **acidulated** infused oils and refrigerate them after opening. COOK • Follow USDA home-canning instructions exactly. • As an added precaution, all home-canned foods can be boiled, covered, for ten minutes to ensure destruction of potential toxin. SELECT • Do not prepare infant formulas with honey or dip pacifiers in honey. • Do not store home-prepared, infused oils. PUBLIC HEALTH development and oversight of commercial canning processes and other food processing systems have reduced incidence of botulism in the United States.
Selected Educational Materials	• Foodborne Illness: What Consumers Need to Know (100) • Botulism (*Clostridium botulinum*): Frequently Asked Questions (107) • Canning, Drying, and Freezing (108)

Sources: References 10, 13, 100, 107–115

Clostridium perfringens	
General Characteristics	*Clostridium perfringens* is an anaerobic, spore-forming bacterium. *C. perfringens* spores are widely distributed in soil and are frequently found in the intestines of humans and many other animals. In the latest foodborne-disease outbreak summaries (1993 to 1997), *C. perfringens* was responsible for 57 confirmed outbreaks, representing 2,772 cases and no deaths (Table 2.4). There is no active surveillance for *C. perfringens*.
Disease	Common perfringens food poisoning is a noninvasive infection caused by *C. perfringens* type A. This form of perfringens poisoning is characterized by intense abdominal cramps and diarrhea that begin 8 to 22 hours after consumption of foods containing large numbers of *C. perfringens* type A bacteria (about 108 vegetative cells). The illness is usually over within 24 hours, but less severe symptoms may persist in the elderly or infirm for 1 or 2 weeks. The rare deaths reported for perfringens poisoning are due to dehydration and other complications. Recoveries are typically without complications.
Implicated Foods	*C. perfringens* poisoning is most common where food is prepared in large quantities hours before serving, often in institutional settings or at outdoor festivals or other celebratory events. Meats, meat products, gravy, and Tex-Mex-style foods are most frequently implicated, in part because this bacterium requires many amino acids for growth. Also, as such foods are cooked and held warm for service or slowly cooled, air is driven off, making the environment perfect for anaerobic growth . Recent outbreaks stemmed from ground-beef-containing fiesta casserole and tacos served in a prison, minestrone soup served at a large banquet, and restaurant-prepared seafood salad, prime rib, turkey, and corned beef. Other outbreaks have occurred in nursing homes, church suppers, schools, and large family gatherings, where large amounts of food were prepared in advance and held at improper temperatures. *C. perfringens* does not grow at recommended refrigerator temperatures (below 41°F/5°C), but it can grow at slightly higher temperatures (43°F/6°C).
Susceptible Populations	All persons are susceptible to perfringens poisoning, but the most frequent victims are those who eat in institutional settings (such as school cafeterias, hospitals, nursing homes, and prisons) where large quantities of food are prepared several hours before serving.
Human Transmission	*C. perfringens* is not transmitted person-to-person. There is no evidence for contamination by food handlers.

TABLE 2.1   Descriptions of Specific Foodborne Bacterial Pathogens *(continued)*

Controls	COOK
	• Cook meat products, especially large roasts and turkeys, and dried beans thoroughly. See Chapter 6 for information on cooking.
	• Do not partially cook for finishing later.
	• Reheat thoroughly (165°F or until steaming).
	• Minimize holding times for cooked foods. Hold foods at appropriate temperatures (above 140°F).
	• Use a thermometer to measure internal temperatures of cooked foods and holding temperatures of foods.
	COOL cooked products quickly in the refrigerator.
Selected Educational Materials	• Foodborne Illness: What Consumers Need to Know (100)

Sources: References 9, 13, 100, 116–118

Escherichia coli **Group**	
General Characteristics	*Escherichia coli* is an aerobic bacterium that does not form spores. It is frequently found in the gastrointestinal tracts of humans and other animals. The bacteria pass through feces to cycle through the environment; for that reason they are also found in soils and in untreated water, such as streams and ponds.
	In the latest foodborne-disease outbreak summaries (1993 to 1997), *E. coli* was responsible for 84 confirmed outbreaks, representing 3,260 cases and 8 deaths (Table 2.4). Current reports from the Foodborne Diseases Active Surveillance Network (FoodNet) show 2.1 laboratory-confirmed cases of disease from *E. coli* O157:H7 per 100,000.
	Currently, there are five recognized strains of enterovirulent *E. coli* (collectively referred to as the EEC group) that cause gastroenteritis in humans. These include enterotoxigenic *E. coli* (ETEC), enteropathogenic *E. coli* (EPEC), enterohemorrhagic *E. coli* (EHEC), enteroinvasive *E. coli* (EIEC), and enteroaggregative *E. coli*.
Disease	Enterotoxigenic *Escherichia coli* O169:H8 causes a gastroenteritis that affects travelers to developing countries (travelers' diarrhea) and infants in developing countries. The syndrome is a noninvasive infection that presents with watery diarrhea, abdominal cramps, low-grade fever, nausea, and malaise. The infective dose is quite high (10^7–10^{10} cells). A similar ETEC has been described in Japan—*Escherichia coli* O169:H41.
	Infantile diarrhea is the infection usually associated with EPEC. EPEC causes either a watery or bloody diarrhea, depending on the tissue destruction caused by a cell-associated shiga-like toxin called **verotoxin.** EPEC is highly infectious for infants, and the infective dose is presumably low. For adults the infective dose is greater than 10^6 cells.
	Hemorrhagic colitis is the invasive infection caused by *E. coli* O157:H7 (EHEC). Other strains of **SLTEC** (Shiga-like toxin-producing *E. coli*) may also cause hemorrhagic *colitis—E. coli* O104:H21 (United States) and *E. coli* O111:H21 (Australia). Like EPEC, *E. coli* O157:H7 produces verotoxin. The illness is characterized by severe cramping (abdominal pain) and diarrhea that is initially watery but frequently becomes grossly bloody. Fever is either low-grade or absent. The illness is usually self-limiting and lasts for an average of 8 days. The infective dose is unknown, but it may be quite low (10 cells), since it is easily passed person-to-person in day-care settings and nursing homes. Some victims, particularly the very young, have developed hemolytic uremic syndrome (HUS), characterized by renal failure and hemolytic anemia. From 0% to 15% of hemorrhagic colitis victims may develop HUS. In the elderly, HUS, plus two other symptoms, fever and neurologic symptoms, constitute thrombotic thrombocytopenic purpura (TTP). This illness can have a mortality rate in the elderly as high as 50%.
	Enteroinvasive *E. coli* (EIEC) produces an invasive infection known as bacillary **dysentery.** Dysentery caused by EIEC usually occurs within 12 to 72 hours after ingestion of contaminated food. The illness is characterized by abdominal cramps, bloody diarrhea, vomiting, fever, and chills. Although the dysentery caused by this organism is generally self-limiting, it can result in secondary hemolytic uremic syndrome (HUS) in pediatric cases. The infectious dose is thought to be small (10 cells).
	Chronic sequelae to *E. coli* infections may include reactive arthritis [strongly associated with people who have the human lymphocyte antigen B27 (HLA-B27)] and Crohn's disease.

TABLE 2.1   Descriptions of Specific Foodborne Bacterial Pathogens *(continued)*

Implicated Foods	Enterotoxigenic *Escherichia coli* is typically found where sewage-contaminated water is consumed. Food handlers can also contaminate food with this organism. It is occasionally found in unpasteurized semisoft cheeses. Recent outbreaks in the United States have been traced to raw vegetable salads prepared from domestic ingredients and to contamination of food by an infected food handler. The Japanese **serotype** has been implicated in outbreaks from pickles and seafood. EPEC outbreaks most often affect bottle-fed infants in developing countries, suggesting that contaminated water is often used to rehydrate the infant formulas. Common foods implicated in EPEC outbreaks are raw beef and chicken, although any food exposed to fecal contamination is strongly suspect. *E. coli* O157:H7 (EHEC) is associated with undercooked ground beef, unpasteurized apple juice made from (presumably) fecal-contaminated apples, undercooked roast beef, raw (unpasteurized) milk, improperly processed cider, contaminated water and mayonnaise, alfalfa sprouts (probably grown from contaminated seed), cut cantaloupe on a salad bar, and vegetables grown in cow manure. A current outbreak from a related SLTEC, *E. coli* O104:H21, was apparently caused by postpasteurization contamination of milk. *E. coli* can grow at refrigerator temperatures.
Susceptible Populations	All persons are susceptible to *E. coli* gastroenteritis, although infants in developing countries are most commonly affected by ETEC and EPEC. Travelers to developing countries are also frequently exposed to ETEC.
Human Transmission	Enterohemorrhagic *E. coli* and enterotoxigenic *E. coli* are occasionally foodborne as a result of contamination by infected food handlers, but they usually contaminate at the source or during processing. Person-to-person transmission in institutions such as child-care centers and hospitals has been reported.
Controls	COOK • Cook foods, especially ground beef, thoroughly to destroy *E. coli.* See Chapter 6 for information on cooking. • Use a thermometer to measure internal temperatures of cooked foods. • If you are served undercooked meat or poultry in a restaurant, send it back. CLEAN • Wash hands and all food contact surfaces before and after preparing food to reduce contamination by *E. coli.* • Wash utensils (including thermometers) between uses. • Wash hands thoroughly after toileting, changing a diaper, or touching pets or pet products. • Do not prepare foods for others if you have diarrhea. SEPARATE cooked and raw foods, and clean used utensils to reduce contamination of cooked food with drip from raw foods. CHILL • Chill meat-containing foods quickly to 34°F to 40°F (1°C to 4°C) to slow the growth of *E. coli.* • Keep refrigerator temperatures at 34°F to 40°F (1°C to 4°C). • Follow label instructions on products that must be refrigerated or that have a "use by" date. This is especially important for foods that might be contaminated with *E. coli,* since it can grow at refrigerator temperatures. SELECT • Select only pasteurized fruit juices. • Avoid alfalfa sprouts. PUBLIC HEALTH • Sewage control and water treatment are important public health measures to reduce presence of *E. coli* in food and water. • On-the-farm and slaughter controls are being investigated to reduce contamination of meats found in the marketplace. • Pasteurization of milk and fruit juices reduces outbreaks caused by *E. coli.*
Selected Educational Materials	• Foodborne Illness: What Consumers Need to Know (100) • *Escherichia coli* O157:H7: Frequently Asked Questions (119) • Use a Meat Thermometer (120)

Sources: References 9, 12–14, 18, 100, 119, 120–136

TABLE 2.1   Descriptions of Specific Foodborne Bacterial Pathogens *(continued)*

Listeria monocytogenes	
General Characteristics	*Listeria monocytogenes* is a bacterium found in the gastrointestinal tracts of mammals, birds, and possibly some species of fish. The bacteria pass through feces to cycle through the environment; for that reason they are also found in soils and in untreated water, such as streams and ponds. *L. monocytogenes* are also found in human nose and throat secretions. *L. monocytogenes* is quite hardy, growing in refrigerated foods and surviving in some dried and cooked foods. In the latest foodborne-disease outbreak summaries (1993 to 1997), *L. monocytogenes* was responsible for 3 confirmed outbreaks, representing 100 cases and 2 deaths (Table 2.4). Current reports from the Foodborne Diseases Active Surveillance Network (FoodNet) show 0.3 laboratory-confirmed cases of listeriosis per 100,000.
Disease	Listeriosis is an invasive infection that presents with gastrointestinal symptoms such as nausea, vomiting, and diarrhea. These symptoms may be the only disease symptoms, or the infection may spread to the nervous system, causing headache, stiff neck, confusion, loss of balance, or convulsions. Serious manifestations of listeriosis include **septicemia,** meningitis, and encephalitis. In pregnant women the gastrointestinal symptoms may precede spontaneous abortion during the second or third trimester or stillbirth. The more serious symptoms occur when the bacterium invades the gastrointestinal epithelium, enters the host's monocytes, begins to grow, and is carried to the brain and placenta. Current research with *Listeria monocytogenes* suggests that this invasion requires a virulence factor called "internalin," which interacts with a protein within the brush border of the intestine to allow admission of *Listeria.* The pathogenesis of *L. monocytogenes* centers on its ability to survive and multiply in phagocytic host cells. The onset time to serious forms of listeriosis is unknown but may range from a few days to three weeks. The infective dose of *L. monocytogenes* is unknown but is believed to vary with the strain and the susceptibility of the victim. It may be as low as 103 cells for healthy individuals. The death-to-case ratio for listeriosis is over 200 deaths per 1,000 cases. While not proven causal, antigens to *L. monocytogenes* have been demonstrated in intestinal tissue from persons with Crohn's disease.
Implicated Foods	Typically, foods that cause listeriosis are ready-to-eat foods contaminated with large numbers of cells and held (refrigerated or at room temperatures) for extended periods to allow for growth. *L. monocytogenes* has been associated with such foods as raw (unpasteurized) milk, supposedly pasteurized fluid milk, cheeses (particularly soft-ripened varieties), ice cream, raw vegetables, fermented raw-meat sausages, raw and cooked poultry, raw meats (all types), and raw and smoked fish. The source for a recent large multistate (22 states) outbreak was hotdogs and deli meats; this outbreak had more that 100 cases, with 21 deaths—15 adults and 6 miscarriages or stillbirths. *L. monocytogenes* can grow at refrigerator temperatures.
Susceptible Populations	All persons are susceptible to listeriosis, but pregnant women and persons with AIDS have more severe infections that are often fatal to the person with AIDS or to the fetus of the infected pregnant woman. Pregnant women are about 20 times more likely than other healthy adults to get listeriosis; about one-third of listeriosis cases happen during pregnancy. Persons with AIDS are almost 300 times more likely to get listeriosis than people with normal immune systems. Also, persons who are immunocompromised by therapy for cancer, organ transplants, and other conditions are at greater risk than the general population. The elderly are more susceptible than younger adults, and antacids or cimetidine may predispose individuals to susceptibility to listeriosis.
Human Transmission	There are no published examples of contamination of food with *L. monocytogenes* by infected food handlers. Cross-contamination of food by food handlers with poor hygiene is possible.
Controls	SELECT • Select pasteurized dairy products. • If you are at high risk (pregnant, immunosuppressed), avoid soft cheeses, such as Mexican-style, feta, brie, camembert, and blue. Mexican-style cheeses are soft, white, ethnic (Hispanic–Latin American) cheeses such as queso blanco and queso fresco. There is no need to avoid hard cheese (aged for 60 days or longer), processed slices, cottage cheese, or yogurt.

TABLE 2.1   Descriptions of Specific Foodborne Bacterial Pathogens *(continued)*

Controls *(cont.)*	COOK
	• Cook meat, poultry, and seafood thoroughly to destroy *L. monocytogenes*. See Chapter 6 for further information on cooking temperatures.
	• Thorough reheating to 165°F (or until steaming) of leftovers, hotdogs, and cold cuts destroys *L. monocytogenes*. Those at high risk may choose to avoid cold cuts (or to reheat them thoroughly).
	• Use a thermometer to measure internal temperatures of cooked foods.
	CHILL
	• Chill food quickly and keep refrigerator temperatures at 34°F to 40°F (1°C to 4°C) to slow the growth of *L. monocytogenes*.
	• Divide leftovers into small, shallow, covered containers before refrigerating, so that they chill rapidly and evenly.
	• Follow label instructions on products that must be refrigerated or that have a "use by" date. This is especially important for foods that might be contaminated with *L. monocytogenes*, since it can grow at refrigerator temperatures.
	CLEAN
	• Clean all fruits and vegetables with water to help reduce contamination by *L. monocytogenes*.
	• Thorough cleaning of potential food contact surfaces, such as counter tops, cutting boards, and the insides of the refrigerator, especially after contact with food, will help reduce contamination of food with *L. monocytogenes*.
	• Wash hands with warm soapy water after handling raw foods.
	• Wash hands thoroughly after toileting, changing a diaper, or touching pets or pet products.
	• Do not prepare foods for others if you have diarrhea.
	SEPARATE raw and cooked foods when shopping, preparing, cooking, and storing foods to help reduce contamination of cooked foods.
	PUBLIC HEALTH
	• Pasteurization of milk and other dairy products reduces public exposure to *L. monocytogenes*.
	• Sewage control and water treatment reduce public exposure to *L. monocytogenes*.
Selected Educational Materials	• Foodborne Illness: What Consumers Need to Know (100)
	• Food Safety for Persons with AIDS (101)
	• *Listeria monocytogenes* and Listeriosis (137)
	• Keep Your Baby Safe: Eat Hard Cheeses instead of Soft Cheeses during Pregnancy (138)
	• Preventing Foodborne Listeriosis (139)
	• Listeriosis: Frequently Asked Questions (140)

Sources: References 9, 11–14, 17–18, 100–101, 137–147

Salmonella spp	
General Characteristics	*Salmonellae* are widespread in animals, especially in poultry and swine. The bacteria pass through feces to cycle through the environment; for that reason they are also found in untreated water, such as streams and ponds. There are many species of *Salmonellae*, all of which are thought to be pathogenic to humans. Preliminary 1999 data from FoodNet show 24% of the serotyped *Salmonella* isolates were Typhimurium, 10% were Enteritidis, 7% were Heidelberg, 9% were Newport, and 6% were Muenchen.
	In the latest foodborne-disease outbreak summaries (1993 to 1997), Salmonellae were responsible for 357 confirmed outbreaks, representing 32,610 cases and 13 deaths (Table 2.4). Current reports from the Foodborne Diseases Active Surveillance Network (FoodNet) show 14.4 laboratory-confirmed cases of salmonellosis per 100,000.
Disease	Salmonellosis is a common foodborne invasive infection in the United States. It can be caused by ingestion of as few as 15 to 20 cells, depending on the susceptibility of the host and the species of bacteria. Typical symptoms are abdominal cramps, diarrhea, fever, and headache. The typical onset for symptoms is 12 to 72 hours, and symptoms usually last for 4 to 7 days. The disease is caused by penetration and passage of *Salmonella* organisms into epithelium

TABLE 2.1 Descriptions of Specific Foodborne Bacterial Pathogens *(continued)*

Disease (*cont.*)	of small intestine, where inflammation occurs. There is evidence that the bacteria produce an enterotoxin, perhaps within the enterocyte.
	S. typhi and *S. paratyphi* A, B, and C produce typhoid and typhoidlike fever in humans. Various organs may be infected, leading to lesions. The fatality rate of typhoid fever is 10%, compared to less than 1% for most forms of salmonellosis. *S. dublin* has a 15% mortality rate when septicemic in the elderly, and *S. enteritidis* has a 3.6% mortality rate in hospital/nursing home outbreaks, with the elderly being particularly affected.
	Salmonellosis is associated with a rare, short-term, reactive arthritis [strongly associated with people who have the human lymphocyte antigen B27 (HLA-B27)] in about 2% of culture-confirmed cases. It has also been associated with Reiter's syndrome, characterized by joint pains, conjunctivitis, and painful urination. These sequelae may follow 3 to 4 weeks after the initial infection. Septic arthritis, subsequent or coincident with septicemia, also occurs and can be difficult to treat.
Implicated Foods	Foods of animal origin, including raw poultry, meat, (unpasteurized) milk, and eggs, may be contaminated with *Salmonellae*. Raw produce and other uncooked foods may become contaminated through contact with feces, raw animal products, or infected food handlers. Recent outbreaks have been caused by:
	• Cut melons contaminated with *S. chester, S. Poona,* and *S. javiana*
	• Mozzarella cheese contaminated by *S. javiana* and *S. oranienberg*
	• Potato salad contaminated with *S. newport* (probably by an infected food handler)
	• Turkey contaminated with *S. agona*
	• Salad bar ingredients cross-contaminated by uncooked meat and poultry contaminated with *S. montevideo*
	• Beef jerky contaminated with *S. montevideo*
	• Chicken and beef fajitas contaminated by *S. heidelberg*
	• Undercooked eggs and products containing undercooked eggs with *S. enteritidis*
	• Sandwiches and ice contaminated by an infected food handler with *S. typhi*
	• Rice pudding contaminated with *S. infantis*
	• Homemade ice cream contaminated with *S. typhimurium*
	• Toasted oat cereal contaminated with *S. agona*
	• Powdered milk products and infant formula contaminated with *S. tennessee*
	• Potato salad, macaroni salad, and ziti prepared with water contaminated by *S. hartford*
	• Cottage cheese contaminated with *S. fetus*
	The vehicle for *S. enteritidis* is intact, **disinfected** grade A eggs and undercooked products containing them. The reason for this is that *S. enteritidis* colonizes the ovaries of healthy hens and contaminates the eggs before the shells are formed. Vehicles of current outbreaks include egg-containing bread pudding, stuffing, sauces and dressings, batters, banana pudding, drinks, noncommercial mayonnaise, both commercial and homemade ice cream, and sandwiches, in addition to egg entrees prepared from raw shell eggs. Salad ingredients cross-contaminated in a mixer used to prepare raw egg mixtures caused one outbreak. Sandwiches and ice contaminated by an infected food handler also caused an outbreak.
	Salmonellae do not grow at recommended refrigerator temperatures (below 41°F/5°C), but they can grow at slightly higher temperatures (44°F/6.5°C).
Susceptible Populations	Salmonellosis can affect anyone, but occurs almost 100 times more frequently in persons with AIDS than in otherwise healthy persons. Also, salmonellosis occurring in persons with AIDS can be particularly difficult to treat and is more likely to lead to serious complications. In typically healthy populations children are the most likely victims of salmonellosis, and the elderly are typically more susceptible than other adults. Most deaths from *S. enteritidis* infections have been in elderly nursing home populations.
Human Transmission	*S. typhi* can be transmitted person-to-person and by infected food handlers. Nontyphoidal *Salmonellae* are occasionally foodborne as a result of contamination by infected food handlers, but they usually contaminate food at the source or during processing.
Controls	SELECT
	• Select pasteurized dairy products.

TABLE 2.1   Descriptions of Specific Foodborne Bacterial Pathogens *(continued)*

Controls *(cont.)*	• For institutional use or for persons with AIDS you may prefer to select pasteurized egg products. COOK • Cook meat, poultry, and eggs thoroughly to destroy *Salmonellae*. See Chapter 6 for information on cooking. • Use a thermometer to measure internal temperatures of cooked foods. • If you are served undercooked meat, poultry, or eggs in a restaurant, send the food back. CHILL • Chill food quickly. • Keep refrigerator temperatures at 34°F to 40°F (1°C to 4°C) to retard the growth of *Salmonellae*. • Purchase only refrigerated eggs, and keep them refrigerated at home. CLEAN • Clean all fruits and vegetables with water to help reduce contamination by *Salmonellae*. • Thorough cleaning of potential food contact surfaces, such as counter tops, sinks, and cutting boards, especially after contact with food, will help reduce contamination of food with *Salmonellae*. • After handling raw foods, wash your hands with warm soapy water. • Wash hands thoroughly after toileting, changing a diaper, or touching pets or pet products. • Do not prepare foods for others if you have diarrhea. SEPARATE raw and cooked foods when shopping, preparing, cooking, and storing foods to help reduce contamination of cooked foods. PUBLIC HEALTH • Pasteurization of milk reduces exposure of the public to *Salmonellae*. • Sewage control and water treatment reduce exposure of the public to *Salmonellae*.
Selected Educational Materials	• Foodborne Illness: What Consumers Need to Know (100) • Food Safety for Persons with AIDS (101) • Salmonellosis: Frequently Asked Questions (148) • *Salmonella enteritidis* Infection: Frequently Asked Questions (149)

Sources: References 9, 11, 13–14, 100–101, 148–169

***Shigella* spp**	
General Characteristics	Shigellae pass through feces to cycle through the environment; for that reason they are also found in untreated water, such as streams and ponds. They are frequently found in waters polluted by human feces. In the latest foodborne-disease outbreak summaries (1993 to 1997), Shigellae were responsible for 43 confirmed outbreaks, representing 1,555 cases and no deaths (Table 2.4). Current reports from the Foodborne Diseases Active Surveillance Network (FoodNet) show 7.9 laboratory-confirmed cases of shigellosis per 100,000, one of the highest rates of foodborne illness caused by a single toxic agent in the United States. Preliminary 1999 FoodNet data show that, among the *Shigella* isolates with known species, most were *S. sonnei*.
Disease	Shigellosis is the third most common foodborne invasive infection in the United States. It is characterized by fever, abdominal pain and cramps, and diarrhea containing blood, pus, or mucus. Depending on the susceptibility of the host, the infective dose is as few as 10 cells. Onset time is 12 to 50 hours, and symptoms usually subside in 5 to 7 days. The disease is caused when **virulent** *Shigella* organisms penetrate the intestinal mucosa, multiply intracellularly, and spread to contiguous epithelial cells, destroying tissue. Some strains produce enterotoxin and Shiga toxin, which resembles the verotoxin of *E. coli* O157:H7. Two recent cases of acute myocarditis have been reported in children with *S. sonnei* gastroenteritis. Extreme dehydration is often a cause of death, which may be as high as 10% to 15% with some strains. Reiter's disease, reactive arthritis [strongly associated with people who have the human lymphocyte antigen B27 (HLA-B27)], and hemolytic uremic syndrome (HUS) are possible sequelae for shigellosis. These sequelae may follow 3 to 4 weeks after the initial infection.

TABLE 2.1   Descriptions of Specific Foodborne Bacterial Pathogens *(continued)*

Implicated Foods	Traditionally, shigellosis is described as being transmitted by the four Fs—food, fingers, feces, and flies. Contamination of foods is usually through the fecal-oral route or by fecally contaminated water. A low infectious dose and multiple transmission possibilities—food, water, person-to-person—make shigellosis a common problem in disasters, such as earthquakes, floods, famines, and wars. Recent outbreaks have been caused by: • Lettuce in the United States and during Operation Desert Shield (possibly washed, cooled, or irrigated with fecally contaminated water) • Salads (potato, tofu, tuna, shrimp, macaroni, and chicken) • Raw vegetables • Raw shellfish • Milk and dairy products Several outbreaks were traced to infected food handlers; others were traced back to fecally contaminated water or soils. Shigellae do not grow at recommended refrigerator temperatures (below 41°F/5°C), but they can grow at slightly higher temperatures (46°F/8°C).
Susceptible Populations	Everyone is susceptible to shigellosis. It occurs almost 100 times more frequently in persons with AIDS than in otherwise healthy persons, and the symptoms are more severe in those with AIDS or other immune-suppressing conditions. Children, especially toddlers, are the most likely to contract shigellosis. Infants, the elderly, and the infirm are most susceptible to the severest symptoms of shigellosis.
Human Transmission	Shigellae are highly infectious. They can be transmitted person-to-person, and unsanitary handling by food handlers is one of the most common factors contributing to foodborne shigellosis.
Controls	CLEAN • Clean all fruits and vegetables with **potable** water to help reduce contamination by shigellae. • Wash hands thoroughly after toileting, changing a diaper, or touching pets or pet products. • Do not prepare foods for others if you have diarrhea. PUBLIC HEALTH • Pasteurization of milk reduces exposure of the public to shigellae. • Sewage control and water treatment reduce exposure of the public to shigellae.
Selected Educational Materials	• Foodborne Illness: What Consumers Need to Know (100) • Food Safety for Persons with AIDS (101) • Shigellosis: Frequently Asked Questions (170)

Sources: References 9, 11, 13–14, 100–101, 125, 156, 170–177

Staphylococcus aureus	
General Characteristics	*Staphylococcus aureus* is a toxin-producing bacterium that is frequently carried in the nose and throat secretions and on the hair and skin of people. In the latest foodborne-disease outbreak summaries (1993 to 1997), *S. aureus* was responsible for 42 confirmed outbreaks, representing 1,413 cases and 1 death (Table 2.4). There is no active surveillance for *S. aureus* in the United States.
Disease	Staphylococcal food poisoning is an intoxication that typically presents with nausea, vomiting, and abdominal cramping. Transient changes in blood pressure and pulse rate may occur in severe cases. The onset of symptom is usually rapid, and recovery usually takes 2 days. Staphylococcal toxin is heat-stable. A toxin dose of less than 1.0 microgram in contaminated food will produce symptoms of staphylococcal intoxication. This toxin level is reached when *S. aureus* levels in food exceed 10^5 cells per gram. Recovery from staphylococcal food poisoning is usually complete, and no sequelae have been demonstrated. Death is rare, but may occur from dehydration among the elderly, infants, and severely debilitated persons.

TABLE 2.1   Descriptions of Specific Foodborne Bacterial Pathogens *(continued)*

Implicated Foods	Foods that require a lot of handling during preparation and that are kept at slightly elevated temperatures after preparation are frequently involved in staphylococcal food poisoning. Foods that are frequently incriminated in staphylococcal food poisoning include meat and meat products (especially ham); poultry and egg products; salads such as egg, tuna, chicken, potato, and macaroni; bakery products such as cream-filled pastries, cream pies, and chocolate eclairs; sandwich fillings; and milk and dairy products. *S. aureus* does not grow at recommended refrigerator temperatures (below 41°F/5°C), but it can grow at slightly higher temperatures (45°F/7°C).
Susceptible Populations	All people are susceptible to the intoxication, although severity of symptoms may vary.
Human Transmission	Food handlers are usually the main source of food contamination in staphylococcal food poisoning outbreaks. Fifty percent or more of healthy individuals carry *S. aureus.* This percentage is even higher for those who associate with or who come in contact with sick individuals and hospital environments.
Controls	CLEAN • Clean hands often, especially after touching your face, hair, other people, or pets. • Keep all potential food contact surfaces clean. COOK meat, poultry and eggs thoroughly to destroy *S. aureus* before it grows on food and produces toxin. Cooking will not destroy the toxin once it is produced. CHILL • Chill food quickly. • Keep refrigerator temperatures at 34°F to 40°F to retard the growth of *S. aureus.*
Selected Educational Materials	• Foodborne Illness: What Consumers Need to Know (100)

Sources: References 9, 13–14, 100, 178–181

Streptococcus	
General Characteristics	Streptococci are microaerophilic bacteria. Groups A and D are foodborne. Group A includes *S. pyogenes.* Group D includes *S. avium, S. bovis, S. durans, Enterococcus faecalis,* and *E. faecium.* In the latest foodborne-disease outbreak summaries (1993 to 1997), *Streptococcus* group A was responsible for 1 confirmed outbreak, representing 122 cases and no deaths (Table 2.4). There is no active surveillance for streptococci in the United States.
Disease	Foodborne *Streptococcus pyogenes* (*Streptococcus* group A) causes an invasive infection (GAS disease) characterized by high fever, sore throat, and tonsilitis. The onset of symptoms occurs in 1 to 3 days, and the infectious dose is low (less than 10^3 cells). Rare, severe infections may result in scarlet fever or rheumatic fever. Two other severe forms of GAS, necrotizing fasciatus (destructive infection of muscle and fat tissue) and toxic shock syndrome, are not foodborne. While not proven causal, antigens to streptococci have been found in intestinal tissue from persons with Crohn's disease. Of the 10,000 to 15,000 severe cases of invasive GAS disease that occur in the United States each year, 10% to 20% are fatal. *Streptococcus* group D (*E. faecalis, E. faecium, S. durans, S. avium,* and *S. bovis*) organisms cause an infection that presents with diarrhea, abdominal cramps, nausea, vomiting, fever, chills, and dizziness in 2 to 36 hours after ingestion of contaminated food. The infectious dose is probably high (greater than 10^7 cells).
Implicated Foods	Group A: Food sources include milk, ice cream, eggs, steamed lobster, ground ham, potato salad, egg salad, custard, rice pudding, and shrimp salad. Recent outbreaks have been caused by food prechewed by parents for their young children and by macaroni and cheese contaminated by bacteria from a food handler's skin lesion. Group D: Food sources include sausage, evaporated milk, cheese, meat croquettes, meat pie, pudding, raw (unpasteurized) milk, and pasteurized milk. Streptococci do not grow at recommended refrigerator temperatures (below 41°F/5°C), but they can grow at slightly higher temperatures (50°F/10°C).
Susceptible Populations	All are susceptible. Streptococcal sore throats are relatively common, especially in children. Persons who are receiving immunosuppressive medications or who have diabetes are at higher risk for severe GAS disease.

TABLE 2.1 Descriptions of Specific Foodborne Bacterial Pathogens *(continued)*

Human Transmission	Contamination of food with *S. pyogenes* is commonly due to poor hygiene of food handlers.
Controls	CLEAN • Clean hands often, especially after toileting or touching your face, hair, other people, or pets. • Do not prepare or serve food to others if you are sick. SELECT • Select only pasteurized dairy products. • Purchase pre-prepared salads and desserts only from reputable vendors with verified quality assurance **(Hazard Analysis Critical Control Point [HACCP])** plans. COOK foods thoroughly. CHILL foods quickly if they will not be consumed within 2 hours of preparation to reduce growth of streptococci in foods. PUBLIC HEALTH • Pasteurization of milk greatly reduced the number of cases of foodborne streptococcal illness in the United States. • Educate parents not to prechew foods for infants.
Selected Educational Materials	• Foodborne Illness: What Consumers Need to Know (100) • Group A Staphylococcal (GAS) Disease: Frequently Asked Questions (182)

Sources: References 9, 12–14, 18, 100, 182–184

Vibrio spp	
General Characteristics	Vibrios are water-dwelling organisms that cause infections (some invasive, some noninvasive) that present with mild to severe diarrhea. Some strains are **halophilic** and require salt. Environmental studies show that vibrios are present in marine and estuarine waters of the United States and in the fish and shellfish that inhabit those waters. In the latest foodborne-disease outbreak summaries (1993 to 1997), vibrios were responsible for 6 confirmed outbreaks, representing 42 cases and no deaths (Table 2.4). Current reports from the Foodborne Diseases Active Surveillance Network (FoodNet) show 0.2 laboratory-confirmed cases of *Vibrio* infection per 100,000.
Disease	*Vibrio cholerae* O1 is responsible for Asiatic or epidemic cholera, a noninvasive infection that occurs when the bacteria attach to the small intestine and produce toxin. Symptoms vary from mild diarrhea to severe diarrhea producing rice-water stools. The infective dose is large (10^6 cells), but antacid consumption markedly lowers the infective dose. Onset varies from 6 hours to 5 days. Death may occur after severe fluid and electrolyte loss. No major outbreaks of this disease have occurred in the United States since 1911, but sporadic cases from consumption of raw, undercooked, or recontaminated shellfish have been recorded since 1971. *Vibrio cholerae* serogroup 01 causes an infection with symptoms that are less severe than cholera. The primary symptoms of the infection are diarrhea (occasionally bloody), abdominal cramps, and fever. These symptoms usually occur within 48 hours of ingestion and last 6 to 7 days. Septicemia can occur in individuals who have cirrhosis of the liver or who are immunosuppressed, but this is relatively rare. *Vibrio parahaemolyticus*-associated gastroenteritis is a noninvasive infection that presents with diarrhea, abdominal cramps, and fever. Onset of symptoms occurs 4 to 96 hours after consuming the organism (usually about 15 hours), and the illness usually lasts 2.5 days. The infective dose is greater than 10^6 and is markedly lowered by antacids. *Vibrio vulnificus* causes gastroenteritis or a syndrome known as "primary septicemia." The ingestion of *V. vulnificus* by healthy individuals can result in a noninvasive gastroenteritis within 16 hours of exposure. The primary septicemia (invasive) form of the disease occurs in individuals with underlying chronic disease, particularly liver disease or hemochromatosis. In such individuals, the bacteria enter the blood stream, causing septic shock and distinctive blistering skin lesions, rapidly followed by death in many cases (about 50%). The infective dose for gastrointestinal symptoms in healthy individuals is unknown, but for predisposed persons septicemia can presumably occur with doses of fewer than 100 cells. Recoveries from *Vibrio* infections are complete. There are no recorded sequelae.

TABLE 2.1   Descriptions of Specific Foodborne Bacterial Pathogens *(continued)*

Implicated Foods	Contaminated crustacean and molluscan shellfish (raw, undercooked, recontaminated after cooking) are the primary food vehicles for *Vibrio* infections. In developing countries untreated water can be a source of vibrios. Most recent outbreaks involve seafoods:
	• Raw oysters from all coastal areas of the United States.
	• Frozen and raw shrimp
	• Reef fish from contaminated waters in Guam and fish from Chesapeake Bay and Mobile Bay
	• Cooked crabs brought illegally into the United States in a suitcase from Ecuador during a cholera epidemic
	• Undetermined foods (probably home-canned palm fruit) brought into the United States illegally from El Salvador during a cholera epidemic
	A more unusual outbreak was caused by frozen coconut milk imported from Thailand.
	Vibrios do not grow at recommended refrigerator temperatures (below 41°F/5°C), but they can grow at slightly higher temperatures (46°F/8°C).
Susceptible Populations	All people are susceptible to infection, but individuals with liver cirrhosis, AIDS, or other forms of immunosuppression are 80 times more likely to develop *V. vulnificus*-caused primary septicemia than are healthy people. Persons with reduced gastric acidity are also more likely to be affected by *Vibrio* infections.
Human Transmission	Person-to-person transmission is not likely. However, food handlers infected with *V. cholerae* can contaminate food with the bacterium.
Controls	SELECT only shellfish (oysters, clams, mussels) harvested from approved waters (approved vendors). Although oysters can be harvested legally only from waters free from fecal contamination, even legally harvested oysters can be contaminated with vibrios because the bacterium is naturally present in marine environments. Vibrios do not alter the appearance, taste, or odor of oysters.
	COOK
	• Cook all shellfish thoroughly. For shellfish in the shell, either (1) boil until the shells open and continue boiling for 5 more minutes, or (2) steam until the shells open and then continue cooking for 9 more minutes. Boil shucked oysters at least 3 minutes, or fry them in oil at least 3 minutes at 375°F.
	• Do not eat those shellfish that do not open during cooking.
	• Do not eat raw shellfish or products that contain raw seafoods, such as **ceviche.**
	SEPARATE juices and cooked foods (including cooked seafoods) from raw seafood.
	CHILL
	• Chill shellfish promptly after cooking for holding.
	• Refrigerate leftovers within 2 hours of cooking.
	PUBLIC HEALTH
	• Sewage control and water treatment reduce public exposure to vibrios.
	• Monitoring harvesting waters reduces likelihood of shellfish contamination.
	TRAVELERS to areas with cholera outbreaks (check with your health department or the CDC):
	• Drink only water that has been boiled or treated with chlorine or iodine. Other safe beverages include tea and coffee made with boiled water and served steaming hot, and carbonated, bottled, or canned beverages with no ice.
	• Eat only foods that have been thoroughly cooked and are still steaming hot, or fruit that you have peeled yourself.
	• Avoid foods and beverages from street vendors.
	• Do not bring perishable seafood back to the United States.
Selected Educational Materials	• If You Eat Raw Oysters, You Need to Know . . . (185)
	• Cholera: Frequently Asked Questions (186)
	• *Vibrio vulnificus:* Frequently Asked Questions (187)
	• *Vibrio parahaemolyticus:* Frequently Asked Questions (188)

Sources: References 9, 13–14, 185–201

TABLE 2.1   Descriptions of Specific Foodborne Bacterial Pathogens *(continued)*

Yersinia spp	
General Characteristics	*Y. enterocolitica* is often isolated from clinical specimens such as wounds, feces, and sputum. *Y. pseudotuberculosis* has been isolated from infected appendices. Neither is a part of normal human flora. Only *Y. enterocolitica* is found in the environment. Most isolates are not pathogenic. In the latest foodborne-disease outbreak summaries (1993 to 1997), yersiniae were responsible for 2 confirmed outbreaks, with 27 cases, and 1 death (Table 2.4). Current reports from the Foodborne Diseases Active Surveillance Network (FoodNet) show 0.4 laboratory-confirmed cases of yersiniosis per 100,000.
Disease	Yersiniosis is an invasive infection that presents 1 to 2 days after ingestion as gastroenteritis with diarrhea and fever. The characteristic symptom of yersiniosis is abdominal pain that mimics appendicitis or Crohn's disease. *Y. enterocolitica* is the only yersiniae that has caused foodborne outbreaks in the United States, but *Y. pseudotuberculosis* has caused foodborne illness in Japan, and *Y. pestis* is the causative agent of "the plague" (not foodborne). Yersiniae may cause infections of wounds, joints, or the urinary tract. Reactive arthritis [strongly associated with people who have the human lymphocyte antigen B27 (HLA-B27)] is a possible sequelae for 3 to 4 weeks after the initial infection.
Implicated Foods	Most outbreaks of yersiniosis have been traced to raw (unpasteurized) milk or milk that was recontaminated after pasteurization. Some outbreaks have also occurred after contamination of food (tofu and bean sprouts) and with untreated water. One outbreak occurred when individuals preparing chitterlings transferred the organism from the food via their hands to children. Yersiniae can grow at refrigerator temperatures.
Susceptible Populations	The most susceptible populations for the initial disease and for its complications are the very young, the very old, and individuals with weakened immune systems.
Human Transmission	*Y. enterocolitica* is occasionally foodborne as a result of contamination by infected food handlers, but it usually contaminates at the source or during processing.
Controls	SELECT • Select only pasteurized milk and other dairy products. • Use only treated water for drinking and for food preparation. COOK foods thoroughly. See Chapter 6 for information on cooking. SEPARATE cooked foods from raw foods, especially sausages in natural casings and chitterlings. CLEAN • After handling raw foods, wash your hands with warm soapy water. • Wash hands thoroughly after toileting or changing a diaper. • Do not prepare foods for others if you have diarrhea. PUBLIC HEALTH • Sewage control and water treatment reduce public exposure to yersiniae. • Pasteurization of milk destroys yersiniae.

Sources: References 9, 11, 13–14, 100, 202–205

TABLE 2.2   Descriptions of Specific Foodborne and Waterborne Parasites

Anisakida spp	
General Characteristics	The anisakids are nematodes (roundworms). To date, only *A. simplex* and *P. decipiens* are reported to cause human disease in North America. Anisakiasis incidence is not reported in CDC's foodborne-disease outbreak summaries or in FoodNet.
Disease	Symptoms of anisakiasis occur within 1 hour to 2 weeks after consuming the parasite (usually one organism). The symptoms may be as simple as a tickling sensation in the throat that causes the victim to cough up the nematode as it travels from the esophagus into the pharynx after digestion of the food vehicle. More severe cases present with nausea and acute abdominal

TABLE 2.2   Descriptions of Specific Foodborne and Waterborne Parasites *(continued)*

Disease *(cont.)*	appendicitis-like pain that occur when larval nematodes burrow into the intestinal mucosa. The larva can detach and reattach to other mucosal sites, causing additional pain and damage that can persist after the nematode dies. Because anisakiasis is so rare in the United States, it is often misdiagnosed as appendicitis, Crohn's disease, gastric ulcer, or gastrointestinal cancer. Anisakids are usually eliminated spontaneously from the digestive tract lumen within 3 weeks of infection, and worms that die in the tissues are eventually removed by phagocytosis. However, severe cases may require surgical intervention.
Implicated Foods	The only implicated foods are raw or undercooked seafood. Anisakidae are sometimes called "sushi parasites."
Susceptible Populations	All people are susceptible to anisakiasis. The population most at risk is consumers of raw or underprocessed seafood.
Human Transmission	There is no documented evidence for human transmission of anisakidae.
Controls	COOK • Cook all fish thoroughly. See Chapter 6 for information on cooking. • Do not eat raw fish or products that may contain raw fish, such as ceviche, sushi, sashimi, or lomi-lomi. SEPARATE juices and cooked foods (including cooked seafoods) from raw seafood. CLEAN all surfaces (including hands) that have held raw fish thoroughly before using them to prepare other foods. For example, food contact surfaces used to prepare sushi can contaminate foods that do not contain raw fish. Watch for this in sushi and sashimi restaurants and bars.

Sources: References 9, 206

Ascaris lumbricoides	
General Characteristics	*Ascaris lumbricoides* is a nematode (roundworm) frequently found in feces. The eggs are sticky and can adhere to hands and clothing. Ascariasis incidence is not reported in CDC's foodborne-disease outbreak summaries or in FoodNet.
Disease	Ascariasis is commonly called the "large roundworm infection." Infection with a few of these worms may not be serious; they may simply exit the body through feces, mouth, or nose. Infection with many worms may cause **pneumonitis** when hatched larvae penetrate the intestine and travel to the lungs, where they break out of the pulmonary capillaries into the air sacs. From the lungs they can ascend into the throat and descend to the small intestine again where they grow, becoming as large as 12 x 1.5 inches (31 x 4 cm). Because they grow to be so large, they can cause intestinal blockage, especially in small children. The worms may also wander to other body sites to cause tissue damage. For example, they may block bile ducts. Allergic symptoms (especially but not exclusively of the asthmatic sort) are common in long-lasting infections or upon reinfection in ascariasis.
Implicated Foods	*Ascaris* can contaminate crops grown in soil fertilized with insufficiently treated sewage-fertilizer. *Ascaris* eggs are resistant to drying, freezing, and chemical treatment and can remain viable in soil for years.
Susceptible Populations	All people are susceptible.
Human Transmission	There is no documented evidence in the United States for transmission of *A. lumbricoides* to food by infected food handlers. Cross-contamination of food by food handlers with poor hygiene is possible.
Controls	CLEAN • Clean raw produce thoroughly before eating it. • Wash hands thoroughly before preparing or serving food and after handling raw foods. PUBLIC HEALTH water treatment reduces risk of ascariasis.

Sources: References 9, 206

TABLE 2.2   Descriptions of Specific Foodborne and Waterborne Parasites *(continued)*

Cryptosporidium parvum	
General Characteristics	*Cryptosporidium parvum* is a protozoan parasite that is usually transmitted via oocysts in fecally contaminated water. The oocysts are resistant to chemical treatment, such as chlorination. *C. parvum* is not reported in foodborne-disease outbreak data from the Centers for Disease Control and Prevention, but it is one of the selected pathogens for the Foodborne Diseases Active Surveillance Network (FoodNet). Current reports from FoodNet show 1.5 laboratory-confirmed cases of **cryptosporidiosis** per 100,000.
Disease	Foodborne cryptosporidiosis is caused by consuming oocysts from feces. The disease presents with severe diarrhea 2 to 10 days after consumption. This diarrhea frequently results in dehydration, although colonized persons may be asymptomatic. The infectious dose is fewer than 10 cells, and presumably 1 cell can initiate the infection. In immunocompetent persons the disease is self-limiting (1 to 2 weeks), but it is life-threatening in immunocompromised persons and may recur sporadically.
Implicated Foods	Fecally contaminated water is the typical vehicle. Foods contaminated by this water or by fecally contaminated soils would be contaminated as well. Recent outbreaks have been reported for unpasteurized apple cider, chicken salad prepared in a licensed day-care home, foods containing uncooked green onions, raw (unpasteurized) milk (cow's and goat's), frozen tripe, and sausage.
Susceptible Populations	All persons are apparently susceptible to cryptosporidiosis. The persons who exhibit the most serious symptoms are persons with AIDS, persons receiving immunosuppressive medications, and young children. Outbreaks are more common in day-care settings among caregivers and diaper-aged children than in other settings.
Human Transmission	Cryptosporidiosis can be transmitted person-to-person (especially by diaper-aged children and their caregivers) and by infected food handlers.
Controls	CLEAN • Clean all raw produce thoroughly before eating it; peel after cleaning, if possible. • Wash hands thoroughly before preparing or eating food, especially after toileting, diapering, playing with pets, or gardening. COOK • Cook foods thoroughly. See Chapter 6 for information on cooking. • During outbreaks or in other situations in which a community **boil-water advisory** is issued, boiling water for 1 minute (covered, at sea level; 3 minutes, covered, at higher altitudes) will eliminate the risk of cryptosporidiosis. • During boil-water advisories, use only ice made from boiled water and stored in clean trays. During boil-water advisories, empty and thoroughly clean ice and water-dispensing machines in institutional settings. SELECT • Select only treated water. *Cryptosporidium* is present in over half the rivers, lakes, and streams in the United States. Also, several outbreaks of cryptosporidiosis have been linked to municipal water supplies. Nationally distributed brands of bottled or canned carbonated soft drinks and commercially packaged, noncarbonated soft drinks and fruit juices that do not require refrigeration until after they are opened (e.g., those that can be stored unrefrigerated on grocery shelves) are safe to drink. Pasteurized fruit juices are also safe to drink. • If you wish to filter water at home to remove potential oocysts, call NSF International at (800) 673-4357 to check on the filtration system you are considering (Note: Filtration does not replace boiling as a preventive measure during boil-water advisories, and filters should be handled and changed according to manufacturer's instructions). PUBLIC HEALTH • Use of appropriate filtration in water treatment reduces contamination of public water supplies by *C. parvum*. • Pasteurization of milk and dairy products, juices, and ciders reduces the risk of *C. parvum* contamination.

TABLE 2.2   Descriptions of Specific Foodborne and Waterborne Parasites *(continued)*

Selected Educational Materials	• Fact Sheet: Cryptosporidiosis (207) • Cryptosporidiosis: A Guide for Persons with HIV/AIDS (208) • Cryptosporidiosis: Control and Prevention (209) • Guidance for People with Severely Weakened Immune Systems (210) • Fact Sheet On Childhood Diseases And Conditions: What You Should Know about . . . Cryptosporidiosis in the Child Care Setting (211) • Preventing Cryptosporidiosis: A Guide to Water Filters and Bottled Water (212)

Sources: References 9, 14, 125, 136, 207–223

Cyclospora cayetanensis	
General Characteristics	*Cyclospora cayetanensis* is a one-celled parasite. *C. cayetanensis* is not reported in foodborne-disease outbreak data from the Centers for Disease Control and Prevention, but it is one of the selected pathogens for the Foodborne Diseases Active Surveillance Network (FoodNet). Current reports from FoodNet show 0.1 laboratory-confirmed cases of cyclosporiasis per 100,000 annually since 1998, but they show 0.4 confirmed cases of cyclosporiasis per 100,000 during 1997, when there were several outbreaks from imported raspberries, fresh basil, and mesclun.
Disease	Cyclosporiasis symptoms usually begin about a week after infection. The primary symptoms are watery, explosive diarrhea, abdominal cramps, and low-grade fever. Symptoms may last a month or longer, and some individuals suffer relapses. Some carriers are asymptomatic.
Implicated Foods	Outbreaks of cyclosporiasis have been linked to various types of raw produce, including imported raw raspberries, mesclun, and fresh basil, all apparently contaminated by feces or feces-contaminated soil. *Cyclospora* has also been identified in chicken feces, although there have been no reported outbreaks of cyclosporiasis from poultry.
Susceptible Populations	All people are susceptible to cyclosporiasis.
Human Transmission	*Cyclospora* must sporulate in the environment to become infectious. Because this takes time (days or weeks) after being passed in a bowel movement, it is unlikely that it is passed directly from one person to another or that contamination by food handlers is a problem.
Controls	CLEAN fresh fruits and other raw produce well, especially if they are to be eaten raw. COOK produce to kill *Cyclospora*. PUBLIC HEALTH sewage control and water treatment reduce the risk of waterborne cyclosporiasis.
Selected Educational Materials	Fact Sheet: *Cyclospora* Infection (224)

Sources: References 9, 14, 224–232

Diphyllobothrium	
General Characteristics	*Diphyllobothrium* are parasitic cestodes (tapeworms). Diphyllobothriasis incidence is not reported in CDC's foodborne-disease outbreak summaries or in FoodNet.
Disease	Diphyllobothriasis is characterized by abdominal distention, flatulence, intermittent abdominal cramping, and diarrhea. Symptoms begin about 10 days after consumption. *D. latum* often grows to lengths between 3 and 6 feet (1 and 2 meters) and may grow to 30 feet (10 meters). *D. pacificum* is found in marine mammals (seals) and typically grows to about 1 meter. Because it is so large, the organism can cause tissue damage as it moves. It can also cause pernicious anemia by competing with its host for vitamin B_{12}. The disease is now rare in the United States. At one time it was common around the Great Lakes, where it was known as "Jewish housewife's disease" or the "Scandinavian housewife's disease" because the preparers of gefilte fish or fish balls tended to taste those dishes before they were fully cooked.
Implicated Foods	The typical vehicle is raw or insufficiently cooked freshwater fish.
Susceptible Populations	All people are susceptible to diphyllobothriasis, especially those who eat raw or undercooked fish.
Human Transmission	There is no person-to-person transmission. Diphyllobothriasis is foodborne.
Controls	COOK raw fish to 160°F or until it flakes easily.

Source: Reference 9

TABLE 2.2   Descriptions of Specific Foodborne and Waterborne Parasites *(continued)*

Entamoeba histolytica	
General Characteristics	*Entamoeba histolytica* is a one-celled protozoan parasite. Amebiasis incidence is not reported in CDC's foodborne disease outbreaks or in FoodNet.
Disease	Most people who are infected with *E. histolytica* do not become ill or they develop only mild cases of amebiasis. Amebiasis may occur within 1 to 4 weeks of ingestion of a single **cyst.** The primary symptoms of the mild cases include abdominal pain and cramping with loose or watery stools. Amebic dysentery is a severe form of amebiasis associated with more severe abdominal pain, bloody stools, and fever. In rare instances *E. histolytica* spreads outside the intestines to the liver and forms an abscess. Even less commonly, it spreads to other parts of the body, such as the lungs or brain.
Implicated Foods	Contaminated water is the most common vehicle.
Susceptible Populations	All people are believed to be susceptible to infection. Individuals with AIDS or who are receiving immunosuppressive medications are much more vulnerable than healthy individuals.
Human Transmission	Amebiasis is occasionally foodborne as a result of contamination by infected food handlers, but *E. histolytica* usually contaminates at the source or during processing.
Controls	PUBLIC HEALTH • Sewage control and water treatment protect the public. • Pasteurization of milk destroys *E. histolytica*.
Selected Educational Materials	Fact Sheet: Amebiasis (233)

Sources: References 9, 233–234

Eustrongylides spp	
General Characteristics	Larval *Eustrongylides* spp are large, bright red roundworms (nematodes), 25 to 150 mm long, 2 mm in diameter. They occur in fish from fresh, brackish, and marine waters. Incidence of infection from *Eustrongylides* is not reported in CDC's foodborne-disease outbreak data or in FoodNet.
Disease	The larvae can penetrate the gut wall, causing severe pain. The nematodes can perforate the gut wall and probably other organs. If the nematodes perforate the gut wall, septicemia results. One larva can initiate an infection. The disease is very rare in the United States.
Implicated Foods	Undercooked fish is the only implicated food. The only reported infections in the United States are from fishers who consumed live minnows and one case from contaminated sashimi.
Susceptible Populations	All people are susceptible to infection by *Eustrongylides*.
Human Transmission	There is no documented evidence for human transmission of *Eustrongylides*.
Controls	COOK raw fish to 160°F or until it flakes easily.

Sources: References 9, 235

Giardia lamblia	
General Characteristics	*Giardia lamblia* is a one-celled protozoan parasite that lives in the gastrointestinal tracts of humans and other animals. In the latest foodborne-disease outbreak summaries (1993 to 1997), *G. lamblia* was responsible for 4 confirmed outbreaks, representing 45 cases and no deaths (Table 2.4). There is no active surveillance for *G. lamblia* in the United States.
Disease	Giardiasis presents with foul-smelling, greasy diarrhea, abdominal cramps, and nausea 1 to 2 weeks after infection. In otherwise healthy persons the symptoms may last as long as 1 to 2 months, although 1 to 2 weeks would be more typical. Giardiasis is the most common parasitic diarrheal disease in North America. The disease can be started with a single cyst. Some carriers are asymptomatic. Lactose intolerance is common (40% of victims) during infection and up to 6 months after the infection. Severe hypothyroidism may result from chronic giardiasis due to poor intestinal thyroid hormone absorption.

TABLE 2.2 Descriptions of Specific Foodborne and Waterborne Parasites *(continued)*

Implicated Foods	Giardiasis is most frequently associated with the consumption of contaminated water. Recent foodborne outbreaks include sliced vegetables, fruit salad, sandwiches, noodle salad, and ice contaminated by food handlers. It is also possible for vegetables that come into contact with contaminated soils, water, or workers to be contaminated during production.
Susceptible Populations	All persons are apparently susceptible to giardiasis. Outbreaks are more common in day-care settings among caregivers, diaper-aged children, and their families than in other settings. Other persons at increased risk for giardiasis include international travelers, hikers, campers, and others who drink untreated water from contaminated sources.
Human Transmission	Food handlers infected with *G. lamblia* can contaminate food with the organism. More commonly, contamination occurs at the source.
Controls	CLEAN • Clean all raw produce thoroughly before eating it; peel after cleaning, if possible. • Wash hands thoroughly before preparing or eating food, especially after toileting, diapering, playing with pets, or gardening. PUBLIC HEALTH • Sewage control and water treatment protect people from giardiasis.
Selected Educational Materials	• Fact Sheet: Giardiasis (236) • Fact Sheet on Childhood Diseases and Conditions: What You Should Know about . . . Giardiasis in the Child Care Setting (237)

Sources: References 9, 12–13, 125, 215, 219, 236–241

Nanophyetus spp	
General Characteristics	*Nanophyetus* spp are trematodes (flukes)—parasitic flatworms. Nanophyetiasis incidence is not reported in CDC's foodborne-disease outbreak data or in FoodNet.
Disease	Nanophyetiasis is characterized by diarrhea, abdominal discomfort, and nausea.
Implicated Foods	Raw, underprocessed, and smoked salmon and steelhead are currently the only implicated foods. Other raw or underprocessed freshwater or anadromous fish, especially salmonids, are potential vehicles.
Susceptible Populations	All people are thought to be susceptible to *Nanophyetus* spp. Consumers of raw or underprocessed freshwater or anadromous fish, especially salmonids, are most at risk for infection.
Human Transmission	There is no documented evidence for human transmission of *Nanophyetus*.
Controls	COOK raw fish to 160°F or until it flakes easily.

Source: Reference 9

Taenia spp	
General Characteristics	*Taenia* spp are cestodes—parasitic tapeworms. Taeniae infections are not reported in CDC's foodborne-disease outbreak data or in FoodNet.
Disease	Cysticercosis is a serious and sometimes fatal pork tapeworm disease. After a person ingests the *Taenia solium* eggs, the larvae penetrate the stomach wall and invade the tissues—particularly skeletal muscle and the brain—where they mature to cystlike masses. After several years, the cysts begin to degenerate and produce an inflammatory reaction and fibrous lesions. At this stage, epileptic convulsions may occur or, occasionally, more diffuse visual disturbances or late-onset epilepsy will occur.
Implicated Foods	*Taenia saginata* is in beef. *Taenia solium* is in pork.
Susceptible Populations	All persons are believed to be susceptible to *Taenia* infections.
Human Transmission	*T. solium* is occasionally foodborne as a result of contamination by food handlers. Recent outbreaks have been caused by infected housekeepers and by infected seasonal farm workers. More commonly, food is contaminated at the source or during processing. There is no documented evidence for contamination of food with *T. saginata* by infected food handlers.
Controls	COOK meat to a minimum internal temperature of 160°F.

Sources: References 9, 242–243

TABLE 2.2 Descriptions of Specific Foodborne and Waterborne Parasites *(continued)*

Toxoplasma gondii	
General Characteristics	*Toxoplasma gondii* is a single-celled protozoan parasite found worldwide. Over a quarter of the people in the United States probably carry the parasite, but very few have symptoms because the immune system usually keeps the parasite from causing illness. Toxoplasmosis incidence is not reported in CDC's foodborne disease outbreak data or in FoodNet.
Disease	Toxoplasmosis is an infection. Most people who become infected with toxoplasmosis are asymptomatic. In otherwise healthy individuals it usually presents with flu-like swollen lymph glands or muscle aches and pains that last for a few days to several weeks. Severe infections cause damage to the eyes and late-onset epilepsy.
Implicated Foods	Raw or partly cooked meat, especially pork, lamb, or venison, are the primary food vehicles.
Susceptible Populations	All are susceptible to infection, although most are asymptomatic. However, individuals with AIDS and those receiving immunosuppressive medications may develop severe toxoplasmosis from new or reactivated infections, causing damage to the eye or the brain. Pregnant women who are first infected several months before pregnancy or during pregnancy can pass the infection to their infants, who can be born retarded or with other serious mental or physical problems.
Human Transmission	There are no documented cases of food handlers infected with *T. gondii* contaminating food. Cross-contamination of food by food handlers with poor hygiene is possible.
Controls	CLEAN • Clean hands thoroughly after toileting, gardening, handling cats or their litter, or raw meat. • Thoroughly clean cutting boards, sinks, knives, and other utensils that have touched raw meat. COOK all meat thoroughly— to at least 160°F throughout. SEPARATE raw meat and meat juices from other foods.
Selected Educational Materials	• Fact Sheet: Toxoplasmosis (244)

Sources: References 9, 23, 244

Trichinella spiralis	
General Characteristics	*Trichinella spiralis* is a parasitic nematode (roundworm). In the latest foodborne-disease outbreak summaries (1993–97), *T. spiralis* was responsible for 2 confirmed outbreaks, representing 19 cases and no deaths (Table 2.4). There is no active surveillance for *T. spiralis*.
Disease	Trichinosis (trichinellosis) first presents with gastrointestinal symptoms such as nausea, diarrhea, vomiting, fatigue, fever, and abdominal discomfort 1 to 2 days after infection. Additional symptoms, such as headaches, chills, coughs, eye swelling, aching joints and muscle pains, itchy skin, and/or constipation follow 2 to 8 weeks later. In mild infections symptoms subside within a few months. In severe cases victims may experience difficulty coordinating movements and may have heart and breathing problems. In the most severe cases, death can occur.
Implicated Foods	Raw and undercooked pork and wild game products are the primary food vehicles. Currently infection through consumption of undercooked game is the most common route. A recent outbreak implicated cougar jerky. All commercial hams are specifically processed to USDA guidelines to kill trichinae.
Susceptible Populations	All peoples are susceptible to infection by *T. spiralis*.
Human Transmission	There is no person-to-person transmission of *T. spiralis*. The only transmission occurs from eating muscle (meat).
Controls	COOK • Cook all meats to a uniform internal temperature of 170°F or greater. Curing (salting), drying, smoking, or microwaving meat does not consistently kill infective worms. • If you are feeding farm animals or pets, cook their feed too, or buy commercially prepared food. CLEAN meat grinders thoroughly if you prepare your own sausage or other ground meats.

TABLE 2.2   Descriptions of Specific Foodborne and Waterborne Parasites *(continued)*

Controls *(cont.)*	PUBLIC HEALTH • Regulations require that food fed to animals be pasteurized to kill *T. spiralis*. • Commercially prepared hams and other processed meats are prepared to be *Trichinella*-free.
Selected Educational Materials	• Fact Sheet: Trichinosis (Trichinellosis) (245)

Sources: References 9, 13, 179, 245–248

TABLE 2.3   Descriptions of Specific Foodborne and Waterborne Viruses

Hepatitis	
General Characteristics	Hepatitis viruses are typically bloodborne. Only hepatitis A is foodborne. In the latest foodborne-disease outbreak summaries (1993 to 1997), hepatitis A was responsible for 23 confirmed outbreaks, representing 729 cases and no deaths (Table 2.4). Hepatitis A is not included in FoodNet active surveillance.
Disease	Hepatitis A is a liver disease that presents with jaundice, fatigue, abdominal pain, loss of appetite, intermittent nausea, and diarrhea. Remission usually occurs in less than 2 months; a few persons are ill for as long as 6 months. The average incubation period for hepatitis A is 28 days (range: 15 to 50 days). Relapse after remission occurs in about 15% of cases. About a third of Americans have immunity from past exposure.
Implicated Foods	Most implicated foods are molluscan shellfish or ready-to-eat foods prepared by infected food handlers. Recent outbreaks include: • Lettuce contaminated before distribution to restaurants • Raw oysters from beds contaminated with human feces • Frozen strawberries contaminated by an infected food handler • Raw salad ingredients contaminated by an infected food handler • Sandwiches and cookies contaminated by infected food handlers • An ice-slush beverage contaminated by an infected handler
Susceptible Populations	Hepatitis A can affect anyone who has not acquired immunity.
Human Transmission	Food handlers can contaminate food with the hepatitis A virus, but foodborne outbreaks from hepatitis A transmitted by food handlers are uncommon in the United States. The more likely transmission is through raw or undercooked shellfish.
Controls	CLEAN • Wash hands thoroughly after toileting or changing a diaper. • Do not prepare foods for others if you have diarrhea. COOK shellfish. See Chapter 6 for information on cooking. Cooking may not destroy all viruses contaminating shellfish. PUBLIC HEALTH • Sewage control and water treatment reduce exposure of the public to hepatitis A. • Surveillance of fishing waters and oyster beds reduces contamination of shellfish.
Selected Educational Materials	• Hepatitis A Fact Sheet (249)

Sources: References 9, 13, 19, 20–22, 125, 249–252

Norwalk Virus Group	
General Characteristics	The Norwalk virus is one of a heterogenous group of viruses also called small round structured viruses (SRSVs) or the Norwalk-like family of agents (NLV). In the latest foodborne-disease outbreak summaries (1993 to 1997), Norwalk and Norwalk-like virus were responsible

TABLE 2.3   Descriptions of Specific Foodborne and Waterborne Viruses *(continued)*

General Characteristics (*cont.*)	for 9 confirmed outbreaks, representing 1,233 cases and 0 deaths (Table 2.4). There is no active surveillance for Norwalk agents in the United States.
Disease	Common symptoms of NLV disease—nausea, vomiting, nonbloody diarrhea, and abdominal cramps—occur after an incubation period of 12 to 48 hours and typically last 12 to 60 hours. Adults have died during illness caused by Norwalk-like viruses, presumably from electrolyte imbalance. No long-term sequelae of NLV infection have been reported.
Implicated Foods	Shellfish that grow in fecally contaminated water concentrate enteric viruses in their tissues. Steaming these shellfish for as long as 10 minutes may fail to inactivate all viral agents.
	When foods other than shellfish are implicated in viral gastroenteritis outbreaks, the contamination usually comes from food handlers or contaminated water, and the foods at greatest risk are those that require handling without subsequent cooking, such as salads and other ready-to-eat foods. One example comes from the U.S. Air Force Academy, where celery stalks were washed in contaminated water and used in chicken salad.
Susceptible Populations	Presumably, all persons are susceptible to initial infections. Immunity appears to be transient. About half of the adults in the United States have some level of immunity.
Human Transmission	Viruses in the Norwalk virus group can be transmitted person-to-person. Infected food handlers can contaminate food.
Controls	CLEAN hands thoroughly before preparing or serving food.
	COOK foods thoroughly. See Chapter 6 for information on cooking. The Norwalk agent is stable at lower cooking temperatures, including steaming; boiling for 10 minutes probably inactivates it, but boiling is not a popular preparation method for shellfish.

Sources: References 9, 13, 21–26, 250, 253–255

Rotavirus	
General Characteristics	Unlike most viruses, which contain a single strand of RNA, rotaviruses contain double-stranded RNA surrounded by a double protein coat. Rotavirus incidence is not reported in CDC's foodborne-disease outbreak data, and there is no active surveillance of rotavirus in the United States.
Disease	After an incubation period of about 2 days, rotavirus infection may present with vomiting for 3 days followed by watery diarrhea for 3 to 8 days. Fever and abdominal pain frequently accompany the gastrointestinal symptoms. In some cases temporary lactose intolerance is a sequela. Some children will be asymptomatic.
	Rotavirus is the most common cause of severe diarrhea among children. Approximately 3.5 million cases occur in the United States each year. It infects virtually every child in the United States by the age of 4 years. Rotavirus infection accounts for 35% of diarrheal hospital stays and an estimated 75 to 125 child deaths annually in the United States. Worldwide the toll is much higher—an estimated 140 million cases and over a half-million deaths annually.
Implicated Foods	One outbreak has been specifically confirmed; the vehicle was sandwiches.
Susceptible Populations	Children are typically the most susceptible to rotavirus infection. In the United States most persons have been infected by age 4 and develop an immunity. The immunity can be overridden by exposures to very high levels of the virus.
Human Transmission	Rotavirus is usually transmitted person-to-person. Infected food handlers can contaminate ready-to-eat foods with rotavirus.
Controls	CLEAN hands thoroughly and frequently, especially after any contact with a child who has diarrhea or after diapering a child.
Selected Educational Materials	• Fact Sheet on Childhood Diseases and Conditions: What You Should Know about . . . Rotavirus in the Child Care Setting (256)
	• Rotavirus (257)

Sources: References 9, 22, 256–258

Major **acute** gastrointestinal symptoms include diarrhea and vomiting. Agents that disrupt electrolyte balance in the intestinal tract by interfering specifically with electrolyte transport or by damaging the intestinal mucosa cause diarrhea. Severe diarrhea occurs when the ratio of water to solids in feces is very high and many gastrointestinal cells are sloughed, causing **rice-water stools.** The most severe **cases** of diarrhea occur when the mucosa is badly damaged. In those cases stools may be black or red because they contain blood and may be particularly foul smelling because of fat malabsorption or degradation of bile acids. Vomiting is a neural reflex triggered by activation of receptors in the intestine. These receptors stimulate the brain to signal the diaphragm and abdominal muscles to eject the offending food. Abdominal cramps, nausea, and headache often accompany diarrhea and/or vomiting.

In addition to acute symptoms, some foodborne infections have chronic **sequelae,** or secondary symptoms. These may occur years after the initial infection. Examples of these sequelae are **reactive arthritis** (11) and Guillain-Barre syndrome (9). It is difficult to link these sequelae to the original infections because data are not systematically collected, the acute symptoms may not have presented with the original infection, and the sequelae may occur as an **autoimmune** response (12). Additionally, the chronic sequelae may be different in different hosts (11).

Characteristic onset times and the presence or absence of fever are important in differentiating foodborne infections from foodborne intoxications, because many other symptoms are similar for both. Symptoms from foodborne infections typically take eight hours to several weeks to present. It takes this amount of time for microorganisms to penetrate body defenses, reproduce, and cause symptoms. Also, infections usually produce fever as an inflammatory response. By contrast, acute symptoms from foodborne intoxications typically occur within one to seven hours of consuming the offending food and do not produce fevers.

One way of describing the severity of foodborne illness is the **death-to-case ratio** for the toxic agent. A low death-to-case ratio indicates that an illness is not life-threatening. A high death-to-case ratio means that an illness is life-threatening. The death-to-case ratio is a calculated value based on 1,000 cases. To compute this ratio the number of deaths from known cases is adjusted to reflect the number of deaths that would have occurred proportionally in 1,000 cases; for example, if 2 deaths occurred in 100 cases, the death-to-case ratio would be 20. Intoxication caused by *Bacillus cereus* has a death-to-case ratio of 0, meaning that it has caused no known deaths over the most recent 5-year reporting period (13). Intoxication caused by *Clostridium botulinum* has a death-to-case ratio of 18 for the same reporting period, indicating that 18 per 1,000 cases of known outcome resulted in death. The death-to-case ratio may change for different reporting periods.

TYPES OF TOXIC AGENTS

Bacteria

Bacteria cause more confirmed foodborne illness and more confirmed deaths from foodborne illness in the United States than all other agents combined (13–14; see Table 2.4). These illnesses and deaths result in very large productivity

TABLE 2.4 Number of Reported Foodborne-Disease Outbreaks, Cases, and Death, by **Etiology**—United States,[a] 1993–1997[b]

Etiology	Outbreaks		Cases		Deaths	
	No.	%	No.	%	No.	%
Bacterial						
Bacillus cereus	14	0.5	691	0.8	0	0.0
Brucella	1	<0.1	19	<0.1	0	0.0
Campylobacter	25	0.9	539	0.6	1	3.4
Clostridium botulinum	13	0.5	56	<0.1	1	3.4
Clostridium perfringens	57	2.1	2,772	3.2	0	0.0
Escherichia coli	84	3.1	3,260	3.8	8	27.6
Listeria monocytogenes	3	0.1	100	0.1	2	6.9
Salmonella	357	13.0	32,610	37.9	13	44.9
Shigella	43	1.6	1,555	1.8	0	0.0
Staphylococcus aureus	42	1.5	1,413	1.6	1	3.4
Streptococcus, group A	1	<0.1	122	0.1	0	0.0
Streptococcus, other	1	<0.1	6	<0.1	0	0.0
Vibrio cholerae	1	<0.1	2	<0.1	0	0.0
Vibrio parahaemolyticus	5	1.8	40	<0.1	0	0.0
Yersinia enterocolitica	2	<0.1	27	<0.1	1	3.4
Other Bacterial	6	0.2	609	0.7	1	3.4
Total Bacterial	655	23.8	43,821	50.9	28	96.6
Chemical						
Ciguatoxin	60	2.2	205	0.2	0	0.0
Heavy metals	4	0.1	17	<0.1	0	0.0
Monosodium glutamate	1	<0.1	2	<0.1	0	0.0
Mushroom poisoning	7	0.3	21	<0.1	0	0.0
Scombrotoxin	69	2.5	297	0.3	0	0.0
Shellfish	1	<0.1	3	<0.1	0	0.0
Other Chemical	6	0.2	31	<0.1	0	0.0
Total Chemical	148	5.4	576	0.7	0	0.0
Parasitic						
Giardia lamblia	4	0.1	45	<0.1	0	0.0
Trichinella spiralis	2	<0.1	19	<0.1	0	0.0
Other Parasitic	13	0.5	2,261	2.6	0	0.0
Total Parasitic	19	0.7	2,325	2.7	0	0.0
Viral						
Hepatitis A	23	0.8	729	0.8	0	0.0
Norwalk	9	0.3	1,233	1.4	0	0.0
Other Viral	24	0.9	2,104	2.4	0	0.0
Total Viral	56	2.0	4,066	4.7	0	0.0
Confirmed Etiology	878	31.9	50,788	59.0	28	96.6
Unknown Etiology	1,873	68.1	35,270	41.0	1	3.4
Total 1993–1997	2,751	100.0	86,058	100.0	29	100.0

Source: Compiled from Olsen SJ, MacKinnon LC, Goulding JS, et al. Surveillance for foodborne-disease outbreaks—United States, 1993–1997. *MMWR.* 2000;49(SS-01):1–51. Available at: ftp://ftp.cdc.gov/pub/Publications/mmwr/SS/SS4901.pdf. Accessed May 12, 2001.

[a]Includes Guam, Puerto Rico, and the U.S. Virgin Islands.

[b]Totals might vary from summed components because of rounding.

losses to the American public (15). Foodborne bacterial illnesses may be intoxications, invasive infections, or noninvasive infections **(toxicoinfections),** depending on the bacterium and the conditions of exposure. Table 2.1 outlines characteristics of major foodborne bacterial pathogens and educational materials that are useful in dietetic practice.

The number of viable bacterial cells required to cause foodborne illness vary according to the susceptibility of the host and the characteristics of the bacterium. Some bacteria have very low **infectious doses (ID$_{50}$)** and are easily transmitted person-to-person or in foods with low levels of contamination. Examples of bacteria with low infectious doses are *Salmonella typhi* and *Shigellae*. Bacteria that **colonize** individuals require much larger doses to cause illness—usually in the range of 10^6 active cells. Usually these bacteria must grow in foods before there are enough organisms to cause disease. *Clostridium perfringens* is an example of these bacteria.

Some bacteria have both vegetative (growing) and **spore** (protective) forms. The vegetative forms are destroyed during appropriate cooking processes. The spore forms are harder to destroy during typical cooking processes and may not be destroyed even by boiling temperatures. *B. cereus*, *C. botulinum*, and *C. perfringens* are spore-forming bacteria. *C. botulinum* spores can outgrow and produce a potentially lethal toxin in inappropriately processed canned foods. For that reason, canning temperature-time recommendations for meats, vegetables, and other low-acid foods are developed to destroy *C. botulinum* spores. These recommendations require pressures above atmospheric pressure (pressure canners or retorts) to reach high enough temperatures to destroy the spores.

Bacteria must have appropriate nutrients and environmental conditions to grow in foods (9, 16). Typical growth requirements for foodborne pathogenic bacteria are:

- **pH** above 4.6
- **Water activity (a$_w$)** above 0.85
- Temperatures in the range of 40°F to 140°F (4°C to 60°C; **danger zone**)
- Oxygen requirements depending upon the organism
- Nutrient requirements depending upon the organism

Foods that support the rapid growth of bacteria are called "potentially hazardous foods" (16). They must be kept refrigerated or frozen during marketing and home storage. Some bacteria grow outside the typical requirements for growth. For example, while most foodborne pathogenic bacteria require oxygen for growth (aerobes), some can grow at low levels of oxygen **(facultative anaerobes)** or without oxygen (anaerobes). Both facultative anaerobes and anaerobes can grow in foods packaged to exclude air. As another example, while most bacteria do not grow at recommended refrigerator temperatures (below 41°F/5°C), *Clostridium botulinum* (types B-nonproteolytic, E and F), *Escherichia coli*, *Listeria monocytogenes,* and *Yersinia enterocolitica* do grow slowly at those temperatures (9). These growth characteristics make some bacteria particularly problematic for some foods.

BACTERIAL INTOXICATIONS. *B. cereus*, *C. botulinum*, and *S. aureus* cause foodborne intoxications by producing toxins when they grow in food. Although streptococci are usually associated with foodborne infections, they can produce toxic monoamines, including tyramine and 2-phenylethylamine, when they contaminate milk used in cheese manufacture or other foods. Foodborne intoxications are different from foodborne infections because ingestion of the preformed toxin can cause injury, even if the pathogen itself is not consumed. Bacterial intoxications are confirmed more often than other chemical intoxications in the United States (13). However, they are confirmed less often and cause fewer deaths than bacterial infections (13). The only bacterial intoxication with a high death-to-case ratio is **botulism,** caused by *C. botulinum*.

Most bacterial toxins are **enterotoxins** that cause vomiting or diarrhea within hours of consuming contaminated food. When vomiting is the primary gastrointestinal symptom, onset time is usually from one to seven hours. This would be typical for staphylococcal and *B. cereus* **emetic** intoxications. Diarrhea and other symptoms take longer to present. *C. botulinum* produces a neural toxin that prevents the release of acetylcholine produced by nerve endings, resulting in weakened muscle response that leads to paralysis and respiratory failure unless treated successfully with antitoxin.

BACTERIAL INFECTIONS. Foodborne bacterial infections cause more cases of confirmed foodborne illness in the United States than all other agents combined (13–14). In addition, foodborne bacterial infections are responsible for more deaths than all other agents combined (13–14). Based on the FoodNet active surveillance system (14), foodborne infectious disease incidence was highest for **salmonellosis, campylobacteriosis,** and **shigellosis** for all reporting sites.

Most infectious bacteria are invasive, causing serious illnesses that present with fever, common **gastroenteritis,** and occasional characteristic symptoms when the bacteria invade other tissues. Infections that involve organs outside the gastrointestinal tract are usually more severe. Current research with *Listeria monocytogenes* suggests that invasion requires a "virulence factor" called "internalin," which interacts with a protein within the brush border of the intestine to allow admission of *Listeria* (17). When the virulence factor is missing, the bacterium is not invasive and cannot cause serious foodborne disease. Similar virulence factors may exist for other invasive organisms.

Campylobacteriosis, salmonellosis, shigellosis, **yersiniosis,** and some *E. coli* infections present largely with fever and severe gastroenteritis. In fact, abdominal pain from yersiniosis is so severe that it is often mistaken for appendicitis. Infections caused by streptococci also cause tonsillitis, scarlet fever, and rheumatic fever when they penetrate the circulatory system. **Listeriosis** can cause a range of symptoms in pregnant women and their infants, including pharyngitis, granulomatosis infantisepticum, meningitis, **encephalitis,** stillbirth, or abortion. *Listeria*-caused pharyngitis and meningitis have also been noted in adults with weakened immune systems.

Foodborne infections may present with sequelae three to four weeks after the acute infection. Infections from five foodborne pathogens—*Campylobacter jejuni, Salmonellae, Shigellae, Yersiniae,* or *E. coli*—may lead to reactive arthritis after the infection is over, especially for individuals carrying the gene responsible for producing the human leucocyte **antigen** HLA-B27 (11–12). The antigens from the bacteria mimic the HLA antigen. Individuals with the HLA-B27 gene are eighteen times more likely to develop reactive arthritis than those who do not carry the gene (12). Another sequela for salmonellosis, shigellosis, campylobacteriosis, yersiniosis, and *E. coli* infection is Reiter's syndrome. Individuals with the HLA-B27 gene are thirty-seven times more likely to develop Reiter's syndrome than those who do not carry the gene (12). Campylobacteriosis can lead to Guillain-Barre syndrome. While not proven to cause Crohn's disease, antigens to *L. monocytogenes, E. coli,* and *Streptococci* have been demonstrated in intestinal tissues from persons with Crohn's disease (18).

Bacteria that cause noninvasive infections produce chemical toxins that actually cause the disease symptoms. Noninvasive bacterial infections are also called toxicoinfections because symptoms result from toxins formed in the host and not preformed in food. *Clostridium perfringens,* some strains of *E. coli, Vibrio cholerae,* and *V. parahaemolyticus* produce toxic chemicals inside their hosts. Infant botulism is also a noninvasive infection, because *C. botulinum* spores from honey-containing formula or on honey-coated pacifiers outgrow and produce botulinum toxin in the less acidic gastrointestinal tract of infants. Of these, *C. perfringens* infections are the most common and the least severe, with diarrhea onset typically in eight to fourteen hours. The vibrio infections cause severe dehydration, occasionally resulting in death. Infection with enterotoxigenic *E. coli* results in fever and severe gastrointestinal distress. **Enterohemorrhagic** *E. coli* infections result in hemorrhagic colitis, a bloody diarrhea. More severe syndromes caused by enterohemorrhagic *E. coli* include **hemolytic uremic syndrome (HUS),** a leading cause of acute kidney failure in children, and **thrombotic thrombocytopenic purpura (TTP),** which can result in blood clots in the brain, largely in the elderly.

Parasites

Parasites are different from most foodborne infectious organisms because they have complicated life cycles that require specific hosts for survival. They do not multiply outside their specific hosts, even in nutrient-rich foods. Human foodborne and waterborne parasites multiply in humans to cause disease symptoms. The major classes of human foodborne parasites important in the United States are helminths (worms) and **protozoa.** The helminths include nematodes (roundworms), cestodes (tapeworms), and trematodes (flukes). Specific species are described in Table 2.2.

Although trichinosis and **giardiasis** are the only parasitic foodborne diseases reported in CDC outbreak reports (13), several additional parasites—*Cryptosporidium parvum* and *Cyclospora cayetanensis*—have been responsible for large foodborne and waterborne outbreaks recently and are included in FoodNet reports (14). Foodborne parasitic diseases are much more common in areas of the world where overcrowding, poor sanitation, and malnutrition are **endemic** and in populations that commonly consume raw or undercooked flesh foods.

In general, parasites damage tissue during their reproduction and growth. They also reduce nutrient absorption by competing for nutrients in the host's gastrointestinal tract. When parasites damage the intestinal mucosa, they usually cause diarrhea and may cause severe pain, mimicking a perforating ulcer or acute appendicitis. When parasites circulate in the bloodstream, they may cause damage to other organs.

Viruses

Viruses are noncellular parasites that cannot carry out any life processes on their own. They consist of nucleic acids and protein. Viruses do not contain the cellular organelles required to produce energy, and they must enter a susceptible **host cell** to replicate. Those that cause human diseases cannot multiply in food. The original inoculum determines infectivity. Viruses become foodborne when they are transmitted to food by human food handlers or human waste (for example, sewage-contaminated water). They cause foodborne infections only when there are receptors for them on human gastrointestinal mucosal cell membranes. Viral diseases result from death of infected cells. This can occur during the replication process or by destruction of the infected cells by the host's immune response. Table 2.3 outlines characteristics of major foodborne viral pathogens and educational materials that are useful in dietetic practice.

Viral control of a host cell begins when nuclear protein from the virus directs the host cell to cease making its own RNA from its DNA template. The virus then begins its own replication. Although the total viral mass produced is small compared to the total cell contents, the normal activities of the host cell stop for viral replication. Often the host cell is not permanently affected; however, if enough cells are affected, metabolic abnormalities or tissue damage may result.

Hepatitis A virus and the Norwalk virus group are both reported in CDC outbreak data. In the most recent reporting period (1993 to 1997), hepatitis A was the ninth leading cause of foodborne-disease outbreaks, and **Norwalk-like** viruses were the twelfth leading cause (13). The only other virus that has been implicated in foodborne acute gastroenteritis in the United States is rotavirus. Transmission of polio virus can be foodborne, although there have been no outbreaks in the United States in several decades. The viruses that cause genital herpes and AIDS are not foodborne. They cannot survive outside the living primate host and are not viable in food.

Two principal modes of transmission are associated with viral foodborne outbreaks: contamination of food during preparation by an infected food handler and contamination of food, such as shellfish or produce, before it reaches the retail establishment. Outbreaks of viral infections may be unifocal or multifocal. In a unifocal outbreak one food handler contaminates food or there is one retail source of contaminated foods. In a multifocal outbreak food is contaminated at a source and distributed to many retail outlets. Examples of unifocal outbreaks are a Florida restaurant outbreak involving sixty-one people from five states who had consumed raw oysters, raw scallops, or baked oysters, apparently harvested illegally from outside approved waters, and a 1988 North Carolina outbreak of thirty-two cases of hepatitis traced to a single restaurant where iced tea prepared by an infected food handler was the vehicle (19). An example of a multifocal outbreak is a hepatitis outbreak traced to lettuce that was apparently contaminated with human waste before distribution to several restaurants (20).

Viruses in molluscan shellfish, such as clams, mussels, oysters, and cockles, contribute prominently to gastroenteritis outbreaks (13, 21–26). It is difficult to assure virus-free shellfish because shellfish concentrate **enteric** viruses from fecally contaminated water in their tissues when they filter feed and because their potentially pathogen-containing gastrointestinal tracts are not removed prior to consumption. Waters meeting bacteriologic standards may still contain viral agents, which are poorly removed by **depuration** (a technique in which shellfish are flushed with clean saline water treated with ultraviolet light to remove pathogens). Also, popular cooking methods do not inactivate the viruses, if they are present. Shellfish are typically eaten raw or lightly cooked, and they may protect viruses from thermal inactivation; steaming for as long as ten minutes may fail to inactivate all viral agents.

Prions

Prions are PROteinaceous INfectious agents. Prion proteins (PrP) are small glycosylated protein molecules found in brain cell membranes. An infective prion is not a complete living organism because it has no associated nucleic acid. It is an agent that replicates by distorting other prions. This process, sometimes called **"recruitment,"** may occur when a distorted molecule reaches the prions in the brain cell membranes of a host and acts as a template. Instead of having a helical tertiary structure, infective prions have flattened sheetlike shapes that are very heat resistant and protease resistant (27). Although prions are considered infective, they do not cause fevers or inflammatory responses in their hosts (28–32).

Current research suggests that several **Transmissible Spongiform Encephalopathies (TSEs),** including Bovine Spongiform Encephalopathy (BSE), scrapie in sheep, and **Creutzfeldt-Jacob disease (CJD)** in humans, are caused by infective prions (27–28). While brain cell proteins of different species have different compositions, research suggests that a new variant of CJD (nvCJD) may have been transmitted from beef to humans before 1989 when bovine offal was used in animal feed (27–28, 32–33). Because it takes a long time for foreign prions to "recruit" host prions, it takes almost a decade for TSEs to present after exposure.

The disease course for nvCJD in humans includes behavioral changes, ataxia, progressive dementia, and death. On autopsy, PrP plaques are found throughout the cerebrum and cerebellum. Although cases of BSE and nvCJD have been found in Europe (27–28, 32–33), no cases of BSE or nvCJD have been found in the United States, even with eight years of active surveillance (28–32, 34). However, the following TSEs have been found in the United States: scrapie in sheep and goats, transmissible mink encephalopathy, and chronic wasting disease of deer and elk (28). Also, reports confirm iatrogenic transmission of CJD from a corneal transplant, electroencephalographic depth electrodes, neurosurgical procedures, cadaveric dura mater grafts, and pituitary hormone administration, although no CJD deaths have been reported for persons with hemophilia A, hemophilia B, thalassemia, or sickle cell disease who routinely receive blood products (31–32).

Emerging Pathogens

Emerging pathogens are microorganisms that are newly recognized as causes of foodborne disease within a specific context (35–39). They include both microorganisms not previously identified as public health threats that begin to cause disease and microorganisms that cause foodborne disease in a new way. One example of a microorganism that emerged to become a foodborne pathogen is *Escherichia coli*. *E. coli* was used in school science labs as a harmless bacterium in experiments for years. At some point strains of *E. coli* began producing **shiga-like toxins** and causing foodborne infections. Examples of microorganisms that cause diseases in new ways include microorganisms that are associated with new foods or that appear in new geographic locations; for example, *Cyclospora cayetanensis* was a previously unknown pathogen in the United States until 1996, when imported raspberries became a vehicle for this parasite.

Each emergence is characteristic, and emergence is hard to predict (39). Past emergence of foodborne pathogens has been associated with bacterial mutations; changes in food production, marketing, and consumption patterns; and improvements in clinical diagnostics. Further, strategic planning for emerging pathogens is challenging because the agent, vehicle, and location of the threat are unknown. *Emerging Infectious Diseases*, a free, searchable, online journal from the Centers for Disease Control and Prevention (http://www.cdc.gov/ncidod/eid) focuses on this issue.

Chemicals in Food

All foods are made up of chemicals. Some chemicals in food, such as vitamins, minerals, cyanide, caffeine, fungal toxins, and bacterial toxins, are **biologically active**. This means that they affect body processes. Some chemical effects are beneficial and some are harmful. While most chemicals in food are biologically inert, there are both naturally occurring and added chemicals that are potentially toxic.

Testing Chemicals for Use in Foods

Chemicals that will become a part of food are tested prior to their approval by government agencies. These chemicals include **food additives,** pesticides, and cleaning aids. The testing methods examine both short-term (acute) and long-term (chronic) potential risks. They also consider total exposure to a chemical, not simply the exposure from a single food.

Chemicals may cause many different types of toxic effects. These include **physiological, biochemical,** and mutagenic effects. Common examples of physiological effects are diarrhea and vomiting. Potential biochemical effects include inhibition of cellular-level energy cycles. **Mutagens** cause changes in genetic material; therefore, they may be **teratogens** or carcinogens. Teratogens cause birth defects. Carcinogens cause or promote cancer. Mutagens that change DNA in germ cells (eggs or sperm) or fetal tissues during development are usually teratogens. Mutagens that change DNA in somatic cells (liver, kidney, and so forth) may be carcinogens. Typically, scientists test suspect chemicals **in vitro** to determine mutagenicity. Then they test mutagen-positive agents in laboratory animals to determine teratogenicity and carcinogenicity. Toxicity statements describe all of these harmful effects.

BOX 2.1   Units of Measurement in Food Safety

Different units of measurement may be used to describe different aspects of food safety. Dosages state the amount of a toxic agent consumed by an individual. They can be expressed as the amount of chemical per unit of body mass or as numbers of pathogen per individual. For example, 25 mg/kg of body mass (1,875 mg for a 75 kg person), might be the dosage of sodium in a special diet. Actual numbers of organisms consumed may be given. For example, an individual drinking creek water on a camping trip might consume ten *Cryptosporidium* **oocysts.**

Scientists describe the amount of a chemical in food as a part of its weight, 1 ppm (parts per million), for example. The level of pathogen contamination in food is the number of organisms per unit of weight, for example, 10^5 *Salmonella*/g. The level of microbial contamination on a surface is the number of organisms per unit of area, for example, 10 *Salmonella*/cm^2.

Example

SR, who weighs 154 lb, consumed 100 g of a milkshake that contained 10^5 *Salmonella*/g and 189 ppm of vanillin.

1. How many *Salmonella* are in 1 g of milkshake?
   1 gram of milkshake has:
   10^5 *Salmonella* = (10)(10)(10)(10)(10)
    = 100,000 *Salmonella*

2. How many *Salmonella* did SR consume?
   (100 g milkshake)(10^5 *Salmonella*/g milkshake) = 10,000,000 *Salmonella*

3. How much vanillin did SR consume?
   (100 g milkshake)(189 ppm vanillin) = (100 g)(0.000189)
    = 0.0189 g vanillin
    = 18.9 mg vanillin

4. What was SR's dose of vanillin?
   Dose = 18.9 mg vanillin/154 lb
    = 18.9 mg vanillin/70 kg
    = 0.27 mg vanillin/kg
    = 270 µg vanillin/kg

The amount of a chemical used in safety testing is described by dosage—the amount of the chemical per unit of body mass (Box 2.1). In safety testing, special names are given to marker dosages:

- The **no observable adverse effect level (NOAEL)** is the largest dose of a chemical to which an individual may have acute exposure with no observable adverse effects.
- The **effective dose (ED)** is the minimum amount of a chemical required to produce an observable effect in an individual after short-term (acute) exposure. It is also called the threshold for a chemical effect. ED_{50} is the amount of the chemical required to produce an effect in a population; that is, an intake of the chemical at the ED_{50} will produce an effect in half the population. The ED_{50} is, therefore, always greater than the NOAEL. A single chemical can cause different effects; each of those effects will have an ED_{50}.
- The **maximum tolerated dose (MTD)** is the largest amount of a chemical that causes an adverse effect without causing a severe health problem.
- The **lethal dose (LD)** is the lethal dose for acute exposure, and the LD_{50} is the intake that will cause death to half the population.
- The **reference dose (RfD)** and the **acceptable daily intake (ADI)** are the largest amounts of a chemical to which an individual may have

chronic exposure with no observable adverse effects. These levels are usually calculated to be about $1/100$ of the NOAEL and are the daily dose that is acceptable over time. This margin of safety allows for species differences between the animals in which the chemical was tested and for differences among humans. Some chemicals may accumulate in body tissues and cause an individual to exceed the NOAEL. Their RfDs/ADIs would typically be even lower than 1 percent of the NOAEL.

- The **lifetime average daily dose (LADD)** is the estimated dose to an individual averaged over a lifetime of seventy years. It is used primarily in assessments of carcinogenic risk.

Table 2.5 describes the typical acute biological actions of chemicals for populations. Populations can consume a potentially toxic chemical with no harmful effect up to the NOAEL. The NOAEL is exceeded when an adverse effect is mea-

TABLE 2.5   Characteristics of Foodborne Allergens

Food	Identified Allergenic Proteins	Label Identifiers	Heat Stability
Peanuts	alpha-arachin conarachin I peanut agglutinin (minor phospholipase D (minor) Ara h 1 (glycoprotein) Ara h 2 (glycoprotein)	peanuts, peanut flour, peanut meal, peanut oil	Peanut allergenic proteins are stable to heat; therefore, people will react to both raw and cooked peanuts.)
Fish	Gad c 1 (parvalbumin from codfish)	Name of fish must be on label.	Fish allergenic proteins are stable to heat; therefore, people will react to both raw and cooked fish.
Crustaceans	Pen a 2 (tropomyosin from shrimp) Pen a 1	Name of seafood must be on label.	Crustacean allergenic proteins are stable to heat; therefore, people will react to both raw and cooked crustaceans.
Tree nuts	methionine-rish 2S albumin (Brazil nuts)	Name of nut must be on label.	
Eggs	Gal d 2 (ovalbumin) Gal d 1 (ovomucoid) Gal d 3 (conalbumin) Gal d 4 (lysozyme) alpha-livetin	albumin, egg whites, egg yolks, lecithin	Ovomucoid, the major allergenic protein, is very heat stable; therefore, most people will react to both raw and cooked egg products.
Milk	beta-lactoglobulin alpha-casein bovine serum albumin alpha-lactalbumin	casein, caseinate, calcium, caseinate, cream, actalbumin, lactose, nonfat milk solids, sodium caseinate, whey	Beta-casein and bovine serum albumin are not stable to heat, but beta-lactoglobulin and alpha-lactalbumin are heat stable. Some people may react to fresh milk but not to cooked milk. Most people will be allergic to all forms of milk.

Sources: Adapted from Bindslev-Jensen C, Poulsen LK. *In vitro* diagnostic methods in the evaluation of food hypersensitivity. In: Metcalfe DD, Sampson HA, Simon RA, eds. *Food Allergy: Adverse Reactions to Foods and Food Additives.* 2nd ed. Cambridge, MA: Blackwell Science Ltd; 1997; and Reference 259.

surable (the ED_{50}). With continued levels of exposure, the population consumes the maximum tolerated dose (MTD), then the lethal dose (LD_{50}). Scientists describe the effects of chemicals for populations instead of for individuals because biological variability within the population and factors such as overall health status determine response differences, although such individual differences are greater for infections than for intoxications.

Table 2.5 can be adapted to apply to longer-term effects. For longer exposures, the terms "reference dose" (RfD) or "acceptable daily intake" (ADI) are used instead of NOAEL.

New food ingredients and compounds that will come into contact with foods must be approved by FDA prior to their use in foods (40). Before approval for use of such compounds occurs, FDA reviews the following information and holds public hearings:

- Results of acute toxicity tests in at least two species of animals to determine the LD_{50}
- Results of subacute toxicity tests in at least two species of animals to determine the NOAEL and the ADI
- Results of chronic toxicity testing in at least two species of animals throughout their lifetimes to determine potential carcinogenicity
- Results of pharmokinetic studies to determine the absorption, distribution, metabolism, and elimination of the chemical and its metabolites
- Results of reproductive studies to determine the effect on litter size, litter weight, number of viable young, and teratogenicity

In granting approval for use of a food additive or food contact surface, the FDA sets limits not only on the amount of the additive that can be included in a particular food or package, but also on the types of foods in which an additive or packaging material can be used. This decision is based on typical food consumption patterns and is designed to minimize the likelihood that an individual will consume the ED_{50}. A more detailed explanation of the approval process for food additives can be found in FDA's *Food Additives and Premarket Approval* (40). The Environmental Protection Agency (EPA) uses similar tests for its approval of pesticides and cleaning aids that may become a part of food during production or marketing (41).

Although tests for approval are rigorous, testing methods themselves are not direct measures that answer all questions about use. The data are extrapolated and interpreted by scientists to estimate risk. Examples of problems in collecting appropriate data and interpreting data appropriately include:

- Applying laboratory data to human exposure. Scientists determine potential toxic effects on humans using tests on experimental animals or in vitro. This information is useful but is not directly applicable to human beings. It also does not reflect the situation that faces a free-living human being who eats a mixed diet. In laboratory tests chemicals are purified and are tested alone or in combination with only one or two other factors. In addition, the dosage of the chemical is much higher than normal exposure levels. Exposure may be at a level higher than can be detoxified by the laboratory animals or may not reflect actual or expected exposure. However, information from laboratory observations is the basis of conservative policy decisions to protect the public's safety.

- Appropriateness of tests used to determine the carcinogenicity of a compound. Carcinogenicity is the ability of a compound to induce cancer in animals or humans. The most frequently used method for determination of the carcinogenicity of a compound is the Ames test, which is based on the ability of a compound to cause mutations in bacteria. Other tests used for determining the carcinogenicity of a food product include various cell culture tests, short-term animal-feeding trials, and long-term animal-feeding trials. The long-term animal-feeding trials are the most accurate. However, in such feeding trials, the level of the suspected carcinogen fed to the animals is the highest one that is not overtly toxic. This maximum tolerated dose frequently represents a large percentage of the diet and reflects an unrealistic eating pattern for human beings. The HERP (human exposure/rodent potency) index has been developed to address the issues that arise when results of animal testing are extrapolated using standard risk assessment calculations. HERP indexes are calculated by dividing human exposure to a substance by the amount of that substance that causes neoplasia in half the test animals.

- Effects of chronic exposures. Small chronic exposures to a chemical may result in large lifetime exposures or accumulations. Scientists cannot reliably determine effects of chronic exposure over the life span of a single individual. Therefore, scientists feed very large doses of test chemicals to laboratory animals over several generations to predict chronic toxicity. Petitions for new food additives must include predictions for lifetime exposure.

- Effects of chemical exposures over the life cycle. Scientists report physiological age at the time of exposure because smaller dosages of a chemical may be hazardous during periods of rapid growth for fetuses and small children. Petitions for new food additives include data through several generations to help predict teratogenic effects. Also the Food Quality Protection Act of 1996 focuses on effects of pesticides on pregnant women, fetuses, and children.

- Cumulative effects. Dosages of different chemicals may be cumulative. Chemicals that have similar effects or structures may be more toxic when consumed together than would be predicted from their individual dosages. The FDA and EPA consider this potential cumulative effect when evaluating new food additive or pesticide applications (40–41). That is one reason that approvals are for single food or crop categories and not for general use.

Food Additives

There are currently over three thousand food additives approved for use in the United States. The Food Additive Amendment was added to the Food, Drug, and Cosmetic Act in 1958. Part of this amendment defined a food additive as any substance the intended use of which results or may reasonably be expected to result, directly or indirectly, in its becoming a component or otherwise affecting the characteristics of any food (including any substance intended for use in producing, manufacturing, packing, processing, preparing, treating, packaging, transporting, or holding food; and including any source of radiation intended for any such use), if such substance is not generally recognized among experts qualified by scientific training and experience to evaluate its safety, as having been adequately shown through scientific procedures (or in the case of a substance used in food prior to January 1, 1958, through either scientific procedures, or experience based on common use in food) to be safe under the conditions of its intended use (42).

Based on this amendment, food additives must be evaluated for safety prior to inclusion in foods and periodically thereafter (43–44). Approved additives are considered to be either **generally recognized as safe (GRAS)** or regulated additives. GRAS additives are those that have been shown to be safe, usually based on a history of common usage in foods. They include such compounds as table salt, spices, and flavoring agents. The so-called regulated additives are permitted in foods under specified conditions and levels of use. These additives include such categories as preservatives, special dietary and nutritional additives, anticaking agents, flavoring agents, gums, specific-use additives, multipurpose additives, radiation, and processing aids. Approval for these additives follows the process outlined above. The FDA constantly monitors the safety of food additives and can withdraw approval for any food additive that is found to cause cancer or to be unsafe in other ways.

Color additives are not strictly considered to be food additives and are covered under the Color Additives Amendment to the Food, Drug, and Cosmetic Act (45). In general, color additives that are from natural sources may be added to foods without specific approval. Color additives that are from synthetic sources must be certified, which means that samples from that batch of color must be analyzed by the FDA to determine that they meet the chemical criteria for that color additive. These color additives are designated on the label as "FD&C" colors. In no instance can a color additive be used to color foods in an attempt to mislead the consumer about the wholesomeness of that product.

Toxic Chemicals in the Food Supply

Most chemicals can cause harm at exaggerated consumption levels. However, there are some chemicals that cause foodborne intoxications frequently enough to be tracked in CDC's foodborne-disease outbreak data or that are included in the *Healthy People 2010* objectives. These include seafood toxins, mushroom toxins, pesticide residues, and **heavy metals.** Additionally, mycotoxin levels in foods and animal feeds are monitored in the United States and are a problem in many developing countries.

SEAFOOD TOXINS. Most naturally occurring seafood toxins are produced by marine algae (**dinoflagellates;** Box 2.2). These toxins accumulate in fish and shellfish when they feed on the algae or on algae-consuming fish. The toxins are not detectable by sensory methods and are stable to normal cooking processes.

BOX 2.2   Dinoflagellate-Caused Seafood Poisoning Syndromes

The dinoflagellate-caused seafood poisoning syndromes are particularly hard to predict because the source algae vary in their distribution, and the toxin is progressively acquired through the food chain. Toxin levels are highest in filter-feeding shellfish and in large finfish. Seafood guides that describe safe harvesting areas are based on historical occurrences. Although proliferation of algae (bloom) causes water to turn reddish brown (red tide), shellfish can become toxic without bloom. Shellfish can destroy or excrete the toxins over time, but this detoxification takes one week to many months, depending on the amount of the toxin and the species of shellfish.

Of the five major seafood poisoning syndromes caused by marine algae (dinofla-gellates)—**amnesic shellfish poisoning (ASP), ciguatera fish poisoning (CFP),** diarrhetic shellfish poisoning (DSP), **neurotoxic shellfish poisoning (NSP),** and **paralytic shellfish poisoning (PSP)**—all except DSP have been found in fish or shellfish harvested from U.S. waters (46). Scombrotoxin, another seafood toxin complex, forms as bacteria grow on fish flesh during storage (47–48), making it a **spoilage** problem and not a naturally occurring toxin. **Tetrodotoxin** is a heat-stable neurotoxin found in puffer fish species, which may be produced by marine bacteria or by the fish itself (46, 48–49). **Haff disease,** caused by eating certain fish (buffalo fish in the United States), results in an unexplained destruction of skeletal muscle cells (50).

Amnesic shellfish poisoning (ASP) is also called **domoic acid poisoning (DAP;** 51–52). Typical ASP/DAP symptoms include vomiting, nausea, diarrhea, and abdominal cramps within twenty-four hours of consumption. Severe cases can include headaches, dizziness, confusion, disorientation, loss of short-term memory, motor weakness, seizures, cardiac arrhythmia, coma, and possibly death (51). Thus far, all deaths have been in the elderly (9). The characteristic symptom—short-term memory loss—resembles Alzheimer's disease and may be permanent. The mechanism of action is from release of excitatory amino acids and adenosine from neurons related to cell swelling and reversal of glutamate transporters (53) that allows the toxin to cross into the brain and interfere with nerve signal transmission. The toxin responsible for ASP/DAP has been found in shellfish from the northeast and northwest coasts of North America; viscera of Dungeness crab, tanner crab, red rock crab, and anchovies along the west coast of the United States; and in algae in the Gulf of Mexico (although not Gulf shellfish at this time; 46).

Ciguatera toxin contaminates more than four hundred species of tropical and subtropical fish caught in Pacific and Atlantic waters, largely from the extreme southeastern United States, Hawaii, and subtropical and tropical areas world-wide. The species most important to the U.S. mainland that may be contaminated with the toxin include amberjack, barracuda, moray eel, grouper, jack, Spanish and king mackerel, pompano, snapper, and triggerfish (9, 46). Ciguatera toxin is a mixture of neurotoxins, making symptoms of CFP variable. The most toxic part of the fish is usually the liver, then the gonads, then the muscle. Ciguatera toxin acts by increasing membrane permeability to sodium ions of excitable neurons. Symptoms usually present within six hours of consuming the toxin. First symptoms include tingling and numbness of the lips, tongue, and throat. Another neurological symptom that may present is reversal of temperature sensation—cold stimuli may feel hot or stinging or painful. Gastrointestinal distress, headache, and general muscle and joint pain usually follow and resolve in twenty-four hours. In severe cases, individuals may present with hypotension and bradycardia (that can change to tachycardia and hypertension) and/or paralysis, occasionally resulting in coma and death. Other nonspecific symptoms may include ataxia, depression, blisters, loss of hair and nails, headache, chills, blurred vision, metallic taste, loose or painful teeth, and ocular muscle pain. Recovery from CFP is slow and may take several weeks or longer (9, 48, 54). There has been one case of CFP in a pregnant woman (sixteen weeks of pregnancy); the mother recovered after eight weeks, and her newborn had normal neurological and respiratory reflexes at birth and developed normally in his first ten months (55). In the latest foodborne-disease outbreak summaries (1993 to 1997), ciguatoxin was responsible for 60 confirmed outbreaks, representing 205 cases and no deaths (13; see Table 2.4).

Neurotoxic shellfish poisoning (NSP) in the United States is usually associated with consumption of molluscan shellfish harvested along the coasts of the Gulf of Mexico or the southern Atlantic (46). NSP is characterized by paresthesia, reversal of hot and cold temperature sensation, myalgia, and vertigo. In one North Carolina outbreak from oysters, the symptoms took about three hours to present and resolved in a day with no lasting symptoms or deaths (56). Thus far, no deaths have been reported (9).

Paralytic Shellfish Poisoning (PSP) is generally associated with consumption of molluscan shellfish from the northeast and northwest coastal regions of the United States, although it has been found recently in the viscera of mackerel, lobster, Dungeness crabs, tanner crabs, and red rock crabs (46). There are many chemicals that contribute to PSP, the most toxic being saxitoxin, neosaxitoxin, and gonyautoxins (52). Saxitoxin, which blocks nerve conduction, is the best-characterized neurotoxin in this group. It can impair sensory, cerebellar, and motor functions. Typical symptoms of saxitoxin poisoning begin within an hour. The first symptoms include numbness in the lips, tongue, and fingertips. Numbness in the arms and legs with general muscle weakness, lower back pain, and lack of muscle coordination follow. In severe cases, respiratory distress and skeletal muscle paralysis result in death (57). In the latest foodborne-disease outbreak summaries (1993 to 1997), PSP was responsible for one confirmed outbreak, representing three cases and no deaths (13; see Table 2.4).

Tetrodotoxin prevents nerve conduction by blocking the inward movement of sodium ions through the cell membrane of an activated neuron. Symptoms begin within ten minutes to three hours of consumption (48–49). Tetrodotoxin is found in members of the order *Tetraodontiformes* (puffers or fugu, porcupinefish, sharp-nosed puffers, and ocean sunfish). It is most concentrated in the skin, liver, gonads, and intestine of the fish (9, 48–49). Most poisonings from tetrodotoxin have been associated with consumption of puffers from Indo-Pacific waters, but several reported poisonings (and deaths) have involved puffers from the Atlantic Ocean, Gulf of Mexico, and Gulf of California (46). The origin of the toxin is unclear, but marine bacteria may play a role in its biosynthesis (9). These fish may also carry ciguatera toxins, making it difficult to distinguish symptoms. The first symptom of tetrodotoxin intoxication (pufferfish poisoning) is a tingling sensation in the lips and tongue, which may account for the unique texture experience described by individuals who eat pufferfish. This sensation may be followed by numbness in the extremities or over the entire body, hypersalivation, profuse sweating, headache, subnormal temperatures, hypotension, pupil changes (both constriction and dilation), respiratory distress, tremor leading to paralysis, and, frequently, death (9, 48). The entire range of symptoms occurs within twenty minutes to eight hours (9). Although many pufferfish victims die, the intoxication is treatable. One U.S. case report describes mild tetrodotoxin intoxication in a forty-five-year-old man with diabetes who ate the cooked liver of a pufferfish twenty-four hours before receiving treatment in the emergency room of a local hospital; he enjoyed a complete recovery after six days of aggressive therapy (58). In another episode three California chefs shared contaminated pufferfish (fugu) brought without customs declaration from Japan as a prepackaged, ready-to-eat product. The chefs each consumed less than two ounces of the product, and symptoms began three to twenty minutes after consumption; all recovered within twenty-four hours of treatment (49). Persons who travel to countries where fugu is served should be aware of the potential risk; it remains a common cause of fatal food poisoning in Japan, where its consumption results in about fifty deaths each year (49).

Scombroid poisoning is caused by histamine in combination with other biogenic amines, such as putrescine and cadaverine, produced by bacterial decomposition during temperature abuse (9, 47). The toxicity of histamine is enhanced by the biogenic amines, which act by inhibiting histamine-metabolizing enzymes in the host's intestine (48). The name "scombrotoxin" derives from a group of fish most commonly contaminated, the suborder *Scombroidea*, which includes tuna and related species. The most common U.S. sources of scombroid poisoning are tuna, mahimahi, and bluefish, but abalone, amberjack, anchovy, bonito, herring, jack, mackerel, marlin, sardine, shad, and snapper have also been contaminated (9, 47). Many victims state that scombroid toxic fish taste sharp or peppery. Major symptoms of scombroid poisoning include headache, gastrointestinal distress, hypotension, rashes, or hives. These symptoms usually present within an hour of eating the contaminated fish and subside within twelve hours without treatment (9, 59), although severe cases may lead to respiratory distress and shock or death (48). Scombrotoxin was responsible for 69 confirmed outbreaks, representing 297 cases and no deaths in the most recent foodborne-disease outbreak reports (13; see Table 2.4).

MUSHROOM TOXINS. There are thousands of species of mushrooms, but commercial sources usually provide only a few varieties. Of mushroom species that have been tested, about one hundred are known to elicit harmful effects, and a dozen or so have caused deaths (60). In general, commercially raised and processed mushrooms are considered safe. Gathering wild mushrooms is a risky activity, because edible and poisonous species are often indistinguishable (9). Additionally, there are variations in accumulations of toxins in the mushrooms, making a "safe" species toxic at other times.

Scientists have identified and characterized over fifty different toxins from mushrooms (60–62). Mushrooms toxins are generally categorized by their physiological effects: protoplasmic poisons that destroy cells and cause organ failure, neurotoxins, gastrointestinal irritants, and disulfiram-like toxins that produce no symptoms unless they are consumed with alcohol (9). Mushroom toxins are tasteless and odorless. There is no reliable way to determine whether wild mushrooms contain toxins or to remove toxins if they are present. While the most current outbreak data (1993 to 1997) show seven outbreaks representing twenty-one cases and no deaths (13; see Table 2.4), there are an estimated one to five deaths from mushroom poisonings each year in the United States (63). Mushroom toxins have been grouped into categories based on their chemical structures and common symptoms (9, 60):

- Protoplasmic poisonings result from consumption of amanitins, gyromitrin, or orellanine.
- Mushroom neurotoxins include muscarine, ibotenic acid, muscimol, and psilocybin-psilocin. Common symptoms for these poisonings are profuse sweating, convulsions, hallucinations, excitement, depression, blurred vision, and dizziness.
- Many mushrooms produce gastrointestinal irritants; these are not well characterized because their effects are not severe or long lasting when replacement fluids are given.
- Disulfiram-like poisoning results from consumption of mushrooms that contain the amino acid coprine. Coprine is converted to cyclo-propanone hydrate in humans and blocks metabolism of ethanol consumed within seventy-two hours of eating the mushrooms.

The most toxic mushrooms are those that contain amatoxins, a group of complex alkaloids. Amatoxins are responsible for about 90 percent of deaths from mushroom poisoning (60). The amatoxin-containing mushroom species most noted for fatal mushroom poisonings is *Amanita phalloides* (death cap). Related species are common in grassy areas and woodlands in the United States, especially during wet periods. The initial symptoms of amatoxin poisoning, largely gastrointestinal distress (severe seizures of abdominal pain, persistent vomiting and watery diarrhea, extreme thirst, and lack of urine production), typically occur within six to twenty-four hours of consumption. After about twenty-four hours the gastrointestinal effects are replaced by dehydrative shock. Liver, kidney, cardiac and skeletal muscle dysfunction occur about three days after consumption. Death, which occurs in about half of untreated cases, typically occurs within three to eight days after consumption (9, 60). Recovery, if it occurs, generally takes at least a month and is accompanied by liver enlargement (9).

MYCOTOXINS. Toxins produced by molds (fungi) growing on food or feed are mycotoxins. The term "mycotoxin" describes more than fifty different toxic chemicals having a wide variety of complex molecular structures and exhibiting many different toxic actions (9). Because many foods are susceptible to mold growth and mycotoxin production and because mycotoxins can carry over from feed to animal products such as eggs and milk, it is difficult to guarantee that a food is mycotoxin-free. Additionally, animal species respond differently to mycotoxins, and natural exposure is probably to a combination of mycotoxins and not to a single chemical (64).

In recent history, acute mycotoxicoses have occurred largely in developing countries during periods of limited food availability (9). Victims of acute aflatoxicosis episodes in Taiwan, Uganda, and India have presented with changes in liver function and with liver necrosis. They had consumed heavily contaminated grains during food shortages.

In the United States concern for mycotoxins focuses on chronic, low-level exposures to **aflatoxins,** fumonisin, deoxynivalenol (DON, vomitoxin), and patulin—mycotoxins produced primarily by *Aspergillus, Fusarium,* and *Penicillium.* It is unlikely that individuals in developed countries would consume enough mycotoxin to cause an acute intoxication (9).

Aflatoxins produce acute liver necrosis and cirrhosis in a number of animal species, probably including humans (9). Chronic aflatoxin consumption is also associated with liver cancer (9), a leading cause of cancer in areas of the world where aflatoxin contamination is high. For these populations high alcohol intakes and high incidences of hepatitis B, which may predispose to additional cellular injury, are also associated with liver cancer. Aflatoxins require metabolic activation to become carcinogens (9). Aflatoxins occur naturally in soybeans, rice, corn, peanuts, figs, cottonseed, various tree nuts, and milk of cattle consuming contaminated feed (9, 64).

Fumonisins are produced by *Fusarium moniliforme* growing on corn (65). These toxins have been linked to fatalities in horses and swine, to human esophageal cancer in South Africa and China, and to liver cancer in rats. Fumonisins block the enzyme ceramide synthase, possibly decreasing levels of sphingolipids and causing accumulations of sphingamine. There is concern that chronic, low-level exposure to fumonisin may compromise immune status.

Deoxynivalenol (vomitoxin, DON) is produced by *Fusarium* spp growing on grains, including barley, corn, rye, and wheat (65–66). This toxin is implicated in Scabby Grain Intoxication (SGI), caused by eating the grain or bread made from the grain. SGI has been reported in Japan, Korea, China, and India. SGI symptoms include abdominal pain, abdominal "fullness," throat irritation, diarrhea, bloody stools, anorexia, weight loss, and physical weakness. Cereal grains worldwide are contaminated with deoxynivalenol.

Penicillium expansum produces patulin in rotting apples and pears (67). Using inferior fruit to make cider or juice results in high levels of patulin in the finished product. Patulin has produced acute gastrointestinal intoxication in humans, but it is no longer considered a carcinogen.

HEAVY METALS. The term "heavy metals" includes the minerals copper, zinc, cadmium, tin, lead, arsenic, and mercury. Most minerals in the body, whether **essential** or nonessential, are biologically active and are toxic when present at excessive levels. Minerals are most active as ions, radicals, or organic complexes. Food equipment and utensils, environmental contaminants, and agricultural chemicals are sources of heavy metals in foods. Contact of acidic foods with containers made of heavy metals causes heavy metals to dissolve in the food. This is the most common cause of heavy metal poisoning in the United States. Preparation or storage of foods, especially acidic foods, in galvanized buckets (zinc and cadmium), unlined tin containers, refrigerator shelves (cadmium), or glazed pottery made only for decorative purposes (lead) can result in contamination of food by heavy metals. Symptoms of acute heavy metal poisoning present within an hour. Metals irritate the gastric mucosa, causing vomiting that can be accompanied by nausea and diarrhea. Acute toxic reactions to elemental heavy metals require a large dose of the metal, and such large doses usually are not associated with food. Current foodborne-disease outbreak reports (1993 to 1997) show only two outbreaks, representing seventeen cases and no deaths (13; see Table 2.4). Symptoms of chronic heavy metal poisoning are characteristic for each metal. They depend largely on the site of accumulation of the metal in the body. For example, lead intoxication leads to anemia and neurological damage, mercury intoxication leads to neurological damage, and cadmium intoxication leads to kidney damage. Environmental exposures to heavy metals are usually higher than dietary exposures, making it difficult to determine the role of food compared with that of other routes of exposure.

The most common signs and symptoms of chronic lead intoxication occur in the blood and nervous system (68–69). Lead disrupts neurotransmitters by fitting into calcium-binding sites. Children exposed to chronic low levels may develop learning or behavioral problems; in adults severe lead poisoning can cause loss of recently acquired skills, loss of coordination, and bizarre behavior. Higher levels of lead exposure in children can cause anemia and changes in kidney function, and higher levels of exposure in adults can contribute to high blood pressure and damage to the reproductive organs. For children and adults high exposure levels can cause seizures, coma, and death. By the time symptoms appear, damage may be irreversible.

Chronic dietary exposure to lead typically comes from water, canned foods, ceramicware, and glassware (68–71). All of these exposures have been reduced over the past thirty years in response to lead-reduction programs, although older houses and water systems are still significant sources (72). Additionally, some ethnic foods may contain lead (73).

Corroded lead pipes, lead solder on copper pipes, and brass faucets contribute to lead in drinking water. Lead is highest in water left in pipes for a long time, such as when the faucet is not used overnight. Individuals living in older houses with lead pipes should be advised to run their water for a minute before daily use. To meet regulatory standards, bottled water should have less than 5 **ppb** lead (69).

FDA's 1994 to 1996 Total Diet Studies showed that intakes of lead from food have decreased by 96 percent for young children and 93 percent in adults since the early 1980s (69). The major factor in this decrease is that U.S. food processors stopped using lead solder in food cans in 1991. Also, it is illegal to import food in lead-soldered cans.

Serious outbreaks of acute lead poisoning have resulted from storage of acidic and alcoholic beverages in ceramic containers (70). Even safely glazed ceramic containers can become hazardous for food storage as the glaze chips and deteriorates during washing. Lead also migrates from lead crystal containers into alcoholic beverages during long-term storage (71), but drinking from crystal stemware is not hazardous because the time it takes to pour and serve a beverage typically would not be long enough for significant migration to occur. Though not common, the use of crystal baby bottles is not recommended because even small migrations of lead may be significant for an infant (69).

Recent lead poisonings have been associated with illegally imported ethnic foods (73). In one case candy from Mexico packaged in improperly fired ceramic containers contained high lead levels. In another instance, a spice (lozeena) contained about 8 percent lead. Several practices can add lead to ethnic products—adding lead to impart yellow or orange colors, adding lead to increase sweetness, adding lead to increase weight, and using leaded gasoline as a fuel around food.

Methylmercury and related organic mercury complexes cause neurological damage in adults, including numbness of lips, arms, and legs; loss of coordination; and loss of vision and hearing. Methylmercury also disrupts cellular transport of glucose across cell membranes. Although there is no clear evidence that fetuses are more susceptible to methylmercury than adults, exposed fetuses may exhibit developmental delays or symptoms resembling cerebral palsy.

Mercury is released into the air naturally by degassing the Earth's crusts and oceans and by human activities, such as burning wastes. This mercury vapor is deposited on land and water. Environmental bacteria and enzymes in animals alkylate inorganic mercury to form organic complexes, which are absorbed more quickly and are more toxic. Fish absorb methylmercury as water passes over their gills and as they feed. The largest levels of methylmercury occur in very large predator fish through **bioamplification** and in fish that feed in waters that contain higher levels of industrial waste. The top ten seafoods—canned tuna, shrimp, pollock, salmon, cod, catfish, clams, flatfish, crabs, and scallops—make up 80 percent of the seafood market and have very low mercury levels (74). Swordfish, shark, King mackerel, and tilefish are long-lived, larger fish that feed on other fish and contain higher levels of methyl mercury; regulators recommend no more than one serving a week for the general population (74) and avoidance by pregnant women or women who may become pregnant (75). Local advisories alert sport fishers of potential contamination problems.

Mercury can contaminate plant foods in two ways. First, mercury is often used in fungicides that protect seed grains during storage. These grains are colored to warn against consumption. Second, when mercury is found at very high levels in soils, it may contaminate plants grown in the soil. While Japanese rice grown on high-mercury-containing soils contains higher levels of mercury than rices grown in other countries, no mercury poisoning has been reported from consumption of the rice (76). The only reported cases of mercury poisoning from consumption of contaminated plants occurred when mercury-treated seeds were accidently consumed (76–77).

A major food-poisoning disaster occurred as a result of mercury discharges into Minamata Bay in Japan from 1953 to 1970. During this epidemic, symptoms were reported in more than seven hundred people exposed to fish and shellfish harvested in the area. At least forty-six people died as a result of consuming the contaminated food. The Minamata disaster is a classic example of what can happen when industrial wastes enter the food supply. However, there is a major limitation to this model as it applies to other heavy metals. Mercury is the only heavy metal that forms a stable organic complex that can be readily absorbed. Other heavy metals can contaminate fish and shellfish, but they are not converted to more toxic organic forms. Thus, these other metals are less toxic to humans.

Idiosyncratic Reactions: Food Allergies, Intolerances, and Sensitivities

"Idiosyncratic reaction" is the term used to describe reactions to foods or food ingredients that are individualistic. They happen only to people who are physiologically predisposed to them either because of immune sensitivity or enzyme deficiencies. Several organizations that focus on allergies have accessible Web sites (78–80) with both consumer and technical information, and FDA has published a general article on food allergies for consumer audiences (81).

FOOD ALLERGIES. Food allergies are immunologically mediated reactions to foods. The reactions may occur within minutes of ingesting the specific food. Target organs include the gastrointestinal tract, skin, respiratory tract, and circulatory system. Food allergies may result in systemic shock or anaphylaxis.

Gastrointestinal symptoms of food allergy include swelling and itching of the oral cavity, nausea, stomach cramps, and diarrhea. Skin symptoms include hives, rashes, and eczema. Respiratory tract symptoms include sneezing, rhinitis, shortness of breath, laryngeal edema, and asthma. Circulatory system reactions include hypotension, angioedema, and systemic anaphylaxis. Of the symptoms, systemic anaphylaxis is the most severe and can result in death (82). About one hundred people die each year from food-induced anaphylaxis (83). *Healthy People 2010* objective 10.4 focuses on reducing deaths from food-induced anaphylaxis (84).

The actual incidence of food allergies is less than frequently reported. Only about 4 percent to 6 percent of infants, 2 percent to 4 percent of children, and 1 percent to 2 percent of adults have reproducible allergic reactions to foods. The higher incidence in infants is probably a result of gut immaturity, which also helps explain the observation that infants and children frequently outgrow their allergies. Children who are allergic to wheat, milk, eggs, crustaceans, and tree nuts are less likely to outgrow their allergies than children who are allergic to other foods (82).

Immunologically, food allergies are initiated when an allergen triggers Immunoglobulin E (IgE) to bind to mast cells. This leads to activation of the mast cells, which includes the release of histamine, chemotactic factors, heparin, prostaglandins, and leukotrienes. These substances produce increases in cell permeability and muscle contraction; stimulate mucus production, gastric acid secretion, and pain fibers; and recruit inflammatory cells.

The foods most frequently associated with food sensitivities are peanuts, fish, crustaceans, tree nuts, eggs, and milk. Table 2.6 describes the allergens that have been identified in those foods, their label identifiers, and their heat stabilities. While the majority of food allergens are heat-stable, in some cases food preparation methods may change the allergenic protein sufficiently that it is no longer reactive. There is some cross-reactivity between food and other allergens and among foods. The following cross-reactivities have been reported (85):

- Ragweed antigen: bananas and melons
- Mugwort pollen: celery
- Grass pollen: potatoes
- Birch pollen: apples, cherries, pears, and peaches
- Natural rubber latex: bananas, avocados, kiwi, apricots, grapes, passion fruit, and pineapple
- Cow's milk: milk from goats, mares, and sheep
- Hen's eggs: eggs from geese, turkeys, and ducks; chicken meat
- Codfish: mackerel, herring, and other fishes
- Peanuts: soybeans, green beans, and lima beans
- Shrimp: crab, crayfish, and lobster

TABLE 2.6   Potential Effects of Increasing Doses of Toxic Agents on Test Animals

NOAEL	ED$_{50}$[a]	ED$_{50}$[b]/ID$_{50}$[c]	MTD[d]	LD$_{50}$[e]
No observable adverse effect level	Beneficial effects (if any)	Detrimental effects	Severe effects	Fatal effect
	Nutritional Therapeutic	Biochemical Physiological Teratogenic Carcinogenic		
Increasing dose of toxic agent———————————————————>				

[a]The ED$_{50}$, or effective dose, for a beneficial effect is the amount of a chemical required to cause such a response in half the population of test animals held under precisely described conditions. Not all chemicals have a beneficial effect at low dosage levels.

[b]The ED$_{50}$ for a detrimental effect is the amount of a chemical required to cause injury in half the population of test animals held under precisely described conditions. The lower the ED50, the more toxic the chemical.

[c]The ID$_{50}$, or infectious dose, for a disease-causing organism is the number of organisms required to establish an infection and cause disease symptoms in half the population of test animals held under precisely described conditions. The severity of the disease is determined by the susceptibility (or resistance) of the host and the characteristics of the infectious organism.

[d]The MTD is the maximum tolerated dose that does not cause death but does cause severe effects. The lower the MTD, the more toxic the chemical.

[e]The LD$_{50}$, or lethal dose, is the amount of a toxic chemical required to kill half the population of test animals held under precisely described conditions. The lower the LD50, the more toxic the chemical.

Diagnosis of food allergies includes conducting medical and dietary histories, physical examinations, prick skin testing, elimination diets, and food challenges. Careful histories include records of timing between eating a particular food and onset of symptoms, frequency with which the reaction occurs, quantity of food eaten, method of food preparation, and presence of other foods and medications. There should be a strong correlation between eating a particular food and onset of symptoms.

Challenge tests are the gold standards for establishing food allergies. Elimination diets are designed to eliminate suspected allergens and to watch for alleviation of symptoms. They are usually followed for at least one to two weeks but should not be followed for prolonged periods of time because they may be nutritionally inadequate. Challenge tests, in which the suspected allergen is given in increasing doses, are the next phase in this diagnostic screening. The ideal challenge test is double-blind and placebo-controlled (82). Because of the possibility of anaphylactic reactions, challenge testing should only be done under direct medical supervision. Once the allergen is identified, management of the chronic condition is avoidance of offending foods. The American Academy for Allergy, Asthma and Immunology (AAAAI) reviews unproved tests for allergies; their findings ar available to the public (86).

Dietetics professionals should counsel clients and their caregivers on food products likely to contain the allergen, names for the allergen that may be used in ingredient labeling, other ways in which the allergen may enter foods, and appropriate use of medications. For example, candies that do not contain peanuts may have some peanut residue from the processing equipment, and ice cream that does not contain nuts may have enough residue from the ice cream scoop at a restaurant or an ice cream parlor to elicit a reaction in a highly sensitive individual. It may be difficult to avoid all food allergens, especially in communal eating situations or when eating commercially prepared menu items. Dietetics professionals who work in those settings need to minimize the risk to their clients by labeling menu items appropriately, making food ingredient labels available to wait staff and clients, and following SSOPs (Standard Sanitary Operating Procedures) that minimize cross-contamination.

One of the concerns surrounding genetic engineering of foods has been the introduction of allergens into other foods. For example, if a gene from brazil nuts were to be incorporated into soybeans, a person allergic to brazil nuts might then become allergic to soybeans or products made from them. The FDA, in approving the use of genetic engineering in foods, clearly states that companies requesting approval for foods must prove that the genes transferred do not code for an allergen (87–88; see Box 2.3).

An additional concern surrounding food allergies addresses anaphylaxis in schools and child care settings. The AAAAI position statement "Anaphylaxis in Schools and Other Child Care Settings" offers suggestions for avoiding this problem (89; see Box 2.4).

Another concern that requires the attention of dietitians who practice in food-service is occupational allergies. Occupational allergies are the conditions that occur in workers who have allergic reactions from working with foods in a food-service setting. Foods most commonly associated with occupational allergies are flours, grains, garlic, onion, and egg whites. Contaminants in food products, such as mold spores and insect parts, may also cause allergic reactions. The prevalence of food-related occupational allergies is not known. Typical manifestations of occupational allergic response are contact urticaria, asthma, and dermatitis. The Americans with Disabilities Act does not allow employers to ask prospective employees about the presence of food allergies or to test them for food allergies. The American Medical Association has reviewed workplace allergies (90).

FOOD INTOLERANCES. Food intolerances are nonimmunologic responses to foods. Lactase deficiency is an example of food intolerance. In lactase deficiency, individuals lack the ability to synthesize lactase, the enzyme responsible for hydrolysis of lactose to glucose and galactose. The undigested and unabsorbed lactose remains in the gut, where it becomes a substrate for bacterial fermentation. Symptoms of lactase deficiency include bloating, cramping, flatulence, and diarrhea. Treatment involves avoidance of foods containing lactose, including milk

BOX 2.3   FDA Statement on Allerginicity of Genetically Engineered Plant Products

In some foods that commonly cause an allergic response, the particular protein(s) responsible for allerginicity is known, and therefore the producer may know whether the transferred protein is the allergen. However, in other cases, the protein responsible for a food's allerginicity is not known, and FDA considers it prudent practice for the producer initially to assume that the transferred protein is the allergen. Appropriate in vitro or **in vivo** allerginicity testing may reveal whether food from the new variety elicits an allergenic response in the potentially sensitive population (that is, people sensitive to the food in which the protein is ordinarily found). Producers of such foods should discuss allerginicity testing protocol requirements with the agency. Labeling of foods newly containing a known or suspect allergen may be needed to inform consumers of such potential.

Source: Reference 88.

BOX 2.4   Suggestions for Avoiding Anaphylaxis in Schools and Other Child-Care Settings

- The most important aspect of the management of patients with life-threatening allergies is avoidance. In the event of contact with the offending allergen, epinephrine (adrenaline) is the treatment of choice for anaphylaxis.
- The diagnosis of allergy with a risk of anaphylactic reactions is made on the basis of the patient's history and confirmed with appropriate skin and/or blood tests done by appropriately trained allergy specialists. Treatment protocols should be physician prescribed for use in the school setting.
- All school personnel should be aware of those students who have been prescribed epinephrine. This information should be readily available and reviewed by all personnel. Furthermore, school personnel should work in partnership with the parents to develop strategies for avoiding a reaction while allowing the student to participate fully in all activities.
- Staff members involved with the child's care should be instructed about the potentially severe nature and proper treatment of the allergic problem. This information should be reviewed with the student's parents before each school year or special activities (e.g., school trips). Any questions and possible treatment strategies should be discussed with the parents, the child's physician, or both.
- All school staff who may be giving allergic students any food or supervising activities involving food should know the technical and scientific words for common foods. Ingredient statements should be carefully read before giving the child any food.
- Strict "no food or eating-utensil trading" rules should be implemented throughout the school.
- Surfaces (e.g., tables and toys) should be washed clean of contaminating foods.
- The food used in lesson plans for math or science, crafts, and cooking classes may need to be substituted depending on the allergies of the students.
- Hand washing before and after food handling should be encouraged.
- If a student is going to eat from the cafeteria menu, the child's parents should inform the cafeteria staff in writing about foods to be avoided and suggest "safe" substitutions.
- Food service personnel should be instructed about measures necessary to prevent cross contact during the handling, preparation, and serving of food.
- Foods brought in for special events should be purchased in stores and contain complete ingredient declarations.

Source: Reference 89.

and products containing whey. Other enzyme deficiencies resulting in food intolerances include sucrase-isomaltase deficiency and celiac disease. Treatment for these conditions also involves removal of the offending food from the diet.

FOOD SENSITIVITIES. The term "food sensitivity" usually refer to an idiosyncratic reaction to a food additive. Sensitivities to food additives are rare. Sensitivities have been clearly associated with a limited number of food additives, and such sensitivities occur in a very small percentage of the population. The three most common food sensitivities are to sulfite, tartrazine (FD&C Yellow No. 5), and monosodium glutamate (MSG).

Sulfite sensitivity was first identified in 1976. It is most common in people who use steroids to manage their asthma. Even so, only about 4 percent to 10 percent of people with asthma are sulfite-sensitive. For those individuals, the reaction can be fatal. Sulfites are used in dried fruits and potato flakes to control non-enzymatic browning, in fresh seafood to inhibit enzymatic browning, and in beer and wine to inhibit microbial growth. Products containing sulfites must declare them on their labels. In 1986, sulfite use in fresh fruits and vegetables (except potatoes) to retard browning was banned. Products that may contain over 100 **ppm** sulfite include dried fruits (except prunes and dark raisins), bottled lemon juice, bottled lime juice, wine, molasses, and grape juice (white, pink, and sparkling). Foods with intermediate levels of sulfites include dried potatoes, wine vinegar, gravies and sauces, fruit toppings, and maraschino cherries. Symptoms of sulfite hypersensitivity include bronchoconstriction, wheezing, dyspnea, nausea, stomach cramps, diarrhea, urticaria, hypotension, shock, and loss of consciousness (91–92).

Tartrazine is a regulated color additive (FD&C Yellow No. 5) used in foods, drugs, and cosmetics. Foods in which FD&C Yellow No. 5 may be used are custards, beverages, ice cream, confections, preserves, and cereals. FDA allows its use "in accordance with good manufacturing practices." If it is used in a food, the label must so declare. FDA's Advisory Committee on Hypersensitivity to Food Constituents concluded in 1986 that FD&C Yellow No. 5 may cause hives in fewer than one out of ten thousand people. The committee found no evidence that the color additive in foods provokes asthma attacks or that aspirin-intolerant individuals may have a cross-sensitivity to the color (93).

Monosodium glutamate (MSG) is a GRAS food constituent that occurs naturally at high concentrations in tomatoes, Parmesan cheese, and soy sauce (94). A small number of people may react to consumption of large amounts of MSG at a single eating occasion. The symptoms associated with this reaction, known as Chinese Restaurant Syndrome, are paresthesia and burning sensations of the neck, chest, and limbs; palpitations; and a sensation of weakness. MSG may be listed on the label as MSG, hydrolyzed vegetable protein (HVP), hydrolyzed plant protein (HPP), kombu extract, natural flavoring, and flavor. Conducting double-blind, placebo-controlled studies of reactions to MSG is complicated because of the unique flavor of MSG. It is the compound associated with unami, a component of taste. In the most recent reports of foodborne-illness outbreaks, MSG was responsible for one outbreak, involving two cases and no deaths (13).

REFERENCES

1. Doyle MP, Beuchat LR, Montville TJ, eds. *Food Microbiology: Fundamentals and Frontiers.* Washington, DC: ASM Press; 1997.
2. Hui YH, Gorham JR, Murrell KD, Cliver DO. *Diseases Caused by Bacteria.* New York, NY: Marcel Dekker Inc; 1994. *Foodborne Disease Handbook, vol. 1.*
3. Hui YH, Gorham JR, Murrell KD, Cliver DO. *Diseases Caused by Viruses, Parasites, and Fungi.* New York, NY: Marcel Dekker Inc; 1994. *Foodborne Disease Handbook, vol. 2.*
4. Hui YH, Gorham JR, Murrell KD, Cliver DO. *Diseases Caused by Hazardous Substances.* New York, NY: Marcel Dekker Inc; 1994. *Foodborne Disease Handbook, vol. 3.*
5. Watson D, ed. *Natural Toxicants in Food.* Boca Raton, FL: CRC Press; 1998.
6. deVries J. *Food Safety and Toxicity.* Boca Raton, FL: CRC Press; 1996.
7. International Commission on Microbiological Specifications for Foods. *Microorganisms in Foods 5: Characteristics of Microbial Pathogens.* Gaithersburg, MD: Aspen Publishers Inc; 1996.
8. Jay J. *Modern Food Microbiology.* 6th ed. Gaithersburg, MD: Aspen Publishers Inc; 2000.
9. US Food and Drug Administration, Center for Food Safety and Applied Nutrition. Bad bug book: foodborne pathogenic microorganisms and natural toxins handbook [FDA Web site]. October 1997. Available at: http://vm.cfsan.fda.gov/~mow/intro.html. Accessed June 5, 2001.
10. Woodburn MJ, Somers E, Rodriguez J, Schantz EJ. Heat inactivation rates of botulinum toxin-A, toxin-B, toxin-E and toxin-F in some foods and buffers. *J Food Sci.* 1979;44:1658–1661.

11. Stanley D. Arthritis from foodborne bacteria? *Agricul Res.* 1996;10:16. Available at: http://www.ars.usda.gov/is/AR/archive/oct96/arthrits.pdf. Accessed June 5, 2001.

12. Lindsay JA. Chronic sequelae of foodborne disease. *Emerg Infect Dis.* 1997;3(4):443–452. Available at: http://www.cdc.gov/ncidod/EID/vol3no4/adobe/lindsay.pdf. Accessed May 25, 2001.

13. Olsen SJ, MacKinnon LC, Goulding JS, et al. Surveillance for foodborne-disease outbreaks—United States, 1993–1997. *MMWR.* 2000;49(SS-01):1–51. Available at: ftp://ftp.cdc.gov/pub/Publications/mmwr/SS/SS4901.pdf. Accessed May 12, 2001.

14. Shallow S, Samuel M, McNees A, et al. Preliminary FoodNet Data on the Incidence of Foodborne Illnesses—United States, 1999. *MMWR.* 2000;49(10):201–205. Available at: ftp://ftp.cdc.gov/pub/Publications/mmwr/wk/mm4910.pdf. Accessed May 26, 2001.

15. Buzby JC, Roberts T, Lin CTJ, MacDonald JM. Bacterial foodborne disease: medical costs and productivity losses. Washington, DC: Food and Consumer Economics Division, Economic Research Service, US Department of Agriculture; 1996. Agricultural Economic Report No. 741. Available at: http://www.ers.usda.gov/publications/Aer741/AER741fm.PDF. Accessed June 6, 2001.

16. US Food and Drug Administration; *1999 Food Code.* Washington, DC: US Department of Commerce, Technology Administration, National Technical Information Service; 1999. PB99-115925. Available at: http://vm.cfsan.fda.gov/~dms/fc99-toc.html. Accessed May 12, 2001.

17. Lecuit M, Vandormael-Pournin S, Lefort J, Huerre M, Gounon P, Dupuy C, Babinet C, Cossart P. A transgenic model for listeriosis: role of internalin in crossing the intestinal barrier. *Science.* 2001;292:1722–1725.

18. Liu Y, van Kruiningen HJ, West AB, et al. Immunocytochemical evidence of Crohn's disease. *Gastroenterology.* 1995;108:1396–1401.

19. Jones ME, Jenkerson SA, Middaugh JP, et al. Epidemiologic notes and reports foodborne hepatitis A—Alaska, Florida, North Carolina, Washington. *MMWR.* 1990;39(14):228–232.

20. Rosenblum LS, Mirkin IR, Allen DT, et al. A multifocal outbreak of hepatitis A traced to commercially distributed lettuce. *Am J Public Health.* 1990;80:1075–1079.

21. Institute of Food Technologists' Expert Panel on Food Safety and Nutrition. Scientific status summary: virus transmission via food. *Food Technol.* 1997;51(4).

22. Centers for Disease Control and Prevention. "Norwalk-like viruses": public health consequences and outbreak management. *MMWR.* 2001;50(RR09):1–18. Available at: http://www.cdc.gov/mmwr/PDF/rr/rr5009.pdf. Accessed June 9, 2001.

23. Conrad C, Hemphill K, Wilson S, et al. Multistate outbreak of viral gastroenteritis related to consumption of oysters—Louisiana, Maryland, Mississippi, and North Carolina. *MMWR.* 1993;42(49):945–948.

24. Davis C, Smith A, Walden R, et al. Viral gastroenteritis associated with consumption of raw oysters—Florida, 1993. *MMWR.* 1994;43(24);446–449. Available at: ftp://ftp.cdc.gov/pub/Publications/mmwr/wk/mm4324.pdf. Accessed May 26, 2001.

25. Farley TA, McFarland L, Estes M, et al. Viral gastroenteritis associated with eating oysters—Louisiana, December 1996–January 1997. *MMWR.* 1997;46(47);1109–1112. Available at: ftp://ftp.cdc.gov/pub/Publications/mmwr/wk/mm4647.pdf. Accessed May 26, 2001.

26. Aristeguieta C, Koenders I, Windham D, et al. Epidemiologic notes and reports: multistate outbreak of viral gastroenteritis associated with consumption of oysters—Apalachicola Bay, Florida, December 1994– January 1995. *MMWR.* 1995;44(02);37–39. Available at: ftp://ftp.cdc.gov/pub/Publications/mmwr/wk/mm4402.pdf. Accessed May 26, 2001.

27. Institute of Food Science and Technology (UK). Current hot topics: Bovine Spongiform Encephalopathy (BSE): part 1/2 [IFST Web site]. Available at: http://www.easynet.co.uk/ifst/hottop5.htm. Accessed June 9, 2001.

28. US Department of Agriculture, Animal and Plant Health Inspection Service. Bovine Spongiform Encephalopathy (BSE) [USDA Web site]. Available at: http://www.aphis.usda.gov/oa/bse/. Accessed June 9, 2001.

29. Centers for Disease Control and Prevention. Questions and answers regarding Bovine Spongiform Encephalopathy (BSE) and Creutzfeldt-Jakob disease (CJD) [CDC Web site]. January 4, 2001. Available at: http://www.cdc.gov/ncidod/diseases/cjd/bse_cjd_qa.htm. Accessed June 9, 2001.

30. Centers for Disease Control and Prevention. Bovine Spongiform Encephalopathy and new variant Creutzfeldt-Jakob disease [CDC Web site]. January 4, 2001. Available at: http://www.cdc.gov/ncidod/diseases/cjd/bse_cjd.htm. Accessed June 9, 2001.

31. Holman RC, Khan AS, Belay ED, Schonberger LB. Creutzfeldt-Jakob disease in the United States, 1979–1994: using national mortality data to assess the possible occurrence of variant cases. *Emerg Infect Dis.* 1996;2:333–337. Available at: http://www.cdc.gov/ncidod/EID/vol2no4/holman2.htm. Accessed May 23, 2001.

32. Brown P, Will RG, Bradley R, Asher DM, Detwiler L. Bovine Spongiform Encephalopathy and variant Creutzfeldt-Jakob disease: background, evolution, and current concerns. *Emerg Infect Dis.* 2001;7:6–16. Available at: http://www.cdc.gov/ncidod/EID/vol7no1/pdfs/brown.pdf. Accessed June 9, 2001.

33. Will RG, Ironside JW, Zeidler M, et al. A new variant of Creutzfeldt-Jakob disease in the UK. *Lancet.* 1996;347:921–925.

34. Koehler J, Toomey K, Danila R, et al. Surveillance for Creutzfeldt-Jakob disease—United States. *MMWR.* 1996;45(31):665–668.

35. Morris JG Jr, Potter M. Emergence of new pathogens as a function of changes in host susceptibility. *Emerg Infect Dis.* 1995;3(4):435–441. Available at: http://www.cdc.gov/ncidod/eid/vol3no4/adobe/morris.pdf. Accessed May 26, 2001.

36. Altekruse SF, Cohen ML, Swerdlow DL. Emerging foodborne diseases. *Emerg Infect Dis.* 1997;3(3):285–293. Available at: ftp://ftp.cdc.gov/pub/EID/vol3no3/adobe/cohen.pdf. Accessed May 26, 2001.

37. Kaplan JK, Roselle G, Sepkowitz K. Opportunistic infections in immunodeficient populations. *Emerg Infect Dis.* 1998;4(3):421–422. Available at: ftp://ftp.cdc.gov/pub/EID/vol4no3/adobe/kaplan.pdf. Accessed May 27, 2001.

38. Collins JE. Impact of changing consumer lifestyles on the emergence/ reemergence of foodborne pathogens. *Emerg Infect Dis.* 1997;3(4):471–479. Available at: http://www.cdc.gov/ncidod/eid/vol3no4/adobe/collins.pdf. Accessed May 26, 2001.

39. Buchanan RL. Identifying and controlling emerging foodborne pathogens: research needs. *Emerg Infect Dis.* 1997;3(4):517–521 (updated June 26, 1999). Available at: http://www.cdc.gov/ncidcd/eid/vol3no4/pdf/buchanan. Accessed May 27, 2001.

40. US Food and Drug Administration, Center for Food Safety and Applied Nutrition. Food additives and premarket approval [FDA Web site]. March 29, 1999. Available at: http://vm.cfsan.fda.gov/~lrd/foodadd.html. Accessed May 27, 2001.

41. US Environmental Protection Administration, Office of Pesticide Programs. Pesticides and food: what you and your family need to know [EPA Web site]. February 1999. Available at: http://www.epa.gov/pesticides/food/. Accessed May 27, 2001.

42. Federal Food, Drug, and Cosmetic Act. Chapter II–definitions. [FDA Web site]. Available at: http://www.fda.gov/opacom/laws/fdcact/fdcact1.htm. Accessed June 5, 2001.

43. US Food and Drug Administration. Food additives and color additives FAQs [FDA Web site]. Available at: http://www.cfsan.fda.gov/~dms/qa-adfq.html. Accessed May 27, 2001.

44. US Food and Drug Administration/International Food Information Council. Food additives [FDA Web site]. 1992. Available at: http://vm.cfsan.fda.gov/~lrd/foodaddi.html. Accessed May 27, 2001.

45. US Food and Drug Administration/International Food Information Council. Food color facts [FDA Web site]. January 1993. Available at: http://vm.cfsan.fda.gov/~lrd/colorfac.html. Accessed May 26, 2001.

46. US Food and Drug Administration, Center for Food Safety and Applied Nutrition. Natural toxins. In: *Fish and Fishery Products Hazards and Controls Guide*. Washington, DC: National Technical Information Service; 1998:65–72. No. 703-487-4650. Available at: http://vm.cfsan.fda.gov/~acrobat/haccpc06.pdf. Accessed May 26, 2001.

47. US Food and Drug Administration, Center for Food Safety and Applied Nutrition. Scombrotoxin (histamine) formation. In: *Fish and Fishery Products Hazards and Controls Guide*. Washington, DC: National Technical Information Service; 1998:73–90. No. 703-487-4650. Available at: http://vm.cfsan.fda.gov/~acrobat/haccpc07.pdf. Accessed May 26, 2001.

48. Halstead BW. Fish toxins. In: Hui YH, Gorham JR, Murrell KD, Cliver DO, eds. *Diseases Caused by Hazardous Substances*. New York, NY: Marcel Dekker Inc; 1994:463–496. *Foodborne Disease Handbook, vol. 3*.

49. Tanner P, Przekwas G, Clark R, et al. Tetrodotoxin poisoning associated with eating puffer fish transported from Japan—California, 1996. *MMWR*. 1996;45:389–391. Available at: ftp://ftp.cdc.gov/pub/Publications/mmwr/wk/mm4519.pdf. Accessed June 3, 2001.

50. Kloss K, Feltmann L, Dodson D, et al. Haff disease associated with eating buffalo fish—United States, 1997. *MMWR*. 1998;47:1091–1093. Available at: http://www.cdc.gov/mmwr/PDF/wk/mm4750.pdf. Accessed June 3, 2001.

51. Todd ECD. Domoic acid and amnesic shellfish poisoning—a review. *J Food Protect*. 1993;56:69–83.

52. US Department of Commerce, National Oceanic and Atmospheric Administration, National Marine Fisheries Service, Northwest Fisheries Science Center. Marine biotoxins and harmful algal blooms [Northwest Fisheries Science Center Web site]. 1999. Available at: http://research.nwfsc.noaa.gov/hab/biotoxins.htm. Accessed May 26, 2001.

53. Berman FW, Murray TF. Domoic acid neurotoxicity in cultured cerebellar granule neurons is mediated predominantly by NMDA receptors that are activated as a consequence of excitatory amino acid release. *J Neurochem*. 1997;69:693–703.

54. Hammond RM, Hopkins RS, Dickey R, et al. Ciguatera fish poisoning—Florida, 1991. *MMWR*. 1993;42(21):417–418. Available at: ftp://ftp.cdc.gov/pub/Publications/mmwr/wk/mm4221.pdf. Accessed May 26, 2001.

55. Senecal P-E, Osterloh JD. Normal fetal outcome after maternal ciguateric toxin exposure in the second trimester. *Clin Toxicol*. 1991;29:473–478.

56. Morris PD, Campbell DS, Taylor TJ, Freeman JI. Clinical and epidemiological features of neurotoxic shellfish poisoning in North Carolina. *Am J Public Health*. 1991;81:471–474.

57. Centers for Disease Control. Paralytic shellfish poisoning—Massachusetts and Alaska, 1990. *MMWR*. 1991(40):157–161.

58. Sims JK, Ostman DC. Pufferfish poisoning: emergency diagnosis and management of mild human tetrodotoxication. *Ann Emerg Med*. 1986;15:149–153.

59. Centers for Disease Control. Scombroid fish poisoning—New Mexico, 1987. *MMWR*. 1988;37:461.

60. Sinden SL, Deahl KL. Alkaloids. In: Hui YH, Gorham JR, Murrell KD, Cliver DO, eds. *Diseases Caused by Hazardous Substances*. New York, NY: Marcel Dekker Inc; 1994:227–259. *Foodborne Disease Handbook, vol. 3*.

61. Concon JM. Toxic mushrooms and other macrofungi. In: Concon JM. *Food Toxicology*. New York: Marcel Dekker Inc; 1988;pt B:463–509.

62. Spoerke DG. Mushrooms: epidemiology and medical treatment. In: Hui YH, Gorham JR, Murrell KD, Cliver DO, eds. *Diseases Caused by Hazardous Substances*. New York, NY: Marcel Dekker Inc; 1994:433–462. *Foodborne Disease Handbook, vol. 3*.

63. Wagstaff DJ. Epidemiology of plant poisoning in humans. In: Keeler RF, Tu AT, eds. *Toxicology of Plant and Fungal Compounds*. New York, NY: Marcel Dekker Inc; 1991:559–574. *Handbook of Natural Toxins, vol. 6*.

64. Koshinsky HA, Khachatourians GG. Mycotoxicoses: the effects of mycotoxin combinations. In: Hui YH, Gorham JR, Murrell KD, Cliver DO, eds. *Diseases Caused by Hazardous Substances.* New York, NY: Marcel Dekker Inc; 1994:463–520. *Foodborne Disease Handbook, vol. 2.*

65. Marasas WFO. *Fusarium.* In: Hui YH, Gorham JR, Murrell KD, Cliver DO, eds. *Diseases Caused by Hazardous Substances.* New York, NY: Marcel Dekker Inc; 1994:521–573. *Foodborne Disease Handbook, vol. 2.*

66. Tanaka T, Hasegawa A, Yamamoto S, et al. Worldwide contamination of cereals by the *Fusarium* mycotoxins nivalenol, deoxynivalenol, and zearalenone. 1. Survey of 19 countries. *J Agric Food Chem.* 1988;36:979–983.

67. Pitt JI. *Penicillium.* In: Hui YH, Gorham JR, Murrell KD, Cliver DO, eds. *Diseases Caused by Hazardous Substances.* New York, NY: Marcel Dekker Inc; 1994:617–630. *Foodborne Disease Handbook, vol. 2.*

68. Centers for Disease Control and Prevention. Current trends childhood lead poisoning—United States: report to the Congress by the Agency for Toxic Substances and Disease Registry. *MMWR.* 1988;37(32):481–485.

69. Farley D. Dangers of lead still linger. *FDA Consumer* [FDA Web site]. January–February 1998. Available at: http://vm.cfsan.fda.gov/~dms/fdalead.html. Accessed May 26, 2001.

70. Raciti KA, Haloukas G, Curran AS, et al. Lead poisoning following ingestion of homemade beverage stored in a ceramic jug—New York. *MMWR.* 1989;38:379–380.

71. Falcone F. Migration of lead into alcoholic beverages during storage in lead crystal decanters. *J Food Protect.* 1991;54:378–380.

72. Lofgren JP, Macias M, Russakow S, et al. Blood lead levels in young children—United States and selected states, 1996–1999. *MMWR.* 2000;49(50):1133–1137. Available at: http://www.cdc.gov/mmwr/PDF/wk/mm4950.pdf. Accessed May 27, 2001.

73. Dorfman JS, Quattrone A, Jacobs RM, et al. Lead poisoning associated with imported candy and powdered food coloring—California and Michigan. *MMWR.* 1998;47(48);1041–1043. Available at: ftp://ftp.cdc.gov/pub/Publications/mmwr/wk/mm4748.pdf. Accessed May 26, 2001.

74. Foulke JE. Mercury in fish: cause for concern? *FDA Consumer* [FDA Web site]. September 1994 (revised May 1995). Available at: http://vm.cfsan.fda.gov/~dms/mercury.html. Accessed May 26, 2001.

75. US Food and Drug Administration, Center for Food Safety and Applied Nutrition. Consumer advisory: an important message for pregnant women and women of childbearing age who may become pregnant about the mercury in fish [FDA Web site]. March 2001. Available at: http://vm.cfsan.fda.gov/~dms/admehg.html. Accessed June 4, 2001.

76. Concon JM. Inorganic and organometallic contaminants in foodstuffs. In: *Food Toxicology.* New York, NY: Marcel Dekker Inc: 1988;pt B:1033–1050.

77. Taylor S. Chemical intoxication. In: Cliver DO, ed. *Foodborne Diseases.* New York, NY: Academic Press Inc;1990:171–182.

78. National Institutes of Health, National Institute of Allergies and Infectious Diseases. Fact sheet: food allergy and intolerances [NIAID Web site]. January 1999. Available at: http://www.niaid.nih.gov/factsheets/food.htm. Accessed May 27, 2001.

79. Food Allergy Network Web site. Available at: http://www.foodallergy.org/. Accessed May 27, 2001.

80. American Academy of Allergy, Asthma, and Immunology Web site. Available at: http://www.aaaai.org. Accessed May 27, 2001.

81. US Food and Drug Administration. Food allergies: rare but risky. *FDA Consumer* [FDA Web site]. May 1994. Available at: http://vm.cfsan.fda.gov/~dms/wh-alrg1.html. Accessed May 26, 2001.

82. Beaudette T. Adverse reactions to food. Chicago, IL: The American Dietetic Association; 1991.

83. Bock SA. The incidence of severe adverse reactions to food in Colorado. *J Allergy Clin Immunol.* 1992;90:683–685.

84. US Department of Health and Human Services. Food safety. In: *Healthy People 2010.* 2nd ed. With Understanding and Improving Health and Objectives for Improving Health. 2 vols. Washington, DC: US Government Printing Office; November 2000:10.3–10.19. Available at: http://www.health.gov/healthypeople/Document/pdf/Volume1/10Food.pdf. Accessed May 12, 2001.

85. Bindslev-Jensen C, Poulsen LK. *In vitro* diagnostic methods in the evaluation of food hypersensitivity. In: Metcalfe DD, Sampson HA, Simon RA, eds. *Food Allergy: Adverse Reactions to Foods and Food Additives.* 2nd ed. Cambridge, MA: Blackwell Science Ltd; 1997.

86. American Academy of Allergy, Asthma, and Immunology (AAAAI). Position statement: unproven procedures for diagnosis and treatment of allergic and immunologic diseases [AAAAI Web site]. 1992. Available at: http://www.aaaai.org/professional/physicianreference/positionstatements/ps14.stm. Accessed May 25, 2001.

87. Astwood JD, Fuchs RL, Lavrik PB. Food biotechnology and genetic engineering. In: Metcalfe DD, Sampson HA, Simon RA, eds. *Food Allergy: Adverse Reactions to Foods and Food Additives.* 2nd ed. Cambridge, MA: Blackwell Science Ltd; 1997.

88. US Food and Drug Administration. Statement of policy: foods derived from new plant varieties [FDA Web site]. August 17, 1998. Docket No. 92N-0139. Available at: http://vm.cfsan.fda.gov/~lrd/bio1992.html. Accessed May 27, 2001.

89. American Academy of Allergy, Asthma, and Immunology (AAAAI). Position statement: anaphylaxis in schools and other child care settings [AAAAI Web site]. Available at: http://www.aaaai.org/professional/physicianreference/positionstatements/ps34.stm. Accessed May 27, 2001.

90. American Medical Association. Allergic reactions to workplace allergens. In: *Primer on Allergic and Immunologic Diseases.* 4th ed. *J Am Med Assoc.* 1997;278:1907–1913. Available at: http://www.ama-assn.org/special/asthma/library/readroom/pr7008.htm. Accessed May 27, 2001.

91. US Food and Drug Administration. A fresh look at food preservatives. *FDA Consumer* [FDA Web site]. 1993. Available at: http://vm.cfsan.fda.gov/~dms/fdpreser.html. Accessed May 21, 2001.

92. Taylor SL, Bush RK, Nordlee JA. Sulfites. In: Metcalfe DD, Sampson HA, Simon RA, eds. *Food Allergy: Adverse Reactions to Foods and Food Additives.* 2nd ed. Cambridge, MA: Blackwell Science Ltd; 1997.

93. US Food and Drug Administration/International Food Information Council. Food color facts [FDA Web site]. January 1993. Available at: http://vm.cfsan.fda.gov/~lrd/colorfac.html. Accessed May 27, 2001.

94. Woessner KM, Simon RA. Monosodium glutamate. In: Metcalfe DD, Sampson HA, Simon RA, eds. *Food Allergy: Adverse Reactions to Foods and Food Additives.* 2nd ed. Cambridge, MA: Blackwell Science Ltd; 1997.

95. Meer RR, Baker J, Bodyfelt FW, Griffiths WM. Psychrotrophic *Bacillus* spp. in fluid milk products: a review. *J Food Prot.* 1991;54:969–979.

96. Luby S, Jones J, Dowda H. A large outbreak of gastroenteritis caused by diarrheal toxin-producing *Bacillus cereus. J Infect Dis.* 1993;167;1452–1455.

97. Granum PE. *Bacillus cereus.* In: Doyle MP, Beuchat LR, Montville TJ, eds. *Food Microbiology: Fundamentals and Frontiers.* Washington, DC: ASM Press; 1997:327–336.

98. Khodr M, Hill A, Perkins L, et al. Epidemiologic notes and reports: *Bacillus cereus* food poisoning associated with fried rice at two child day care centers—Virginia, 1993. *MMWR.* 1994;43(10);177–178. Available at: ftp://ftp.cdc.gov/pub/Publications/mmwr/wk/mm4310.pdf. Accessed May 27, 2001.

99. US Department of Agriculture, Food Safety and Inspection Service. Campylobacter questions and answers [USDA Web site]. November 1997. Available at: http://www.fsis.usda.gov/OA/background/campyq&a.htm. Accessed May 27, 2001.

100. US Department of Agriculture, Food Safety and Inspection Service. Foodborne illness: what consumers need to know [USDA Web site]. August 2000. Available at: http://www.fsis.usda.gov:80/oa/pubs/fact_fbi.htm. Accessed June 6, 2001.

101. US Department of Agriculture, Food Safety and Inspection Service. Food safety for persons with AIDS [USDA Web site]. May 2000. Available at: http://www.fsis.usda.gov:80/oa/pubs/aids.htm. Accessed May 26, 2001.

102. Centers for Disease Control and Prevention, National Center for Infectious Diseases, Division of Bacterial and Mycotic Diseases. Campylobacter: frequently asked questions [CDC Web site]. April 6, 2000. Available at: http://www.cdc.gov/ncidod/dbmd/diseaseinfo/campylobacter_g.htm. Accessed June 6, 2001.

103. Centers for Disease Control and Prevention. Campylobacter isolates in the United States, 1982–1986. *MMWR*. 1988;37:SS–22.

104. Altekruse SF, Stern NJ, Fields PI, Swerdlow DL. *Campylobacter jejuni*— An emerging foodborne pathogen. *Emerg Infect Dis*. 1999;5(1):28–35. Available at: http://www.cdc.gov/ncidod/EID/vol5no1/pdf/altekruse.pdf. Accessed June 6, 2001.

105. Graves TK, Bradley KK, Crutcher JM. Outbreak of *Campylobacter* enteritis associated with cross-contamination of food—Oklahoma,1996. *MMWR*. 1998;47(07):129–131. Available at: ftp://ftp.cdc.gov/pub/Publications/mmwr/wk/mm4707.pdf. Accessed June 6, 2001.

106. Nachamkin I. *Campylobacter jejuni*. In: Doyle MP, Beuchat LR, Montville TJ, eds. *Food Microbiology: Fundamentals and Frontiers*. Washington, DC: ASM Press; 1997:159–170.

107. Centers for Disease Control and Prevention. Botulism [CDC Web site]. Available at: http://www.cdc.gov/ncidod/dbmd/diseaseinfo/botulism_g.htm. Accessed June 7, 2001.

108. Canning, drying, and freezing [National Food Safety Database Web site]. Available at: http://www.foodsafety.ufl.edu/cmenu/preserve.htm. Accessed May 12, 2001.

109. Dodds KL, Austin JW. *Clostridium botulinum*. In: Doyle MP, Beuchat LR, Montville TJ, eds. *Food Microbiology: Fundamentals and Frontiers*. Washington, DC: ASM Press; 1997:288–304.

110. MacDonald KL, Spengler RF, Hatheway CL, et al. Type A botulism from sauteed onions: clinical and epidemiologic observations. *JAMA*. 1985;253:1275–1278.

111. St. Louis ME, Shaun HS, Peck MB. Botulism from chopped garlic: delayed recognition of a major outbreak. *Ann Intern Med*. 1988;108:363–368.

112. Morse DL, Pickard LK, Guzewich JJ, et al. Garlic-in-oil associated botulism: episode leads to product modification. *Am J Public Health*. 1990;80:1372–1373.

113. Knubley W, McChesney TC, Mallonee J, et al. Foodborne botulism—Oklahoma, 1994. *MMWR*. 1995;44(11):200–202. Available at: http://www.cdc.gov/mmwr/pdf/wk/mm4411.pdf. Accessed May 27, 2001.

114. Rifkin G, Sibounheuang K, Peterson L, et al. Foodborne botulism from eating home-pickled eggs—Illinois, 1997. *MMWR*. 2000;49(34):778–780. Available at: http://www.cdc.gov/mmwr/pdf/wk/mm4934.pdf. Accessed June 9, 2001.

115. Notermans SJ, Dufrenne J, Lund BM. Botulism risk of refrigerated, processed foods of extended durability. *J Food Protect*. 1990;86:373–374.

116. McClane BA. *Clostridium perfringens*. In: Doyle MP, Beuchat LR, Montville TJ, eds. *Food Microbiology: Fundamentals and Frontiers*. Washington, DC: ASM Press; 1997:305–326.

117. Zimomra J, Wenderoth T, Snyder A, et al. *Clostridium perfringens* gastroenteritis associated with corned beef served at St. Patrick's Day meals—Ohio and Virginia, 1993. *MMWR*. 1993(08);43:137, 143–144. Available at: ftp://ftp.cdc.gov/pub/Publications/mmwr/wk/mm4308.pdf. Accessed May 27, 2001.

118. Roach RL, Sienko DG. *Clostridium perfringens* outbreak associated with minestrone soup. *Am J Epidemiol*. 1992;136:1288–1291.

119. Centers for Disease Control and Prevention. *Escherichia coli* O157:H7: frequently asked questions [CDC Web site]. Available at: http://www.cdc.gov/ncidod/dbmd/diseaseinfo/escherichiacoli_g.htm. Accessed June 7, 2001.

120. US Department of Agriculture, Food Safety and Inspection Service. Use a meat thermometer [USDA Web site]. June 1997. Available at: http://www.fsis.usda.gov/OA/pubs/cithermo.htm. Accessed May 26, 2001.

121. Buchanan RL, Doyle MP. Institute of Food Technologists' scientific status summary: foodborne disease significance of *Escherichia coli* O157:H7 and other enterohemorrhagic *E. coli*. *Food Tech.* 1997;51(10):69–76.

122. US Department of Agriculture, Centers for Epidemiology and Animal Health. An update: *Escherichia coli* O157:H7 in humans and cattle [USDA Web site]. May 1997. Available at: http://www.aphis.usda.gov:80/vs/ceah/cei/ecoupdat.pdf. Accessed May 27, 2001.

123. Goldwater PN, Bettelheim KA. Hemolytic uremic syndrome due to shiga-like toxin producing *Escherichia coli* O48:H21 in South Australia. *Emerg Infect Dis.* 1995;1(4):132–133. Available at: ftp://ftp.cdc.gov/pub/EID/vol1no4/adobe/goldwate.pdf. Accessed May 27, 2001.

124. Nishikawa Y, Hanaoka M, Ogasawara J, et al. Heat-stable enterotoxin-producing *Escherichia coli* O169:H41 in Japan. *Emerg Infect Dis.* 1995;1(2):61–62. Available at: ftp://ftp.cdc.gov/pub/EID/vol1no2/adobe/letters.vol1no2.pdf. Accessed May 27, 2001.

125. Centers for Disease Control and Prevention. Travelers' health: safe food and water [CDC Web site]. Available at: http://www.cdc.gov/travel/foodwater.htm. Accessed May 26, 2001.

126. Doyle MP, Zhao T, Meng J, Zhao S. *Escherichia coli* O157:H7. In: Doyle MP, Beuchat LR, Montville TJ, eds. *Food Microbiology: Fundamentals and Frontiers.* Washington, DC: ASM Press; 1997:171–191.

127. Besser RE, Lett SM, Weber JT, et al. An outbreak of diarrhea and hemolytic uremic syndrome from *Escherichia coli* O157:H7 in fresh-pressed apple cider. *JAMA.* 1993;269:2217–20.

128. Davis M, Osaki C, Gordon D, et al. Update: multistate outbreak of *Escherichia coli* O157:H7 infections from hamburgers—Western United States, 1992–1993. *MMWR.* 1993;42(14):258–263. Available at: ftp://ftp.cdc.gov/pub/Publications/mmwr/wk/mm4214.pdf. Accessed May 27, 2001.

129. Belongia EA, Osterholm MT, Soler JT, et al. Transmission of *Escherichia coli* O157:H7 infection in Minnesota child day-care facilities. *JAMA.* 1993;269:883–888.

130. Moore K, Damrow T, Abbott DO, et al. Outbreak of acute gastroenteritis attributable to *Escherichia coli* serotype O104:H21—Helena, Montana, 1994. *MMWR.* 1995;44(27);501–503. Available at: ftp://ftp.cdc.gov/pub/Publications/mmwr/wk/mm4427.pdf. Accessed May 27, 2001.

131. Benoit V, Raiche P, Smith MG, et al. Foodborne outbreaks of Enterotoxigenic *Escherichia coli*—Rhode Island and New Hampshire, 1993. *MMWR.* 1994;43(05);81,87–88. Available at: ftp://ftp.cdc.gov/pub/Publications/mmwr/wk/mm4305.pdf. Accessed May 27, 2001.

132. Taylor WR, Schell WL, Wells JG, et al. A foodborne outbreak of enterotoxigenic *Escherichia coli* diarrhea. *N Engl J Med.* 1982;306:1093–1095.

133. Merson MH, Morris GK, Sack DA, et al. Traveler's diarrhea in Mexico: a prospective study of physicians and family members attending a conference. *N Engl J Med.* 1976;294:1299–1305.

134. Feng, P. *Escherichia coli* serotype O157:H7: novel vehicles of infection and emergence of phenotypic variants. *Emerg Infect Dis.* 1995;1(2):47–52. Available at: ftp://ftp.cdc.gov/pub/EID/vol1no2/adobe/feng.vol1no2.pdf. Accessed May 27, 2001.

135. Como-Sabetti K, Reagan S, Allaire S, et al. Outbreaks of *Escherichia coli* O157:H7 infection associated with eating alfalfa sprouts—Michigan and Virginia, June–July 1997. *MMWR.* 1997;46(32):741–744. Available at: ftp://ftp.cdc.gov/pub/Publications/mmwr/wk/mm4632.pdf. Accessed May 23, 2001.

136. Mshar PA, Dembek ZF, Cartter ML, et al. Outbreaks of *Escherichia coli* O157:H7 infection and cryptosporidiosis associated with drinking unpasteurized apple cider—Connecticut and New York, October 1996. *MMWR.* 1997;46(01):4–8. Available at: ftp://ftp.cdc.gov/pub/Publications/mmwr/wk/mm4601.pdf. Accessed May 23, 2001.

137. US Department of Agriculture Food Safety and Inspection Service. *Listeria monocytogenes* and listeriosis [USDA Web site]. February 1999. Available at: http://www.fsis.usda.gov/OA/pubs/listeria.htm. Accessed May 26, 2001.

138. US Food and Drug Administration. Keep your baby safe: eat hard cheeses instead of soft cheeses during pregnancy [FDA Web site]. July 1997. Available at: http://vm.cfsan.fda.gov/~dms/listeren.html. Accessed May 27, 2001.

139. US Food and Drug Administration, Center for Food Safety and Applied Nutrition; US Department of Agriculture, Food Safety and Inspection Service; Centers for Disease Control and Prevention. Draft assessment of the relative risk to public health from foodborne *Listeria monocytogenes* among selected categories of ready-to-eat foods [Foodsafety.gov Web site]. January 2001. Available at: http://www.foodsafety.gov/%7Edms/lmrisk.html. Accessed June 6, 2001.

140. Centers for Disease Control and Prevention. Listeriosis: frequently asked questions [CDC Web site]. January 1999. Available at: http://www.cdc.gov/ncidod/dbmd/diseaseinfo/listeriosis_g.htm. Accessed June 7, 2001.

141. Centers for Disease Control and Prevention. Multistate outbreak of listeriosis—United States, 1998. *MMWR.* 1998;47(50);1085–1086. Available at: ftp://ftp.cdc.gov/pub/Publications/mmwr/wk/mm4750.pdf.

142. Rocourt J, Cossart P. *Listeria monocytogenes.* In: Doyle MP, Beuchat LR, Montville TJ, eds. *Food Microbiology: Fundamentals and Frontiers.* Washington, DC: ASM Press; 1997:337–352.

143. Schuchat A, Deaver KA, Wenger JD, et al. Role of foods in sporadic listeriosis, I: case-control study of dietary risk factors. *JAMA.* 1992;267:2041–2045.

144. Fleming DW, Cochi WL, MacDonald KL, et al. Pasteurized milk as a vehicle of infection in an outbreak of listeriosis. *N Engl J Med.* 1985;312:404–407.

145. Linnan MJ, Mascola L, Lou XD, et al. Epidemic listeriosis associated with Mexican-style cheese. *N Engl J Med.* 1988;319:823–828.

146. Centers for Disease Control and Prevention. Update: multistate outbreak of listeriosis—United States, 1998–1999. *MMWR.* 1999;47(51);1117–1118. Available at: ftp://ftp.cdc.gov/pub/Publications/mmwr/wk/mm4751.pdf. Accessed May 27, 2001.

147. Anderson G, Mascola L, Rutherford GW, et al. Update: foodborne listeriosis—United States, 1988–1990. *MMWR.* 1992;41(15);251,257–258.

148. Centers for Disease Control and Prevention. Salmonellosis: frequently asked questions [CDC Web site]. March 30, 2000. Available at: http://www.cdc.gov/ncidod/dbmd/diseaseinfo/salmonellosis_g.htm. Accessed June 7, 2001.

149. Centers for Disease Control and Prevention. Salmonella enteritidis: frequently asked questions [CDC Web site]. April 25, 2001. Available at: http://www.cdc.gov/ncidod/dbmd/diseaseinfo/salment_g.htm. Accessed June 7, 2001.

150. D'Aoust J-Y. *Salmonella* species. In: Doyle MP, Beuchat LR, Montville TJ, eds. *Food Microbiology: Fundamentals and Frontiers.* Washington, DC: ASM Press; 1997:129–158.

151. Hedberg CW, White KE, Johnson JA, et al. An outbreak of *Salmonella enteritidis* infection at a fast-food restaurant: implications of food handler-associated transmission. *J Infect Dis.* 1991;164:1135–1140.

152. Mishu B, Griffin PM, Tauxe RV, et al. *Salmonella enteritidis* gastroenteritis transmitted by intact chicken eggs. *Ann Intern Med.* 1991;115:190–194.

153. Centers for Disease Control and Prevention. Outbreak of *Salmonella enteritidis* infection associated with consumption of raw shell eggs. *MMWR.* 1991(21);41:369–372.

154. Hedberg CW, Korlath JA, D'Aoust J-Y, et al. A multistate outbreak of *Salmonella javiana* and *Salmonella oranienburg* infections due to consumption of contaminated cheese. *JAMA*. 1992;268:3203–3207.

155. Centers for Disease Control and Prevention. Multistate outbreak of *Salmonella* serotype *Agona* infections linked to toasted oats cereal—United States, April–May 1998. *MMWR*. 1998;47(22);462–464. Available at: ftp://ftp.cdc.gov/pub/Publications/mmwr/wk/mm4722.pdf. Accessed May 23, 2001.

156. Van Houten R, Farberman D, Norton J, et al. *Plesiomonas shigelloides* and *Salmonella* serotype *Hartford* infections associated with a contaminated water supply—Livingston County, New York, 1996. *MMWR*. 1998;47(19);394–396. Available at: ftp://ftp.cdc.gov/pub/Publications/mmwr/wk/mm4719.pdf. Accessed May 27, 2001.

157. Ravenholt O, Schmutz CA, Empey LC, et al. Salmonellosis associated with a Thanksgiving dinner—Nevada, 1995. *MMWR*. 1996;45(46);1016–1017. Available at: ftp://ftp.cdc.gov/pub/Publications/mmwr/wk/mm4546.pdf. Accessed May 27, 2001.

158. Levy M, Fletcher M, Moody M, et al. Outbreaks of Salmonella serotype *Enteritidis* infection associated with consumption of raw shell eggs—United States, 1994–1995. *MMWR*. 1996;45(34);737–742. Available at: ftp://ftp.cdc.gov/pub/Publications/mmwr/wk/mm4534.pdf. Accessed May 27, 2001.

159. Crespin FH, Eason B, Gorbitz K, et al. Outbreak of salmonellosis associated with beef jerky—New Mexico, 1995. *MMWR*. 1995;44(42);785–788. Available at: ftp://ftp.cdc.gov/pub/Publications/mmwr/wk/mm4442.pdf. Accessed May 27, 2001.

160. Centers for Disease Control and Prevention. Emerging infectious diseases outbreak of *Salmonella enteritidis* associated with nationally distributed ice cream products—Minnesota, South Dakota, and Wisconsin, 1994. *MMWR*. 1994;43(40);740–741. Available at: ftp://ftp.cdc.gov/pub/Publications/mmwr/wk/mm4340.pdf. Accessed May 23, 2001.

161. Buckner P, Ferguson D, Anzalone F, et al. Outbreak of *Salmonella enteritidis* associated with homemade ice cream—Florida, 1993. *MMWR*. 1994;43(36);669–671. Available at: ftp://ftp.cdc.gov/pub/Publications/mmwr/wk/mm4336.pdf. Accessed May 27, 2001.

162. Ewert D, Bendana N, Tormey M, et al. Outbreaks of *Salmonella enteritidis* gastroenteritis—California, 1993. *MMWR*. 1993;42(41);793–797. Available at: ftp://ftp.cdc.gov/pub/Publications/mmwr/wk/mm4241.pdf. Accessed May 27, 2001.

163. Louie KK, Paccagnella AM, Osei WD, et al. *Salmonella* serotype *Tennessee* in powdered milk products and infant formula—Canada and United States, 1993. *MMWR*. 1993;42(26);516–517. Available at: ftp://ftp.cdc.gov/pub/Publications/mmwr/wk/mm4226.pdf. Accessed May 23, 2001.

164. Lindsay RE, Krissinger WA, Fields BF. Microwave versus conventional oven cooking of chicken: relationship of internal temperature to surface contamination by *Salmonella typhimurium*. *J Am Diet Assoc*. 1986;86:373–374.

165. De Boer D and Hahne M. Cross-contamination with *Campylobacter jejuni* and *Salmonella* spp. from raw chicken products during food preparation. *J Food Protect*. 1990;53:1067–1068.

166. Lecos C. Of microbes and milk: probing America's worst *Salmonella* outbreak. *Dairy Food Sanit*. 1986;6:136–140.

167. Ryan CA, Nickels MK, Hargrett-Bean NT, et al. Massive outbreak of antimicrobial-resistant salmonellosis traced to pasteurized milk. *JAMA*. 1987;258:3269–3274.

168. Mahon BE, Rohn DD, Pack SR, and Tauxe RV. Electronic communication facilitates investigation of a highly dispersed foodborne outbreak: *Salmonella* on the superhighway. *Emerg Infect Dis*. 1995;1(3):94–95. Available at: ftp://ftp.cdc.gov/pub/EID/vol1no3/adobe/mahon.pdf. Accessed May 26, 2001.

169. Hurd S, Phan Q, Hadler J, et al. Multistate outbreak of listeriosis—United States, 2000. *MMWR*. 2000;49(50);1129–1130. Available at: http://www.cdc.gov/mmwr/PDF/wk/mm4950.pdf. Accessed May 27, 2001.

170. Centers for Disease Control and Prevention. Shigellosis: frequently asked questions [CDC Web site]. May 30, 2000. Available at: http://www.cdc.gov/ncidod/dbmd/diseaseinfo/shigellosis_g.htm. Accessed May 27, 2001.

171. Frost JA, McEvoy MB, Bentley CA, et al. An outbreak of *Shigella sonnei* infection associated with consumption of iceberg lettuce. *Emerg Infect Dis*. 1995; 1(1):26–28. Available at: ftp://ftp.cdc.gov/pub/EID/vol1no1/adobe/frost.vol1no1.pdf. Accessed May 27, 2001.

172. Maurelli AT, Lampel KA. *Shigella* species. In: Doyle MP, Beuchat LR, Montville TJ, eds. *Food Microbiology: Fundamentals and Frontiers*. Washington, DC: ASM Press; 1997:216–227.

173. Rubenstein JS, Noah ZL, Zales VR, Shulman ST. Acute myocarditis associated with *Shigella sonnei* gastroenteritis. *J Pediatr*. 1993;122:82–84.

174. Yagupsky P, Loeffelholz M, Bell K, Menegus MA. Use of multiple markers for investigation of an epidemic of *Shigella sonnei* infection in Monroe County, New York. *J Clin Microbiol*. 1991;29:2850–2855.

175. Hyams KC, Bourgeois AL, Merrell BR, et al. Diarrheal disease during Operation Desert Shield. *N Engl J Med*. 1991;325:1423–1428.

176. Centers for Disease Control and Prevention. Outbreak of *Shigella sonnei* associated with eating a nationally distributed dip—California, Oregon, and Washington, January 2000. *MMWR*. 2000;49(3):60–61. Available at: http://www.cdc.gov/mmwr/PDF/wk/mm4903.pdf. Accessed May 27, 2001.

177. Crowe L, Lau W, McLeod L, et al. Outbreaks of *Shigella sonnei* infection associated with eating fresh parsley—United States and Canada, July–August 1998. *MMWR*. 1999;48(14):285–289. Available at: http://www.cdc.gov/mmwr/PDF/wk/mm4814.pdf. Accessed May 27, 2001.

178. Collins RK, Henderson MN, Conwill DE, et al. Epidemiologic notes and reports: multiple outbreaks of staphylococcal food poisoning caused by canned mushrooms. *MMWR*. 1989;38(24):417–418.

179. US Department of Agriculture, Food Safety and Inspection Service. Focus on: ham [USDA Web site]. March 1995. Available at: http://www.fsis.usda.gov:80/oa/pubs/ham.htm. Accessed May 27, 2001.

180. Jablonski LM, Bohach GA. *Staphylococcus aureus*. In: Doyle MP, Beuchat LR, Montville TJ, eds. *Food Microbiology: Fundamentals and Frontiers*. Washington, DC: ASM Press; 1997:353–375.

181. Ward K, Hammond R, Katz D, Hallman D. Outbreak of staphylococcal food poisoning associated with precooked ham—Florida, 1997. *MMWR*. 1997;46(50);1189–1191. Available at: ftp://ftp.cdc.gov/pub/Publications/mmwr/wk/mm4650.pdf. Accessed May 27, 2001.

182. Centers for Disease Control and Prevention. Group A Streptococcal (GAS) disease [CDC Web site]. December 21, 2000. Available at: http://www.cdc.gov/ncidod/dbmd/diseaseinfo/groupastreptococcal_g.htm. Accessed May 27, 2001.

183. Steinkuller JS, Chan K, Rinehouse SE. Prechewing of food by adults and streptococcal pharyngitis in infants. *J Pediatr*. 1992;120:563–564.

184. Farley TA, Wilson SA, Mahoney F, et al. Direct inoculation of food as the cause of an outbreak of group A streptococcal pharyngitis. *J Infect Dis*. 1993;167:1232–1235.

185. US Food and Drug Administration. If you eat raw oysters, you need to know . . . . [FDA Web site] July 1995; updated January 28, 1999. Available at: http://vm.cfsan.fda.gov/~lrd/oyster.html. Accessed May 27, 2001.

186. Centers for Disease Control and Prevention. Cholera: frequently asked questions [CDC Web site]. November 4, 2000. Available at: http://www.cdc.gov/ncidod/dbmd/diseaseinfo/cholera_g.htm. Accessed May 27, 2001.

187. Centers for Disease Control and Prevention. *Vibrio vulnificus:* frequently asked questions [CDC Web site]. March 29, 2000. Available at: http://www.cdc.gov/ncidod/dbmd/diseaseinfo/vibriovulnificus_g.htm. Accessed May 27, 2001.

188. Centers for Disease Control and Prevention. *Vibrio papahaemolyticus:* frequently asked questions [CDC Web site]. March 29, 2000. Available at: http://www.cdc.gov/ncidod/dbmd/diseaseinfo/vibrioparahaemolyticus_g.htm. Accessed May 27, 2001.

189. Oliver JD, Kaper JB. *Vibrio* species. In: Doyle MP, Beuchat LR, Montville TJ, eds. *Food Microbiology: Fundamentals and Frontiers.* Washington, DC: ASM Press; 1997:228–264.

190. Levine WC, Griffin PM, and the Gulf Coast *Vibrio* Working Group. *Vibrio* infections on the Gulf Coast: results of first year of regional surveillance. *J Infect Dis.* 1993;167:479–483.

191. Eichold BH II, Williamson JR, Woernle CH, et al. Isolation of *Vibrio cholerae* O1 from oysters—Mobile Bay, 1991–1992. *MMWR.* 1993;42(05):91–93. Available at: ftp://ftp.cdc.gov/pub/Publications/mmwr/wk/mm4249.pdf. Accessed May 27, 2001.

192. Rashid HO, Ito H, Ishigaki I. Distribution of pathogenic vibrios and other bacteria in imported frozen shrimps and their decontamination by gamma-irradiation. *World J Microbiol Biotechnol.* 1992;8:494–499.

193. Taylor JL, Tuttle J, Pramukul T, et al. An outbreak of cholera in Maryland associated with imported commercial frozen coconut milk. *J Infect Dis.* 1993;167:1330–1335.

194. Cooper G, Hadler JL, Barth S, et al. Cholera associated with international travel. *MMWR.* 1992;41(36):664–667.

195. Bullen JJ, Spalding PB, Ward CG, Gutteridge JMC. Hemochromatosis, iron, and septicemia caused by *Vibrio vulnificus. Arch Intern Med.* 1991;151:1606–1609.

196. Berry TM, Park DL, Lightner DV. Comparison of the microbial quality of raw shrimp form China, Ecuador, or Mexico at both wholesale and retail levels. *J Food Prot.* 1994;57:150–153.

197. Wechsler E, D'Aleo A, Hill VA, et al. Outbreak of *Vibrio parahaemolyticus* infection associated with eating raw oysters and clams harvested from Long Island Sound—Connecticut, New Jersey, and New York, 1998. *MMWR.* 1999;48(03);48–51. Available at: ftp://ftp.cdc.gov/pub/Publications/mmwr/wk/mm4803.pdf. Accessed May 27, 2001.

198. Fyfe M, Kelly MT, Yeung ST, et al. Outbreak of *Vibrio parahaemolyticus* infections associated with eating raw oysters—Pacific Northwest, 1997. *MMWR.* 1998;47(22);457–462. Available at: ftp://ftp.cdc.gov/pub/Publications/mmwr/wk/mm4722.pdf. Accessed May 27, 2001.

199. Mascola L, Tormey M, Dassey D, et al. *Vibrio vulnificus* infections associated with eating raw oysters—Los Angeles, 1996. *MMWR.* 1996;45(29);621–624. Available at: ftp://ftp.cdc.gov/pub/Publications/mmwr/wk/mm4529.pdf. Accessed May 27, 2001.

200. Hlady WG, Mullen RC, Hopkins RS. *Vibrio vulnificus* infections associated with raw oyster consumption—Florida, 1981–1992. *MMWR.* 1993;42(21);405–407. Available at: ftp://ftp.cdc.gov/pub/Publications/mmwr/wk/mm4221.pdf. Accessed May 27, 2001.

201. Bailey N, Louck M, Hopkins D, et al. Cholera associated with food transported from El Salvador—Indiana, 1994. *MMWR.* 1995;44(20);385–386. Available at: ftp://ftp.cdc.gov/pub/Publications/mmwr/wk/mm4420.pdf. Accessed May 27, 2001.

202. Robins-Browne RM. *Yersinia enterocolitica.* In: Doyle MP, Beuchat LR, Montville TJ, eds. *Food Microbiology: Fundamentals and Frontiers.* Washington, DC: ASM Press; 1997:192–215.

203. Lee LA, Taylor J, Carter GP, Quinn B, et al. *Yersinia enterocolitica* O:3: An emerging cause of pediatric gastroenteritis in the United States. *J Infect Dis.* 1991;163:660–663.

204. Tacket CO, Ballard J, Harris N, et al. An outbreak of *Yersinia enterocolitica* infections caused by contaminated tofu (soybean curd). *Am J Epidemiol.* 1985;121:705–711.

205. Centers for Disease Control. *Yersinia enterocolitica* infections during the holidays in Black families—Georgia. *MMWR*. 1990;39:819–821.

206. Hayunga EG. Helminths acquired from finfish, shellfish, and other food sources. In: Doyle MP, Beuchat LR, Montville TJ, eds. *Food Microbiology: Fundamentals and Frontiers*. Washington, DC: ASM Press; 1997:463–477.

207. Centers for Disease Control and Prevention. Fact sheet: cryptosporidiosis [CDC Web site]. May 2001. Available at: http://www.cdc.gov/ncidod/dpd/parasites/ cryptosporidiosis/factsht_cryptosporidiosis.htm. Accessed June 9, 2001.

208. Centers for Disease Control and Prevention, National Center for Infectious Diseases. Cryptosporidiosis: a guide for persons with HIV/AIDS [CDC Web site]. May 26, 2001. Available at: http://www.cdc.gov/ncidod/diseases/crypto/hivaids.htm. Accessed May 26, 2001.

209. Centers for Disease Control and Prevention. Cryptosporidiosis control and prevention [CDC Web site]. August 15, 1999. Available at: http://www.cdc.gov/ncidod/ dpd/parasites/cryptosporidiosis/crypto_control_prevent.htm. Accessed June 9, 2001.

210. Environmental Protection Agency/Centers for Disease Control and Prevention. Guidance for people with severely weakened immune systems [EPA Web site]. Available at: http://www.epa.gov/ogwdw000/crypto.html. Accessed May 26, 2001.

211. Hale CM, Polder JM. Fact sheet on childhood diseases and conditions: what you should know about . . . cryptosporidiosis in the child care setting. In: *The ABC's of Safe and Healthy Child Care: An On-Line Handbook for Child Care Providers* [CDC Web site]. January 1997. Available at: http://www.cdc.gov/ncidod/hip/abc/facts08.htm. Accessed May 26, 2001.

212. Centers for Disease control and Prevention. Preventing cryptosporidiosis: a guide to water filters and bottled water [CDC Web site]. August 15, 1999. Available at: http:// www.cdc.gov/ncidod/dpd/parasites/cryptosporidiosis/factsht_crypto_prevent _water.htm. Accessed June 9, 2001.

213. Colley DG. Waterborne cryptosporidiosis threat addressed. *Emerg Infect Dis*. 1995;1(2):66. Available at: ftp://ftp.cdc.gov/pub/EID/vol1no2/adobe/ newsandnotes.vol1no2.pdf. Accessed June 9, 2001.

214. Speer CA. Protozoan parasites acquired from food and water. In: Doyle MP, Beuchat LR, Montville TJ, eds. *Food Microbiology: Fundamentals and Frontiers*. Washington, DC: ASM Press; 1997:478–493.

215. LeChevallier MW, Norton WD, Lee RG. Occurrence of *Giardia* and *Cryptosporidium* spp. in surface water supplies. *Appl Environ Microbiol*. 1991;57:2610–2616.

216. Quinn K, Baldwin G, Stepak P, Thorburn K, et al. Foodborne outbreak of cryptosporidiosis—Spokane, Washington, 1997. *MMWR*. 1998;47(27):565–567. Available at: ftp://ftp.cdc.gov/pub/Publications/mmwr/wk/mm4727.pdf. Accessed June 9, 2001.

217. Besser-Wiek JW, Forfang J, Hedberg CW, et al. Foodborne outbreak of diarrheal illness associated with *Cryptosporidium parvum*—Minnesota, 1995. *MMWR*. 1996;45(36):783–784. Available at: ftp://ftp.cdc.gov/pub/Publications/mmwr/wk/ mm4536.pdf. Accessed June 9, 2001.

218. Cordell RL, Addiss DG. Cryptosporidiosis in child care settings: a review of the literature and recommendations for prevention and control. *Ped Infect Dis J*. 1994;13: 310–307.

219. Smith JL. *Cryptosporidium* and *Giardia* as agents of foodborne disease. *J Food Prot*. 1993;56:451–461.

220. Centers for Disease Control and Prevention. 1999 USPHS/IDSA guidelines for the prevention of opportunistic infections in persons infected with human immunodeficiency virus: US Public Health Service (USPHS) and Infectious Diseases Society of America (IDSA). *MMWR*. 1999;48(RR-10):1–82. Available at: http://www.cdc.gov/ mmwr/PDF/RR/RR4810.pdf. Accessed May 26, 2001.

221. Juranek DD. Cryptosporidiosis: Sources of infection and guidelines for prevention. *Clin Infect Dis.* 1995;21(Suppl1)S57–61.

222. Guerrant RL. Cryptosporidiosis: an emerging, highly infectious threat. *Emerg Infect Dis.* 1997;3(1):51–57. Available at: ftp://ftp.cdc.gov/pub/EID/vol3no1/adobe/guerrant.pdf. Accessed June 8, 2001.

223. Centers for Disease Control and Prevention. Travelers' health: safe food and water [CDC Web site]. Available at: http://www.cdc.gov/travel/foodwater.htm. Accessed May 26, 2001.

224. Centers for Disease Control and Prevention. *Cyclospora* infection [CDC Web site]. May 26, 2001. Available at: http://www.cdc.gov/ncidod/diseases/cyclospo/cyclogen.htm. Accessed June 9, 2001.

225. Chambers J, Somerfeldt S, Mackey L, et al. Outbreaks of *Cyclospora cayetanensis* infection—United States, 1996. *MMWR.* 1996;45(25):549–551. Available at: ftp://ftp.cdc.gov/pub/Publications/mmwr/wk/mm4525.pdf. Accessed May 23, 2001.

226. Hofmann J, Liu Z, Genese C, et al. Update: outbreaks of Cyclospora cayetanensis infection—United States, 1996. *MMWR.* 1996;45(28):611–612. Available at: ftp://ftp.cdc.gov/pub/Publications/mmwr/wk/mm4528.pdf. Accessed June 9, 2001.

227. Jacquette G, Guido F, Jacobs J, et al. Outbreaks of *Cyclospora cayetanensis* infection—United States, 1997. *MMWR.* 1997;46(21):461–462. Available at: ftp://ftp.cdc.gov/pub/Publications/mmwr/wk/mm4621.pdf. Accessed May 23, 2001.

228. DeGraw E, Heber S, and Rowan A. Update: outbreaks of *Cyclospora cayetanensis* infection—United States and Canada, 1997. *MMWR.* 1997;46(23):521–523. Available at: ftp://ftp.cdc.gov/pub/Publications/mmwr/wk/mm4623.pdf. Accessed June 9, 2001.

229. Colley DG. Widespread foodborne cyclosporiasis outbreaks present major challenges. *Emerg Infect Dis.* 1996;2(4):354–356. Available at: ftp://ftp.cdc.gov/pub/EID/vol2no4/adobe/letters.pdf. Accessed June 9, 2001.

230. Garcia-Lopez HL, Rodriguez-Tovar LE, Medina-De la Garza CE. Identification of *Cyclospora* in poultry. *Emerg Infect Dis.* 1996;2(4):356–357. Available at: ftp://ftp.cdc.gov/pub/EID/vol2no4/adobe/letters.pdf. Accessed June 9, 2001.

231. Pritchett R, Gossman C, Radke V, et al. Outbreak of cyclosporiasis—Northern Virginia–Washington, D.C.–Baltimore, Maryland, Metropolitan Area, 1997 *MMWR.* 1997; 46(30):689–691. Available at: ftp://ftp.cdc.gov/pub/Publications/mmwr/wk/mm4630.pdf. Accessed June 9, 2001.

232. Health Canada and the Centers for Disease Control and Prevention. Outbreak of Cyclosporiasis—Ontario, Canada, May 1998. *MMWR.* 1998;47(38);806–809. Available at: ftp://ftp.cdc.gov/pub/Publications/mmwr/wk/mm4738.pdf. Accessed June 9, 2001.

233. Centers for Disease Control and Prevention. Fact sheet: amebiasis [CDC Web site]. March 2001. Available at: http://www.cdc.gov/ncidod/dpd/parasites/amebiasis/factsht_amebiasis.htm. Accessed June 9, 2001.

234. Ravdin JI. Amebiasis. *Clin Infect Dis.* 1995;20:1453–1466.

235. Guerin PF, Marapudi S, McGrail L, et al. Epidemiologic notes and reports: intestinal perforation caused by larval *Eustrongylides*— Maryland. *MMWR.* 1982;31(28):383–384,389.

236. Centers for Disease Control and Prevention. Fact sheet: giardiasis [CDC Web site]. May 2001. Available at: http://www.cdc.gov/ncidod/dpd/parasites/giardiasis/default.htm. Accessed June 9, 2001.

237. Hale CM, Polder JM. Fact sheet on childhood diseases and conditions: what you should know about . . . giardiasis in the child care setting. In: *The ABC's of Safe and Healthy Child Care: An On-Line Handbook for Child Care Providers* [CDC Web site]. January 1997. Available at: http://www.cdc.gov/ncidod/hip/abc/facts16.htm. Accessed May 26, 2001.

238. Mintz ED, Hudson-Wragg M, Mshar P, et al. Foodborne giardiasis in a corporate office setting. *J Infect Dis.* 1993;167:250–253.

239. Quick R, Paugh K, Addiss D, et al. Restaurant-associated outbreak of giardiasis. *J Infect Dis.* 1992;166:673–676.

240. Cody MM, Sottnek HM, O'Leary VS. Recovery of *Giardia lamblia* cysts from chairs and tables in child day care centers. *Pediatrics.* 1994;94 (suppl):1006–1008.

241. Osterholm MT, Forfang JC, Ristenen TL. An outbreak of foodborne giardiasis. *N Engl J Med.* 1981;304:24–28.

242. Lettau LA, Gardner S, Tennis J, et al. Locally acquired neurocysticercosis—North Carolina, Massachusetts, and South Carolina, 1989–1991. *MMWR.* 1992;41(01):1–4.

243. Schantz PM, Moore AC, Munoz JL, et al. Neurocysticercosis in an orthodox Jewish community in New York City. *N Engl J Med.* 1992;327:692–695.

244. Centers for Disease Control and Prevention. Fact sheet: toxoplasmosis [CDC Web site]. August 15, 1999. Available at: http://www.cdc.gov/ncidod/dpd/parasites/toxoplasmosis/factsht_toxoplasmosis.htm. Accessed June 9, 2001.

245. Centers for Disease Control and Prevention. Fact Sheet: trichinosis (Trichinellosis) [CDC Web site]. August 15, 1999. Available at: http://www.cdc.gov/ncidod/dpd/parasites/trichinosis/factsht_trichinosis.htm. Accessed June 9, 2001.

246. MacLean JD, Poirier L, Gyorkos TW, et al. Epidemiologic and serologic definition of primary and secondary trichinosis in the Arctic. *J Infect Dis.* 1992;165:908–912.

247. McAuley JB, Michelson MK, Hightower AW, et al. A trichinosis outbreak among Southeast Asian refugees. *Am J Epidemiol.* 1992;135:1404–1410.

248. Vollbrecht A, Sokolowski D, Hollipeter W, et al. Outbreak of trichinellosis associated with eating cougar jerky—Idaho, 1995. *MMWR.* 1996;45(10);205–206. Available at: ftp://ftp.cdc.gov/pub/Publications/mmwr/wk/mm4510.pdf. Accessed June 9, 2001.

249. Centers for Disease Control and Prevention. Viral hepatitis A [CDC Web site]. May 29, 2001. Available at: http://www.cdc.gov/ncidod/diseases/hepatitis/a/index.htm. Accessed June 9, 2001.

250. Cliver DO. Foodborne viruses. In: Doyle MP, Beuchat LR, Montville TJ, eds. Food Microbiology: *Fundamentals and Frontiers.* Washington, DC: ASM Press; 1997:437–446.

251. Niu MT, Polish LB, Robertson BH, et al. Multistate outbreak of hepatitis A associated with frozen strawberries. *J Infect Dis.* 1992;166:518–524.

252. Skala M, Collier C, Hinkle CJ, et al. Foodborne hepatitis A—Missouri, Wisconsin, and Alaska, 1990–1992. *MMWR.* 1993;42(27);526–529. Available at: ftp://ftp.cdc.gov/pub/Publications/mmwr/wk/mm4227.pdf. Accessed June 3, 2001.

253. Warner RD, Carr RW, McCleskey FK, et al. A large nontypical outbreak of Norwalk virus: gastroenteritis associated with exposing celery to nonpotable water and with *Citrobacter freundii. Arch Intern Med.* 1991;151:2419–2424.

254. Arness M, Canham M, Feighner B, et al. Norwalk-like viral gastroenteritis in U.S. Army Trainees—Texas, 1998. *MMWR.* 1999;48(11);225–227. Available at: ftp://ftp.cdc.gov/pub/Publications/mmwr/wk/mm4811.pdf. Accessed June 3, 2001.

255. Daniels NA, Bergmire-Sweat DA, Schwab KJ, et al. Foodborne outbreak of gastroenteritis associated with Norwalk-like viruses: first molecular traceback to deli sandwiches contaminated during preparation. *J Infect Dis.* 2000;181:1467–1470.

256. Hale CM, Polder JM. Fact sheet on childhood diseases and conditions: what you should know about . . . rotavirus diarrhea in the child care setting. In: *The ABC's of Safe and Healthy Child Care: An On-Line Handbook for Child Care Providers* [CDC Web site]. December 1998. Available at: http://www.cdc.gov/ncidod/hip/abc/facts34.htm. Accessed June 3, 2001.

257. Centers for Disease Control and Prevention. Rotavirus [CDC Web site]. June 21, 1999. Available at: http://www.cdc.gov/ncidod/dvrd/nrevss/rotfeat.htm. Accessed June 9, 2001.

258. Fletcher M, Levy ME, Griffin DD. Foodborne outbreak of group A rotavirus gastroenteritis among college students—District of Columbia, March–April 2000. *MMWR.* 2000;49(50):1131–1133. Available at: http://www.cdc.gov/mmwr/PDF/wk/mm4950.pdf. Accessed June 9, 2001.

259. King TP, Hoffman D, Lowenstein H, et al. Allergen nomenclature. *Int Arch Allergy Immunol.* 1994;105:224–233.

CHAPTER 3

THE FOOD IN FOOD SAFETY

Foods are the vehicles for toxic agents that cause foodborne illness. This means that the food "carries" the toxic agent into the body. To serve as a vehicle, a food must be contaminated by a toxic agent, either a pathogen or a chemical. If the toxic agent is a pathogen, the pathogen must remain viable in the food until consumption to cause disease. Bacterial pathogens usually must grow in foods or produce toxins to cause foodborne illness, while parasites and viruses do not grow in foods. Vehicles supply the nutrients and water for the survival, growth, and toxin production of pathogens. In addition, vehicles must meet specific environmental requirements of pathogens for survival and growth, including pH, water activity (a_w), temperature, salt, and oxygen requirements. Food production, processing, storage, and preparation processes also affect the likelihood that a food will become a vehicle of foodborne illness.

A food may contain a toxic agent naturally—for example, as mushrooms contain mushroom toxins. Alternatively, food may become contaminated with a toxic agent during growth, production, marketing, storage, preparation, or service. Further, some toxic agents grow or magnify in foods, such as growth of bacteria in foods, production of aflatoxins by molds growing on stored grains, or increased concentrations of heavy metals caused by food storage in inappropriate containers.

Since bacteria cause most of the cases of foodborne illness in the United States, much of the regulation of commercial food handling focuses on reducing bacterial contamination of food and on reducing bacterial growth in food. The characteristics of the food itself determine whether it will support rapid bacterial growth. If the food can support rapid bacterial growth, it is a potentially hazardous food, which means the environment (temperature) must be controlled to reduce the potential bacterial growth on the food.

POTENTIALLY HAZARDOUS FOODS

According to the FDA's *1999 Food Code* (1), a potentially hazardous food:

(a) is a food that is natural or synthetic and that requires temperature control because it is in a form capable of supporting:
 (i) The rapid and progressive growth of infectious or toxigenic microorganisms;
 (ii) The growth and toxin production of *Clostridium botulinum;* or
 (iii) In raw shell eggs, the growth of *Salmonella enteritidis*
(b) includes an animal food (a food of animal origin) that is raw or heat-treated; a food of plant origin that is heat-treated or consists of raw seed sprouts; cut

melons; and garlic-in-oil mixtures that are not modified in a way that results in mixtures that do not support growth as specified under Subparagraph (a) of this definition.

(c) "Potentially hazardous food" does not include:
  (i) An air-cooled hard-boiled egg with shell intact;
  (ii) A food with an a_w value of 0.85 or less;
  (iii) A food with a pH level of 4.6 or below when measured at 24°C (75°F);
  (iv) A food, in an unopened hermetically sealed container, that is commercially processed to achieve and maintain **commercial sterility** under conditions of nonrefrigerated storage and distribution; and
  (v) A food for which laboratory evidence demonstrates that the rapid and progressive growth of infectious or toxigenic microorganisms or the growth of *S. enteritidis* in eggs or *C. botulinum* cannot occur, such as a food that has an a_w and a pH that are above the levels specified under Subparagraphs (c)(ii) and (iii) of this definition and that may contain a preservative, other barrier to the growth of microorganisms, or a combination of barriers that inhibit the growth of microorganisms.
  (vi) A food that does not support the growth of microorganisms as specified under Subparagraph (a) of this definition even though the food may contain an infectious or toxigenic microorganism or chemical or physical contaminant at a level sufficient to cause illness.

This definition is intended to describe foods prepared or processed for retail sale and is based, in part, on evidence that specific foods have or have not caused foodborne disease. For example, alfalfa sprouts are specifically mentioned because they have caused several foodborne-disease outbreaks. One food that is specifically excluded is air-cooled hard-boiled eggs with shells intact intended for retail sale because they have not caused any recorded foodborne-disease outbreaks. These presumably would be prepared daily and held under sanitary conditions. However, USDA does not recommend consumption of consumer-produced hard-boiled eggs if they are out of refrigeration for longer than two hours (2).

If a food is potentially hazardous, the *Food Code* specifies that it be held at refrigerated temperatures (or frozen) throughout marketing, including during shipping and display in retail establishments. These foods should also be refrigerated at home.

Dietetics professionals can use the definition of potentially hazardous foods to focus client attention on foods that require special handling to protect their safety and to remind clients that once packages are opened or foods are cut to expose their interiors, they become more vulnerable to contamination. Also, specific foods, such as alfalfa sprouts, may not be appropriate choices for immuno-compromised individuals. Additionally, potentially hazardous foods are the primary foods addressed in developing food safety plans for retail foodservice.

SAFETY ISSUES WITHIN FOOD GUIDE PYRAMID GROUPS

Table 3.1 shows the food vehicles for foodborne-disease outbreaks for 1993 to 1997 by Food Guide Pyramid group. This table does not include outbreaks for which the vehicle was not confirmed or specifically noted. Following are brief descriptions of individual Food Guide Pyramid groups and some food safety problems associated with each.

TABLE 3.1 Number of Reported Foodborne-Disease Outbreaks, Cases, and Deaths, by Vehicle—U.S.,[a] 1993–1997[b]

Etiology	Outbreaks		Cases		Deaths	
	No.	%	No.	%	No.	%
Bread, Cereal, Rice, and Pasta Group						
Baked Goods	35	1.3	853	1.0	0	0.0
Fruit and Vegetable Groups						
Fruits and Vegetables	66	2.4	12,357	14.4	2	6.9
Mushrooms	4	0.1	12	<0.1	0	0.0
Potato Salad	14	0.5	555	0.6	2	6.9
Milk, Yogurt, and Cheese Group						
Ice Cream	15	0.5	1,194	1.4	0	0.0
Milk	10	0.4	207	2.4	0	0.0
Cheese	4	0.1	34	<0.1	1	3.4
Unknown Dairy	4	0.1	72	<0.1	0	0.0
Meat, Fish, Poultry, Beans, Eggs, and Nuts Group						
Beef	66	2.4	3,205	3.7	4	13.8
Chicken	30	1.0	1,113	1.3	0	0.0
Eggs	19	0.7	367	0.4	3	10.3
Ham	12	0.4	293	0.3	0	0.0
Fish	140	5.1	696	0.8	0	0.0
Pork	14	0.5	638	0.7	1	3.4
Sausage	2	0.1	57	<0.1	0	0.0
Shellfish	47	1.7	1,868	2.2	0	0.0
Turkey	22	0.8	758	0.9	0	0.0
Unknown Meat	22	0.8	645	0.7	2	6.9
Others, Including Mixed Dishes						
Chinese Food	10	0.4	163	0.2	0	0.0
Mexican Food	32	1.2	1,614	1.9	0	0.0
Multiple Vehicles	262	9.5	25,628	29.8	1	3.4
Carbonated Drink	4	0.1	45	<0.1	0	0.0
Nondairy Beverage	20	0.7	606	0.7	0	0.0
Salads						
Poultry, Fish, or Egg	16	0.6	1,381	1.6	0	0.00
Other Salad	97	3.5	4,547	5.3	0	0.0
Known Vehicle	967	35.2	58,908	68.5	16	55.2
Unknown Vehicle	1,784	64.8	27,150	31.5	13	44.8
Total 1993–1997	2,751	100.0	86,058	100.0	29	100.0

Source: Olsen SJ, MacKinnon LC, Goulding JS, Bean NH, Slutsker L. Surveillance for foodborne-disease outbreaks—United States, 1993–1997. *MMWR.* 2000;49(SS-01):1–51. Available at: ftp://ftp.cdc.gov/pub/Publications/mmwr/SS/SS4901.pdf. Accessed May 12, 2001.

Breads, Cereals, Rice, and Pasta Group

ASSOCIATED TOXIC AGENTS. Current (1993 to 1997) reports of foodborne-disease outbreaks (3) cite 35 outbreaks of foodborne illness from baked goods, resulting in 853 cases and no deaths. *Salmonella* caused 12 outbreaks, *Staphylococcus aureus* caused 3 outbreaks, and *Shigella,* hepatitis A, and Norwalk virus each caused 1 outbreak. The *Salmonella*-caused outbreaks were frequently associated with stuffing or similar products containing undercooked egg. Additionally, some of the outbreaks caused by Chinese-style foods involved cooked rice mixtures. Mycotoxin contamination of grain is a problem worldwide. In addition to causing losses from spoilage, mycotoxins cause damage to various organ systems and are frequently carcinogens (4–5).

FOOD CHARACTERISTICS ASSOCIATED WITH FOOD SAFETY. Foods in the Bread, Cereal, and Pasta Group are derived from grains and include some potentially hazardous foods, although many of these foods are not potentially hazardous in their stored forms. Examples of grains and grain products include raw, minimally processed, frozen, and cooked grains, such as rice; dry, refrigerated, frozen, and cooked pastas; dry flour mixtures; refrigerated doughs, frozen doughs, and baked goods; and ready-to-eat cereals, uncooked cereals, and cooked cereals. Many foods in the grain group—raw grains, dry pastas, dry flours, ready-to-eat cereals, and uncooked cereals—have low water activities until they are cooked and are not potentially hazardous foods. However, the hydration of grains and grain products during cooking increases the a_w sufficiently that the cooked grain food becomes potentially hazardous and should not be held in the danger zone (40°F to 140°F; 4°C to 60°C) for longer than two hours. Batters and doughs used for making breads also have high water activities; however, baking removes much of the free water. The a_w of most of these products is low enough after baking that they are not potentially hazardous, although the a_w remains high enough to support growth of molds.

Fruit and Vegetable Groups

ASSOCIATED TOXIC AGENTS. In the latest reporting period, 1993 to 1997 (3; see Table 3.1), fruits and vegetables were the vehicles for 66 foodborne-disease outbreaks (12,357 cases with 2 deaths), and potato salad was the vehicle for 14 outbreaks (555 cases and 2 deaths). Additionally, mushroom intoxications caused 4 outbreaks (12 total mushroom cases). Agents for fruit and vegetable outbreaks included *Campylobacter* (4 outbreaks), *Clostridium botulinum* (6 outbreaks), *Salmonella* (13 outbreaks), *Escherichia coli* (7 outbreaks), *Shigella* (2 outbreaks), *Staphylococcus aureus* (1 outbreak), viruses (4 outbreaks), and parasites (4 outbreaks). Potato salad was a vehicle for *Staphylococcus aureus* (1 outbreak), *Escherichia coli* (1 outbreak), *Listeria monocytogenes* (2 outbreaks), *Salmonella* (1 outbreak), and *Shigella* (1 outbreak). The most common mycotoxin found in fruit products is patulin, which is found in moldy apples and in ciders and juices pressed from moldy apples (6). While mycotoxin-producing molds can grow on corn, this is primarily a problem for animal feed.

FOOD CHARACTERISTICS ASSOCIATED WITH FOOD SAFETY. Most fruits and vegetables in their raw, unpeeled states are not potentially hazardous foods. One reason is that peels or skins protect the flesh from contamination by pathogenic organisms. However, failure to thoroughly clean the fruit or vegetable prior to removing the peel or skin can result in contamination of the flesh with pathogenic organisms that are on the surface. This route of contamination has occurred with melons and is why cut melons are specifically listed as potentially hazardous foods. Another natural protective mechanism is that many fruits and vegetables have pH values less than 4.6, which retards growth of most bacteria and prevents toxin production by *Clostridium botulinum.*

Once cooked, all fruits and vegetables are potentially hazardous, unless they are protected by a pH less than 4.6 or an a_w less than 0.85. For example, apples and oranges have pH levels below 4.6. Their juices also have pH levels below 4.6 and are not potentially hazardous foods; however, these juices may be vehicles for foodborne illness if they are contaminated by high levels of bacteria, even though the bacteria cannot grow in the juices. Pasteurization destroys the pathogens present in the fresh juices, but juices can be recontaminated after pasteurization if the packaging barrier is compromised or if handling is inappropriate. In another example, cooked potatoes would typically have pH values above 4.6 and water activities above 0.85 and would be potentially hazardous foods; an exception would be commercially produced potato chips, which can be stored at room temperature because of their low water activity.

The traditional storage recommendations for fresh fruits and vegetables are based largely on maintaining quality because those foods are not potentially hazardous. For sustained quality most of them should be stored in a refrigerator or be processed in a way that destroys or reduces the growth of pathogenic and spoilage microorganisms. Exceptions to this include potatoes, onions, and winter squashes, which can be stored at room temperatures for up to ten days before significant losses of quality occur. Shelf life can be extended up to several weeks by storing at 45°F to 50°F (7°C to 10°C). For longer storage, these foods require further processing, such as canning, dehydration, irradiation, or freezing.

Surfaces of fruits and vegetables may be contaminated with pesticide residues. FDA and USDA monitoring programs report that most residues are within EPA established **tolerances** (7). One of the developmental objectives in *Healthy People 2010* focuses on reassessment of pesticide residue tolerances for fruits and vegetables (8). Most pesticide residues can be removed by scrubbing with water.

Milk, Yogurt, and Cheese Group

ASSOCIATED TOXIC AGENTS. The most common pathogen associated with outbreaks from dairy products in the 1993 to 1997 reporting period (3) was *Salmonella* (sixteen outbreaks), followed by *Escherichia coli* in fluid milk (two outbreaks). There was one outbreak each for *Listeria monocytogenes* and *Campylobacter jejuni* in fluid milk, heavy metal contamination and *Giardia lamblia* in ice cream, *Clostridium perfringens* in cheese, and *Shigella* in an unspecified dairy product.

FOOD CHARACTERISTICS ASSOCIATED WITH FOOD SAFETY. Dairy foods are typically potentially hazardous foods and should be handled as though they contain pathogenic organisms. They contain high levels of protein and micronutrients required for microbial growth, but some dairy foods have barriers that retard bacterial growth. Although fresh fluid milk has a high pH and a high a_w, some cultured dairy products have much lower pH values, and some cheeses and non-fat dry milk have low a_w values.

Most of the fluid milk sold in the United States is pasteurized to destroy pathogens, and outbreaks caused by milk are typically from raw (unpasteurized) milk or from inadequately pasteurized milk. Likewise, outbreaks from cheese and other dairy foods usually involve inadequately processed product or product recontaminated after processing. Many of these outbreaks involve large numbers of people since milk is pooled from many farms, processed, and distributed through large networks.

Meat, Poultry, Fish, Beans, Eggs, and Nuts Group

ASSOCIATED TOXIC AGENTS. Foodborne-disease outbreaks in this food group (3; see Table 3.1) result from bacterial, parasitic, viral, and chemical agents. *Salmonella* was the most frequently confirmed pathogen for this food group (fifty-five outbreaks), and it was associated with every product category in the group except sausage and fish (3). *Salmonella* was the only agent found in outbreaks caused by eggs (seventeen outbreaks). *Clostridium perfringens* was associated with eleven outbreaks for beef, one outbreak for pork, one outbreak for turkey, and one outbreak for shellfish. *Staphylococcus aureus* was associated with outbreaks for beef (one outbreak), chicken (one outbreak), ham (seven outbreaks), fish (one outbreak), pork (one outbreak), and turkey (four outbreaks). Ham is frequently a vehicle for staphylococcal intoxication because the organism survives salt concentrations that retard growth of other bacteria. *Trichinella spiralis* caused one outbreak in an unspecified meat. Beef was a vehicle in twenty-one outbreaks caused by *Escherichia coli*. Fish were responsible for outbreaks from botulin toxin (one outbreak), *Staphylococcus aureus* (one outbreak), ciguatera toxin (fifty-four outbreaks), scombrotoxin (sixty-six outbreaks), and an unspecified virus (one outbreak). Shellfish-related outbreaks were caused by bacterial, viral, and chemical agents: *Clostridium perfringens* (one outbreak), *Salmonella* (one outbreak), *Shigella* (two outbreaks), *Campylobacter jejuni* (two outbreaks), vibrios (one outbreak), ciguatera toxin (two outbreaks), paralytic shellfish poisoning (one outbreak), Norwalk virus (four outbreaks), and unspecified viruses (seven outbreaks).

FOOD CHARACTERISTICS ASSOCIATED WITH FOOD SAFETY. Animal foods are typically potentially hazardous foods and should be handled as though they contain pathogenic organisms. First, animal foods have high nutrient levels and few natural barriers. Even eggs with intact shells are potentially hazardous foods because *Salmonella enteritidis* contaminates eggs before they are laid (9). In addition, flesh foods and eggs have high pH and high a_w values. Although beans and nuts have similar nutrient values to those of animal foods, their safety issues are different. For these products, mold contamination and mycotoxin production are more important than bacterial contamination.

In general, the number of cases per outbreak for animal foods in the Meat, Poultry, Fish, Beans, Eggs, and Nuts Group suggests a foodservice or large group gathering, which is consistent with inappropriate food handling and holding practices. Also, it is more likely that an outbreak involving larger numbers of people would be reported.

Animal foods that have been canned or dehydrated can be safely stored at room temperatures until their containers are opened, but all others must be frozen or refrigerated to control growth of microorganisms. Recommended storage times for animal foods can be found in USDA's "Refrigeration in Food Safety" (10) or ADA's "Safe Eating: A Guide to Preventing Foodborne Illness" (11).

Processed meats, such as deli-sliced meats, ham, packaged luncheon meats, pepperoni, and jerky, may have some barriers to microbial growth, depending on the individual product. Deli-sliced meats, in general, are sold as ready to eat, but they may be contaminated with various bacteria, most seriously *Listeria monocytogenes*. For this reason, health and regulatory agencies recommend that these products be reheated to 165°F (73°C) for individuals with compromised immune systems and for pregnant women (12–14). In settings where reheating is undesirable they can be eliminated from menus. Hams are produced with various barriers to microbial growth. Salt, sugar, and nitrite used in curing limit growth of clostridia and other bacteria, depending on concentration used, and heat processing is used to pasteurize or can hams. Also, vacuum-packaging sliced ham limits growth of many bacteria. Although true country-cured hams and canned hams can be stored at room temperature, most of today's hams are not fully cured, are pasteurized instead of canned, and must be refrigerated. After cured hams are cooked or canned hams are opened, the products must be refrigerated. Many ham products, including deli-sliced ham, are treated as cooked meats, not as preserved foods. **Vacuum-packaged** luncheon meats (**modified atmosphere packaging/controlled atmosphere packaging (MAP/CAP)** products) have longer shelf lives than other cooked meats because of the reduced oxygen atmosphere. Once opened, they are treated as cooked meats. Jerky, pepperoni, and similar summer sausages are sufficiently dried and fermented to reduce growth of pathogens. However, their surfaces can be contaminated by food handlers or by environmental contaminants, if they are not packaged.

Seafood products are available raw, cooked, frozen, previously frozen (cooked or raw), canned, dried (salted), and fermented. They have environmental and handling sources of contamination. Raw seafoods may be contaminated with parasites, viruses, bacteria, and chemical toxins that are invisible, odorless, and tasteless. Therefore, consumption of any raw seafood, such as sushi or oysters on the half shell, is a risky behavior. While appropriate cooking will destroy the parasites, viruses, and bacteria, it will not destroy the chemical toxicants. Also, while marinated seafood, such as ceviche, may appear cooked, the marinating process does not destroy microorganisms that may contaminate the product naturally. Most dried or fermented fishes are ethnic speciality foods. Few of these products are produced by regulated processors who can determine critical limits for microbial barriers, such as water activity or pH. Producing and eating these products can be riskier than preparing and consuming cooked products that have standard cooking procedures.

BARRIERS TO FOODBORNE DISEASE

Table 3.2 gives additional details on natural and processing barriers applicable to the different food groups. Natural barriers include chemical factors such as a_w or

TABLE 3.2 Natural and Processing Barriers in Foods

Food Group	Natural Barriers	Processing Barriers
Breads, Cereals, Rice, and Pasta	Low a_w when dry	Baking lowers a_w. Food additives retard microbial growth. Intact packaging protects against contamination.
Fruits and Vegetables	Peels and skins pH less than 4.6 (some) Low a_w (some)	Canning destroys pathogenic microorganisms. Pasteurizing juices destroys pathogenic microorganisms. Refrigerating and freezing slow microbial growth. Acidifying or fermenting slow microbial growth. Dehydrating reduces water available for microbial growth. Adding sufficient sugar for jelly products reduces water available for microbial growth. Waxes and coatings form a physical barrier to microorganisms. MAP/CAP reduce oxygen available for microbial growth. Food additives retard microbial growth. Intact packaging protects against contamination.
Meat, Poultry, Fish, Beans, Eggs, and Nuts		Canning destroys pathogenic microorganisms. Refrigerating and freezing slow microbial growth. MAP/CAP reduce oxygen available for microbial growth. Acidifying or fermenting slow microbial growth. Dehydrating, salting, and sugaring reduce water available for microbial growth. Food additives retard microbial growth. Intact packaging protects against contamination.
Milk, Yogurt, and Cheese	Rinds on cheeses Low pH in yogurt and some other cultured or acidulated products Low a_w in dried products	Canning destroys microorganisms. Pasteurizing destroys pathogenic microorganisms. Refrigerating slows microbial growth. Fermenting (culturing) slows microbial growth. Drying reduces water available for microbial growth. Intact packaging protects against contamination.

Source: Adapted from Reference 33

pH and physical factors such as peels or rinds. Barriers introduced by processing include destruction of microorganisms and reduction in their growth rates. In many instances, packaging forms a physical barrier to prevent recontamination of the food product.

USING TECHNOLOGY TO CONTROL HAZARDS

Most commercial food preservation methods are designed to extend the shelf life of foods by stabilizing the natural degradative changes that occur in foods and by slowing the rate of microbial spoilage. Natural degradative changes may affect development of natural toxicants in foods, and they frequently enhance the growth of pathogenic microorganisms. The most common means of destroying microorganisms in foods employ heat or radiant energy under well-defined conditions. Heat is the energy source used for traditional cooking, canning, and pasteurizing. Radiant energy, such as irradiation and microwaving, offers alternatives for cooking and pasteurizing foods.

The growth of microorganisms in foods is typically controlled by lowering the temperature, pH, available oxygen, or available water. With these food preservation practices, microorganisms are still there, but their growth has been retarded. The microorganisms will resume their normal growth as soon as conditions desirable for microbial growth return. At that point, foods preserved by these methods must be handled as though they contain pathogenic microorganisms. For example, dried fruits can be safely stored at room temperature; however, if the fruit is rehydrated, it should then be refrigerated until consumption to keep the temperature outside the ideal growth range for pathogenic organisms.

Canning

Destruction of microorganisms in food is most commonly achieved by application of heat, as in canning (thermal processing). The total destruction of microorganisms, including spores, is known as sterilization; surgical supplies are sterilized, for example. Achieving such a high level of sterility is not necessary for foods and would result in decreases in food quality. The level of sterility achieved by commercial thermal processing or canning is referred to as commercial sterility. Commercial sterility is achieved when a food has been treated in a way that all pathogenic, spoilage, and toxin-forming organisms have been destroyed. Most bacteria, yeasts, and molds are killed at temperatures of 179°F to 200°F (82°C to 93°C), although all bacterial spores are not destroyed until the temperature reaches 240°F (121°C). The latter temperature can be achieved only by the addition of pressure during canning. The metal or glass container used to hold canned food products provides a physical barrier to prevent recontamination of the contents with microorganisms from the environment. Under normal storage conditions, most commercial thermally processed foods have a shelf life of at least two years before there are significant losses of product quality. Even though there are losses of product quality, commercially canned foods are safe to eat as long as the package remains intact.

Aseptic processing is a modification of conventional canning. It involves heating foods to achieve commercial sterility prior to putting the foods into a commercially sterile package. The food does not require any additional processing to be shelf stable. Examples of products processed in this way include beverages or soups in "box" packages, individual containers of coffee cream and whiteners, and institutional packs of ketchup, soups, and the like. The containers used in aseptic processing also provide a physical barrier to prevent recontamination of the product, and these foods are considered safe as long as the package remains intact.

Processing times for all commercially canned foods are calculated to provide commercial sterility of the product. The FDA requires that all thermal processing be done under good manufacturing practices (GMPs), that manufacturers register their processing plants and their processing times (schedules) with the FDA, that adequate records be kept by the manufacturers, and that facilities be open to inspection by FDA (Box 3.1).

BOX 3.1   Preserving Foods at Home

Even though fewer consumers can, freeze, or dry foods at home, dietetics professionals may be asked to provide information to such consumers. To answer questions on preservation, dietetics professionals may refer to USDA recommended procedures (22) for canning and freezing or to local USDA Cooperative Extension offices. In addition, the National Food Safety Database contains questions and answers for home food preservation (22), and recent references give detailed information on the science of food preservation (23).

Canning foods at home is a more involved procedure than freezing or drying, and consumers who can foods at home need information on appropriate techniques and equipment. High acid foods, those with a pH less than 4.6, can be processed in a boiling water bath. Examples would be most fruits and tomatoes. Low acid foods, those with a pH above 4.6, must be processed in a pressure canner. Low acid foods include most vegetables and all animal products. The pressure gauge on home pressure canners should be calibrated before each canning season. In most states, the USDA Cooperative Extension Service can assist consumers with this calibration. Even though foods processed according to those recommendations are safe, they are not intended for retail sale or use in retail food establishments because they are not processed under FDA supervision.

Pasteurization

There are two primary food preservation techniques that pasteurize foods, conventional heat pasteurization and irradiation. Both reduce the number of microorganisms in foods, but neither produces commercial sterility. In conventional heat pasteurization, foods are sufficiently heated just long enough to destroy the pathogenic microorganisms. Pasteurized foods still contain non-pathogenic microorganisms and spores. These foods should be stored at refrigerator temperatures to slow the growth of microorganisms, and they have limited shelf lives. Pasteurized foods include fluid milk, many "fresh" juices, liquid egg products, and some in-shell eggs.

Irradiation, as it is applied in foods, is also a form of pasteurization. It is frequently called cold pasteurization or radurization. In 1983, FDA approved the use of irradiation for spices sold in the United States. In 1985, they extended that approval to fresh fruits and vegetables, poultry, and ground meat. Shelf life of irradiated foods is extended, but they still must be handled in the home or foodservice facility as other fresh foods. Foods treated with radiation must bear the radura symbol and the words "treated with radiation" (Figure 3.1). Foods prepared from irradiated foods are not required to be labeled with the radura symbol or the words "treated with radiation." Irradiation uses very low-dose radiation, usually from a radioactive cobalt isotope, and does not make the food radioactive. Irradiation does result in formation of so-called radiolytic products in foods; however, any type of food processing (including cooking) results in the creation of compounds with unknown physiological functions and effects. It is simply that much more is known about the types of compounds formed as a result of irradiation. The Institute of Food Technologists (15), the American Dietetic Association (16), and the Council for Agricultural Science and Technology (17) have official papers recognizing the role that irradiation could have in maintaining the safety of the food supply. In addition, the World Health Organization (WHO; 18) and the American Medical Association (AMA; 17) support the use of irradiation as a way to improve the safety of the food supply.

Pasturized products are packaged in containers designed to minimize recontamination of the product with pathogenic microorganisms from the envi-

FIGURE 3.1
Radura Symbol

ronment. Since pasteurized products are not commercially sterile, the containers are not designed to exclude air or to ensure shelf stability. Once these products are opened or the packaging barrier is compromised, they are subject to recontamination.

Refrigeration

Refrigeration is the gentlest food preservation method and results in the fewest structural and organoleptic changes in most foods. Most pathogenic microorganisms do not grow at refrigerator temperatures of less than 41°F (5°C). However, **psychrotrophic microorganisms,** such as *Listeria monocytogenes,* will grow at the 41°F to 45°F (5°C to 7°C) refrigerator temperatures common in home and foodservice settings, which means that refrigeration cannot always be assumed to assure safety of the food. Fact sheets and brochures on safe refrigerator practices with charts detailing the length of time that foods can be safely stored at refrigerator temperatures are available (10,11). In general, most foods should not be stored in the refrigerator for more than one week, and refrigerator temperatures should be monitored regularly to make sure that the temperature of the interior of the refrigerator is above 32°F and below 41°F. Consumers should be encouraged to have appliance thermometers in their refrigerators, to regularly check the temperature, and to discard foods that have been stored longer than recommended times.

Foodservice facilities should monitor refrigerator temperatures at least two times per day; label and date all refrigerated food products; perform regular, random checks of internal temperatures of refrigerated foods; and establish appropriate corrective actions for occasions when refrigerator temperatures or storage times exceed the critical limits set in the food safety plan. For example, an appropriate corrective action would be to discard foods that have been stored longer than recommended times. Dietetics professionals working in facilities with cook-chill or ready-prepared foodservice systems need to be particularly diligent in assuring appropriate refrigeration temperatures, rates of chilling foods, and length of food storage. Cook-chill foodservice systems produce foods designed to have extended shelf lives at refrigerator temperatures. This is comparable to foods that the food industry terms "refrigerated processed foods of extended durability" and includes such technologies as conventional packaging for luncheon meats, *sous vide,* and MAP/CAP. Of particular concern with these systems are growth of pathogenic psychrotrophic and **mesophilic microorganisms,** such as *Clostridium botulinum, Listeria monocytogenes, Yersinia enterocolitica, Bacillus cereus,* and *Vibrio parahaemolyticus.* The potential growth of these microorganisms can be controlled by use of strict standard operating procedures regarding starting materials, sanitation, and hygiene, combined with a mechanism for monitoring **critical control points (CCP).** For additional recommendations on these microbiological concerns and appropriate control measures, see the Institute of Food Technologists' Scientific Status Summary "Extended Shelf Life Refrigerated Foods: Microbiological Quality and Safety" (19).

In client care areas where small or individual refrigerators store client foods, it is important to perform regular temperature checks and to discard food of unknown origin, undated foods, or foods past date. It is also important to clean refrigerators periodically and between clients to reduce potential for pathogen contamination of the refrigerator.

Freezing

Freezing is one of the most popular food preservation methods and has greatly increased the variety of foods available in the home and in foodservice settings. Fruits and vegetables are typically blanched before freezing to halt enzymatic changes that affect quality. Commercial processes for freezing foods are designed to maximize quality. Commercial food processors are expected to follow good manufacturing practices, but they are not required to have those processes on file with FDA.

Dietetics professionals working in foodservice and food management should regard monitoring freezer temperatures and storage times for foods as standard operating procedures. Since freezing merely retards the growth of microorganisms, potentially hazardous foods that have been allowed to thaw should be thoroughly cooked before refreezing. Facility disaster plans should describe handling of frozen foods. Facilities that use cook/freeze foodservice systems should pay particular attention to rates of chilling and freezing foods and recommended storage times for frozen foods (Box 3.2).

BOX 3.2   Disaster Plans

According to the Joint Commission on Accreditation of Healthcare Organizations (JCAHO) standards, facilities must have a plan to provide continuous care for patients or residents and to respond to the needs of others affected by a disaster. This disaster plan must include procedures for treating the injured, providing food and shelter for those seeking refuge, and continuing care of existing patients (24).

Disaster plans for foodservice departments provide instructions for production and service of food for 24, 48, and 72 hours. Adequate food and supplies to implement this plan should be on hand at all times. Plans contain provisions for:

1. Simple menus using those items most likely to spoil
2. Adequate supplies of disposable serviceware, cleaning and disinfecting compounds, garbage bags, and sterile water
3. Continued sanitation with careful attention to checking for spoiled food, sanitizing pots and pans, and cleaning food production work areas
4. Safety of employees, food, and supplies
5. Use and supervision of unskilled workers in defined tasks
6. Setting priorities for service to meet needs of existing patients or residents and disaster victims before those of staff, employees, and visitors

For additional information on food safety during disasters for institutions and for clients, see the following reproducible handouts, which are available on the Internet:

- Hurricane and Flood Food Safety (25)
- Keeping Food Safe during a Power Outage (26)
- Saving Foods during Winter Storms (27)
- Tornado Food Safety (28)
- After a Fire, Is the Food Safe? (29)
- Food and Water in an Emergency (30)
- Hurricane: A Prevention Guide to Promote Your Personal Health and Safety (31)
- Emergency Disinfection of Drinking Water (32)

Acidification/Fermentation

Acidification, or lowering the pH of a food, may be done directly by adding an acid, such as vinegar, or indirectly through fermentation. The basic premise behind the use of acidification to preserve foods is that pathogenic bacteria do not grow at pH levels lower than 4.6. High-acid foods are those that have a pH lower than 4.6; they can be processed for shorter time periods with a milder heat treatment. Low-acid foods have a pH above 4.6 and require a more intensive heat treatment to achieve commercial sterility. Simply lowering the pH of a food to lower than 4.6 does not kill microorganisms, and even high-acid foods require some additional treatment to ensure their safety. For example, unpasteurized apple juice, a high-acid food, has been implicated in an outbreak of *E. coli* food-borne illness (20–21). Apple juice sold in the United States is now required to be pasteurized or to bear a label indicating that it is not recommended for use by immunocompromised individuals.

Fermentation in foods refers to the anaerobic and aerobic metabolism of carbohydrates by microorganisms. Microorganisms usually involved in fermentations are lactic acid bacteria, acetic acid bacteria, and yeasts. Acids such as lactic acid or acetic acid are the end products of microbial metabolism of carbohydrates from the foods. As the concentration of the acids increases, the pH of the food decreases. Many fermented foods are considered high-acid foods and can be made shelf stable with a less intensive heat treatment.

Available Oxygen Levels

Most pathogenic microorganisms require oxygen for growth. Therefore, completely or partially removing free (available) oxygen from the environment can reduce pathogen growth in many foods. In vacuum packaging and in canning most of the atmospheric oxygen is removed, which stops growth of aerobic microorganisms. However, for vacuum-packaged or canned foods that have not received an adequate heat treatment, microorganisms are not necessarily destroyed. Anaerobic bacteria, such as *Clostridium botulinum*, will continue to grow in the absence of oxygen. Foods that are canned or that are heat-treated and vacuum-packaged are shelf stable and have a shelf life measured in months or years rather than days or weeks.

Another food preservation technique that modifies the amount of oxygen available for microbial growth is coating foods with waxes, shellac, or other edible coatings. These coatings serve as physical barriers as well as inhibitors of microbial metabolism. Unless they are prepared from food ingredients, such as cornstarch or soy protein, compounds used as edible coatings for foods are regarded as food additives and, as such, are subject to the same approval processes as other food additives (Chapter 2). Knowledge of types of coatings typically used on foods may help explain some reactions in clients who have certain food allergies. At the present time, edible coatings are primarily in three types of products. Confections may have coatings such as sugar, chocolate, or shellac; fresh fruits and vegetables may have wax coatings to retard moisture loss; and sausages and luncheon meats may have collagen casings. Coatings composed of antimicrobial compounds are being developed to specifically inhibit growth of pathogenic and spoilage organisms.

Modified atmosphere packaging (MAP) or controlled atmosphere packaging (CAP) is another food preservation method that modifies the amount of oxygen available for microbial growth. MAP/CAP is intended to meet consumer demand for minimally processed food that has a longer shelf life than conventional fresh foods. In MAP/CAP, the foods are placed in a package with a known permeability to atmospheric gases. The oxygen in the interior of the package is partially replaced with nitrogen or carbon dioxide. At the lower oxygen levels, most pathogenic and spoilage microorganisms are inhibited, although growth of other microorganisms is unaffected or may be increased. MAP/CAP does not decrease growth rates of all pathogenic microorganisms, and the typical cues that a product is spoiled (off odors, flavors, colors) are not present. The vast majority of these food products are intended to be held at refrigeration temperatures, and, in fact, the permeabilities of the packaging materials are to some extent temperature dependent. Examples of MAP/CAP foods are bagged salad mixtures, fresh pasta products packed in semiflexible bags, and prepacked deli meat and cracker lunch meals. Consumers and foodservice workers need to be instructed on the importance of appropriate storage times and temperatures and safe handling of these products.

Available Water

Removal of water from food either by drying or by binding the water will result in decreased growth of microorganisms, including bacteria, yeasts, and molds. Bacteria and yeasts have higher water requirements than molds; therefore, molds will grow on foods such as dried fruits where bacteria will not. Three of the oldest methods of food preservation involve alterations in the available water within foods. These methods are drying, salt curing, and sugar curing.

The effectiveness of each of these methods of food preservation may be explained by the concept of water activity. Water activity (a_w) is a measure of unbound, free water in a food available to support biological and chemical reactions. It is this water, not the total water content of a food, that determines the rate of microbial growth. Thus, jellies and fruit juices, which have similar total water contents, have very different capacities to support growth of microorganisms because the additional sugar in the jellies binds the water.

As foods are dried, water is physically removed. Dried foods have a water content of about 20 percent, but most of this water is actually bound to components of the cells and is unavailable for metabolic processes (that is, water activity is low). Thus, most dried foods are relatively shelf stable. Storage of dried foods in humid conditions will allow them to accumulate water from the environment and may support microbial growth in at least some areas of the food. For example, nuts should be packed in moisture-resistant containers to minimize water uptake and subsequent mold growth. Also, storage of dried foods in the same container with foods of a higher moisture content may result in microbial growth in the dried food. Again, since molds have a lower water requirement than bacteria and yeasts, molds may be the first microorganisms to grow on dried foods.

When foods are cured with either salt or sugar, the free or available water in the food becomes bound to the sugar or salt and is no longer available to support microbial growth. The most common salt-cured food is country ham, which is cured with a mixture including sodium chloride and sodium nitrate. Hams may also be sugar-cured. The sugar added to jams and jellies also acts to reduce the free or available water in the fruits, making the sugar a preservative. Changing salt and sugar levels in products to reduce dietary sodium and sugar reduces the effectiveness of the compounds as barriers to microbial growth. Most of the modified products require refrigeration either throughout marketing or after opening.

REFERENCES

1. US Food and Drug Administration. *1999 Food Code.* Washington, DC: US Department of Commerce, Technology Administration, National Technical Information Service; 1999. PB99-115925. Available at: http://vm.cfsan.fda.gov/~dms/fc99-toc.html. Accessed May 12, 2001.

2. US Department of Agriculture, Food Safety and Inspection Service. Egg and egg product safety [USDA Web site]. April 2001. Available at: http://www.fsis.usda.gov/oa/pubs/eggfacts.htm. Accessed May 12, 2001.

3. Olsen SJ, MacKinnon LC, Goulding JS, Bean NH, Slutsker L. Surveillance for foodborne-disease outbreaks—United States, 1993–1997. *MMWR.* 2000;49(SS-01):1–51. Available at: ftp://ftp.cdc.gov/pub/Publications/mmwr/SS/SS4901.pdf. Accessed May 12, 2001.

4. US Food and Drug Administration, Center for Food Safety and Applied Nutrition. Bad bug book: foodborne pathogenic microorganisms and natural toxins handbook [FDA Web site}. June 5, 2001. Available at: http://vm.cfsan.fda.gov/~mow/intro.html. Accessed June 5, 2001.

5. Bailey GS, Williams DE. Scientific status summary: potential mechanisms for food-related carcinogens and anticarcinogens. *Food Tech.* 1993;47(2):105–118.

6. Pitt JI. Penicillium. In: Hui YH, Gorham JR, Murrell KD, Cliver DO, eds. *Diseases Caused by Hazardous Substances.* New York, NY: Marcel Dekker Inc; 1994:617–630. *Foodborne Disease Handbook;* vol. 2.

7. US Food and Drug Administration, Center for Food Safety and Applied Nutrition, Pesticide Program. FDA Pesticide Program residue monitoring, 1993–1999 [FDA Web site]. April 2000. Available at: http://vm.cfsan.fda.gov/~dms/pesrpts.html. Accessed May 12, 2001.

8. US Department of Health and Human Services. Food safety. In: *Healthy People 2010.* 2nd ed. With Understanding and Improving Health and Objectives for Improving Health. 2 vols. Washington, DC: US Government Printing Office; November 2000:10.3–10.19. Available at: http://www.health.gov/healthypeople/Document/pdf/Volume1/10Food.pdf. Accessed May 12, 2001.

9. Mishu B, Griffin PM, Tauxe RV. *Salmonella enteritidis* gastroenteritis transmitted by intact chicken eggs. *Ann Intern Med.* 1991;115:190–194.

10. US Department of Agriculture, Food Safety and Inspection Service. Refrigeration and food safety [USDA Web site]. January 1999. Available at: http://www.fsis.usda.gov/OA/pubs/focus_ref.htm. Accessed May 12, 2001.

11. The American Dietetic Association. Safe eating: a guide to preventing foodborne illness. Chicago, IL: The American Dietetic Association; 1997.

12. US Food and Drug Administration, Center for Food Safety and Applied Nutrition; US Department of Agriculture, Food Safety and Inspection Service; Centers for Disease Control and Prevention. Draft assessment of the relative risk to public health

from foodborne *Listeria monocytogenes* among selected categories of ready-to-eat foods. January 2001. Available at: http://www.foodsafety.gov/%7Edms/lmrisk.html. Accessed May 12, 2001.

13. US Departments of Health and Human Services and Agriculture. HHS and USDA release listeria risk assessment and listeria action plan. Release No. 0020.01. January 18, 2001. Available at: http://www.usda.gov/news/releases/2001/01/0020.htm. Accessed May 12, 2001.

14. US Food and Drug Administration, Center for Food Safety and Applied Nutrition; US Department of Agriculture, Food Safety and Inspection Service; Centers for Disease Control and Prevention. Reducing the risk of *Listeria monocytogenes:* joint response to the President. January 2001. Available at: http://www.foodsafety.gov/%7Edms/lmriplan.html. Accessed May 12, 2001.

15. Olson DG. Institute of Food Technologists' scientific status summary: irradiation of food. *Food Tech.* 1998;52(1):56–62.

16. Wood OB, Bruhn CM. Food irradiation—position of ADA. *J Am Diet Assoc.* 1996;96:69 [ADA Web site]. Available at: http://www.eatright.org/airradi.html. Accessed May 12, 2001.

17. Thayer DW, Josephson ES, Brynjolfsson A, Giddings GG. *Issue Paper: Radiation Pasteurization of Food.* Ames, IA: Council for Agricultural Science and Technology; 1996(7):1–10 [CAST Web site]. Available at: http://www.cast-science.org/past_ip.pdf. Accessed May 12, 2001.

18. World Health Organization. *Safety and Nutritional Adequacy of Irradiated Food.* Geneva, Switzerland: WHO Publications; 1994.

19. Marth EH. Institute of Food Technologists' scientific status summary: extended shelf life refrigerated foods: microbiological quality and safety. *Food Tech.* 1998;52(2):57–62.

20. Besser RE, Lett SM, Weber JT. An outbreak of diarrhea and hemolytic uremic syndrome from *Escherichia coli* O157:H7 in fresh-pressed apple cider. *JAMA.* 1993;269:2217–2220.

21. Mshar PA, Dembek ZF, Cartter ML, et al. Outbreaks of *Escherichia coli* O157:H7 infection and cryptosporidiosis associated with drinking unpasteurized apple cider—Connecticut and New York, October 1996. *MMWR.* 1997;46(01):4–8. Available at: ftp://ftp.cdc.gov/pub/Publications/mmwr/wk/mm4601.pdf. Accessed May 12, 2001.

22. Canning, drying, and freezing [National Food Safety Database Web site]. Available at: http://www.foodsafety.ufl.edu/cmenu/preserve.htm. Accessed May 12, 2001.

23. VanGarde SJ, Woodburn M. *Food Preservation and Safety: Principles and Practice.* Ames, IA: Iowa State University Press; 1994.

24. Byers, BA, Shanklin, CW, Hoover LC. *Food Service Manual for Health Care Institutions.* American Hospital Association; 1994.

25. US Department of Agriculture, Food Safety and Inspection Service. Hurricane and flood food safety [USDA Web site]. October 1996. Available at: http://www.fsis.usda.gov/OA/pubs/ciflood.htm. Accessed May 12, 2001.

26. US Department of Agriculture, Food Safety and Inspection Service. Keeping food safe during a power outage [USDA Web site]. January 1999. Available at: http://www.fsis.usda.gov/oa/pubs/pofeature.htm. Accessed May 12, 2001.

27. US Department of Agriculture, Food Safety and Inspection Service. Saving food during winter storms—don't be left out in the cold! [USDA Web site]. May 1998. Available at: http://www.fsis.usda.gov/oa/pubs/coldout.htm. Accessed May 12, 2001.

28. US Department of Agriculture, Food Safety and Inspection Service. Tornado food safety [USDA Web site]. October 1996. Available at: http://www.fsis.usda.gov/oa/pubs/tornado.pdf. Accessed May 12, 2001.

29. US Department of Agriculture, Food Safety and Inspection Service. After the fire, is the food safe? [USDA Web site]. October 1996. Available at: http://www.fsis.usda.gov/oa/pubs/fires.pdf. Accessed May 12, 2001.

30. Federal Emergency Management Agency. Food and water in an emergency [FEMA Web site]. December 1998. Available at: http://www.fema.gov/pte/foodwtr.htm. Accessed May 12, 2001.

31. Centers for Disease Control and Prevention. Hurricane: a prevention guide to promote your personal health and safety [CDC Web site]. 1996. Available at: http://www.cdc.gov/nceh/emergency/Hurricane.pdf. Accessed May 12, 2001.

32. US Environmental Protection Agency, Office of Water. Emergency disinfection of drinking water [EPA Web site]. July 1993. Available at: http://www.epa.gov/ogwdw000/faq/emerg.html. Accessed May 12, 2001.

33. Potter NN, Hotchkiss JH. *Food Science.* 5th ed. New York: Chapman & Hall; 1995:265.

CHAPTER 4

FOOD AND WATER SAFETY SURVEILLANCE SYSTEMS IN THE UNITED STATES

Food safety surveillance systems provide continuous monitoring of data critical to making public food and water safety decisions in the United States. These data include information on chemicals and pathogens in the food and water supplies, on food and water consumption patterns, and on behaviors of consumers and producers. Surveillance systems monitor both domestic and imported foods.

In general, the food safety surveillance systems provide information on the sources and amounts of toxic agents in the food supply. These data must be combined with food consumption patterns to determine the potential risks for specific demographic groups. For example, if pesticide X is found only in food Y, then the people who consume food Y are the consumers at highest risk. Also, knowing the source(s) of pesticide X in the diet makes it possible to develop programs to reduce its level, if necessary, and to educate at-risk consumers.

Food safety surveillance has served to identify and remove contaminated products from the marketplace and to provide decision-making information for development of regulatory, educational, and research programs. While each surveillance system has a specific focus, integration of information from the various surveillance systems drives decisions on approval of pesticides and food additives and on development of other food and water safety regulations. This chapter provides an overview of U.S. surveillance programs that focus specifically on food safety, their functions, and their current findings.

SURVEILLANCE FOR FOODBORNE-DISEASE OUTBREAKS

The Centers for Disease Control and Prevention (CDC) maintains the collaborative surveillance program for collecting and reporting information on foodborne-disease outbreaks caused by pathogens and toxic chemicals in the United States (1). This passive surveillance system focuses on the occurrences and causes of foodborne-disease outbreaks. Outbreaks are reported to CDC on standard reporting forms by state and local health departments, federal agencies, and private physicians. After reviewing the reports to determine whether the specific food vehicle and etiologic agent have been confirmed for the outbreak, CDC compiles the data into summaries that include the food vehicles, etiologic agents, **morbidity**/mortality cases, and practices that contribute to the outbreaks. These summary reports are issued every five years. The most current summary is for 1993 to 1997 (1). Tables 2.4, 3.1, and 4.1 illustrate the data available from the summary.

While the longitudinal data from this program are useful, they have limitations. First and foremost, the reporting is passive. Not all foodborne-disease

TABLE 4.1   Number of Reported Foodborne-Disease Outbreaks, by Etiology and Contributing Factors—United States,[a] 1993–1997

Etiology	Number of Reported Outbreaks	Number of Outbreaks in Which Factors Reported	Contributing Factors: Improper Holding Temps	Inadequate Cooking	Contaminated Equipment	Food from Unsafe Source	Poor Personal Hygiene	Other
Bacterial								
Bacillus cereus	14	12	11	3	2	—	2	1
Brucella	1	0	—	—	—	—	—	—
Campylobacter	25	18	7	5	11	2	8	5
Clostridium botulinum	13	10	6	1	—	3	—	2
Clostridium perfringens	57	46	46	13	5	—	5	11
Escherichia coli	84	39	8	19	8	11	6	11
Listeria monocytogenes	3	2	1	—	1	—	—	1
Salmonella	357	255	153	112	78	33	70	53
Shigella	43	24	4	1	1	3	19	1
Staphylococcus aureus	42	30	25	3	6	4	12	4
Streptococcus, group A	1	1	1	—	—	—	1	—
Streptococcus, other	1	1	1	—	—	—	—	—
Vibrio cholerae	1	0	—	—	—	—	—	—
Vibrio parahemolyticus	5	2	1	1	1	1	—	—
Yersinia entercolitica	2	2	—	—	2	—	1	—
Other Bacterial	6	5	5	1	1	—	1	—
Total Bacterial	655	447	269	159	116	57	125	89
Chemical								
Ciguatoxin	60	35	2	—	—	25	—	16
Heavy metals	4	3	—	—	1	—	—	2
Monosodium glutamate	1	1	—	—	—	—	—	1
Mushroom poisoning	7	4	—	—	—	3	—	1
Scombrotoxin	69	46	38	2	2	11	1	2
Shellfish	1	1	—	—	—	1	—	1
Other Chemical	6	4	—	—	1	2	—	2
Total Chemical	148	94	40	2	4	42	1	25
Parasitic								
Giardia lamblia	4	2	—	—	1	—	2	1
Trichinella spiralis	2	1	—	1	—	—	—	—
Other Parasite	13	5	—	—	—	4	—	2
Total Parasitic	19	8	—	1	1	4	2	3
Viral								
Hepatitis A	23	17	1	1	—	1	15	1
Norwalk	9	7	—	2	—	3	4	—
Other Viral	24	14	2	3	2	5	7	2
Total Viral	56	38	3	6	2	9	26	3
Confirmed Etiology	878	587	312	168	123	112	154	120
Unknown Etiology	1,873	971	626	106	277	41	336	162
Total 1993–1997	2,751	1558	938	274	400	153	490	282

Source: Reference 1
[a]Includes Guam, Puerto Rico, and the U.S. Virgin Islands.

outbreaks are reported. Isolated cases of foodborne illness are not included in outbreak data, because an outbreak requires two or more confirmed cases of similar illness from ingestion of a common food. Also, outbreaks on cruise ships are not included in this system, and outbreaks are not included if the food is eaten outside the United States, even when the symptoms occur in the United States (1). While reported cases of foodborne-disease from outbreaks average fewer than twenty thousand per year (1), estimates of total cases are over seventy-six million per year (2).

FOODBORNE DISEASES ACTIVE SURVEILLANCE NETWORK (FOODNET)

FoodNet is an active surveillance program developed to enhance surveillance and investigation of infections that are commonly foodborne (3). FoodNet collaborators are the CDC, the U.S. Food and Drug Administration (FDA), the U.S. Department of Agriculture (USDA), and Emerging Infections Program (EIP) sites in California, Colorado, Connecticut, Georgia, Maryland, Minnesota, New York, Oregon, and Tennessee. This catchment area represents 33.1 million people, or about 12 percent of the 1999 population in the United States. The number of EIP sites will expand as the program develops further. The primary objectives of FoodNet are to:

1. Determine the frequency and severity of foodborne diseases
2. Determine the proportion of common foodborne diseases that results from eating specific foods
3. Describe the epidemiology of new and emerging bacterial, parasitic, and viral foodborne pathogens
4. Contribute to the public health infrastructure for dealing with emerging foodborne disease

Instead of reviewing case reports filed by agencies or providers (passive surveillance), FoodNet personnel contact each of the clinical laboratories within the surveillance areas, either weekly or monthly, depending on the size of the clinical laboratory. Cases are recorded as the first isolation from a person by the clinic. Using this active method of data gathering, FoodNet can provide a more precise measure of the laboratory-diagnosed cases of foodborne illness than are provided by foodborne-disease outbreak reports. This still includes only cases for which people have sought medical care and submitted laboratory specimens for analysis. However, the pathogens surveyed by FoodNet are those that typically have symptoms that are severe or last several days, increasing the likelihood that individuals would seek care. FoodNet reports do not link pathogens to food vehicles, and they include cases resulting from nonfood routes, such as contaminated water, person-to-person transmission, and direct animal exposures. Also, data are subject to local variations and may not represent national trends.

Timely data retrieval in FoodNet enhances the potential for early warning of food safety emergencies and improves the accuracy of estimates of foodborne illness by specific pathogens. For example, the reduction of cyclosporiasis cases (Table 4.2) follows restrictions on raspberry imports from Guatemala after a large outbreak was traced to the food (4–8).

TABLE 4.2 Rate (Incidence per 100,000 Population) of Diagnosed Infections for Pathogens at the Five Original Sites, 1996–2000, and for All Eight Sites, 2000, by Year and Pathogen—Foodborne Diseases Active Surveillance Network, United States.

Pathogen	Original Five Sites[a]					All Sites[b]
	1996	1997	1998	1999	2000	2000
Campylobacter	23.5	25.2	21.4	17.5	20.1	15.7
Cryptosporidium	NR[c]	3.7[d]	2.9[d]	1.8[d]	2.4[d]	1.5
Cyclospora	NR[c]	0.4[d]	0.1[d]	0.1[d]	0.1[d]	0.1
Escherichia coli 0157	2.7	2.3	2.8	2.1	2.9	2.1
Listeria	0.5	0.5	0.6	0.5	0.4	0.3
Salmonella	14.5	13.6	12.3	13.6	12.0	14.4
Shigella	8.9	7.5	8.5	5.0	11.6	7.9
Vibrio	0.2	0.3	0.3	0.2	0.3	0.2
Yersinia	1.0	0.9	1.0	0.8	0.5	0.4

Reprinted courtesy of Shallow S, Samuel M, McNees A, et al. Preliminary FoodNet data on the incidence of food-borne illnesses—selected sites, United States, 2000. *MMWR.* 2001;50(13):241-246. Available at: http://www.cdc.gov/mmwr/PDF/wk/mm5013.pdf. Accessed May 24, 2001.

[a]Original sites: Minnesota, Oregon, and selected counties in California, Connecticut, and Georgia.

[b]All sites—Connecticut, Georgia, Minnesota, Oregon, and selected counties in California, Maryland, New York, and Tennessee. Data from Colorado are not available for this reporting period.

[c]Not reported.

[d]Urine isolates excluded because they are not reported prior to 1999.

As these data are collected over time, they will help to determine the effectiveness of food safety control measures and provide data to identify future control points and program needs. Preliminary data from the FoodNet surveillance system point to *Salmonella* spp, *Campylobacter jejuni,* and *Shigella* spp as the pathogens in the United States causing the greatest incidence of foodborne illness (Table 4.2). While trend data are complicated by sporadic large outbreaks in local areas and by the addition of larger catchment areas, it is clear that incidence of *Campylobacter, Cryptosporidium,* and *Cyclospora* infections have decreased substantially over the five-year study period (Table 4.2).

NATIONAL MOLECULAR SUBTYPING NETWORK FOR FOODBORNE-DISEASE SURVEILLANCE (PULSENET)

The initial model for PulseNet originated in 1993 when CDC linked food and clinical isolates to verify the food vehicle in a large outbreak caused by *Escherichia coli* O157:H7 in fast-food hamburgers. Rapidly increased demand for subtyping led to decentralization of the laboratory functions with standardization of protocols, equipment, and nomenclature and implementation of a rigorous quality assurance program to ensure integrity of the results of the subtyping. Currently, PulseNet is a network of forty-six state laboratories, public health laboratories in New York City and Los Angeles County, the food safety laboratories of FDA and USDA, and six Canadian provincial food safety laboratories (9).

PulseNet permits rapid comparisons of DNA "fingerprints" for foodborne pathogens via an electronic database maintained at CDC. Since these DNA fingerprints are unique to each strain of bacteria, comparisons of the fingerprints can determine whether an organism isolated from a suspect food and from a human specimen are the same, leading to confirmations of food vehicles in cases or outbreaks of foodborne illness. Comparisons can also determine whether outbreaks caused by the same agent are linked to a common food source, even if they are geographically separated. Also, identification by PulseNet of an increase in a specific subtype of a pathogen may be an early indicator for an outbreak, and a decrease in that subtype can help confirm that an outbreak is over by showing a substantial decrease in circulation of the outbreak subtype in the affected communities (9,10).

PulseNet began tracking *E. coli* O157:H7 in 1996 and has now been used to track three additional foodborne pathogens—nontyphoidal *Salmonella* serotypes, *Listeria monocytogenes,* and *Shigella sonnei.* By 2003 additional bacterial pathogens will be added to the system, including *Clostridium perfringens, Campylobacter jejuni, Vibrio parahaemolyticus, V. cholerae, Clostridium botulinum,* other pathogenic *E. coli,* and *Yersinia enterocolitica.* Viral and parasitic pathogens will be added later, as well (9).

Examples of how PulseNet can help to identify and investigate outbreaks include the following:

- In 1994 the number of cases of *E. coli* O157:H7 increased nearly tenfold. Public health officials suspected a common source outbreak, but seventeen different fingerprints were identified for the twenty-three patients. This meant that expensive outbreak investigation procedures were not used (10).
- In 1996, epidemiologists traced two concurrent outbreaks of *E. coli* O157:H7 infections occurring in Connecticut and Illinois to mesclun lettuce grown on the same California farm. As a result, safer lettuce growing and processing practices are being developed (10).
- In 1996, epidemiologists traced an outbreak of *E. coli* O157:H7 infections in patients from four states and one Canadian province to commercial apple juice. This resulted in a rapid product recall to limit the scope of the outbreak (11).
- In 1998, the state public health departments in both Illinois and Pennsylvania informed CDC about increases in *Salmonella agona* infections. PulseNet surveillance data from other states confirmed similar increases in ten other states, implying a national outbreak with no obvious source. Subsequently, the outbreak was traced to contaminated ready-to-eat toasted-oat cereal. PulseNet was successful in describing the occurrence of this geographically disparate outbreak and in confirming the control of the outbreak as the organism returned to normal levels in the affected populations (12).
- In 1998, PulseNet helped to track a large, multistate outbreak of listeriosis to contaminated hotdogs and sandwich meats produced in a single meat-processing plant. Identification of the food source led to a recall of the implicated product, rapidly ending the outbreak and potentially reducing the death toll from listeriosis (13).

FDA PESTICIDE PROGRAM (REGULATORY COMPONENT)

FDA enforces pesticide tolerances on imported foods and on foods (other than meat and poultry products) that are shipped through interstate commerce (14–17). In the FDA Pesticide Program, products are examined for 366 different pesticides. Of the 36,428 samples examined from 1996 to 1999, only 1.8 percent contained violative residues (0.9 percent domestic, 2.6 percent imported). These violative residues are either contamination levels above the allowable limit or residues of pesticides that are not approved for the particular commodity. Table 4.3 shows the residue data for domestic and imported products from 1996 to 1999. The primary commodities with residues, both violative and nonviolative, are fruits and vegetables. Products are sampled as close to harvest as possible, maximizing the potential for finding residues. These levels do not represent

TABLE 4.3 Percentages of Products with Pesticide Residues in the FDA Pesticide Program, 1996–1999 (Regulatory Samples)

Product Type	Domestic Samples % Non-violative / % Violative	Imported Samples % Non-violative / % Violative
Grains and Grain Products		
1996	45.5 / 1.1 (363 samples)	19.1 / 0.9 (230 samples)
1997	40.6 / 0 (397 samples)	13.0 / 0.9 (322 samples)
1998	36.5 / 0.2 (479 samples)	16.0 / 0 (144 samples)
1999	38.8 / 0.2 (468 samples)	23.9 / 0.7 (276 samples)
Milk / Dairy Products / Eggs		
1996	2.6 / 0 (781 samples)	5.4 / 0 (129 samples)
1997	3.0 / 0 (628 samples)	10.6 / 0 (85 samples)
1998	3.0 / 0 (335 samples)	3.7 / 0 (27 samples)
1999	2.6 / 0 (116 samples)	4.5 / 0 (22 samples)
Fish / Shellfish		
1996	37.7 / 0.4 (520 samples)	12.1 / 0 (124 samples)
1997	32.0 / 0 (369 samples)	6.3 / 0 (158 samples)
1998	21.5 / 0 (260 samples)	3.6 / 0 (194 samples)
1999	28.9 / 0 (218 samples)	5.0 / 0 (296 samples)
Fruits		
1996	52.6 / 1.3 (1,194 samples)	40.2 / 2.8 (1,735 samples)
1997	54.7 / 1.2 (1,171 samples)	38.2 / 1.2 (2,034 samples)
1998	57.6 / 0.9 (1,066 samples)	36.0 / 2.9 (1,257 samples)
1999	60.6 / 0.6 (1,063 samples)	40.7 / 1.8 (2,290 samples)
Vegetables		
1996	34.7 / 1.1 (1,958 samples)	34.2 / 2.8 (2,378 samples)
1997	28.5 / 2.4 (1,707 samples)	34.9 / 2.1 (2,356 samples)
1998	27.7 / 1.4 (1,291 samples)	30.9 / 3.6 (2,010 samples)
1999	29.1 / 1.2 (1,414 samples)	31.3 / 3.9 (2,768 samples)
Other		
1996	25.0 / 0 (144 samples)	14.2 / 3.1 (325 samples)
1997	17.2 / 0 (157 samples)	10.8 / 2.6 (268 samples)
1998	12.7 / 0 (166 samples)	4.8 / 3.1 (228 samples)
1999	23.0 / 1.4 (147 samples)	10.6 / 10.6 (358 samples)

Source: Compiled from References 14–17

residue levels at time of consumption, that is, after washing, peeling, or cooking. Instead, they give the background residues on commodities after harvest. The Total Diet Study is another component of the FDA Pesticide Program, usually reported separately because the objectives, sampling methods, and sample preparation are different.

THE TOTAL DIET STUDY (MARKET BASKET STUDY; TDS)

FDA conducts the market basket study annually to monitor trends in levels of certain nutrients and contaminants in representative diets (14–19). Each market basket contains 261 foods that represent over 3,500 different foods reported in the USDA food consumption surveys. The foods are purchased from consumer markets four times a year—once from each of four geographic regions of the country. Then they are prepared in a home-type kitchen and analyzed for concentrations of nutrients (various minerals, vitamin B_6, and folic acid) and contaminants (pesticide residues, industrial chemicals, radionucleotides, and toxic elements). These data are used in conjunction with USDA food consumption data to estimate dietary intakes of various chemicals. Data from TDS will be used to assess Objective 10-7 in *Healthy People 2010* (Reduce human exposure to **organophosphate** pesticides from food; 20).

The advantage of the Total Diet Study is that the chemical analyses are performed directly on foods in the marketplace that have been prepared as consumers would prepare them. However, sampling is restricted by resource limitations, reducing the generalization of the results for all populations across all regions.

Over three hundred different chemicals can be detected using the study methods, although only one hundred or so are typically found in a given year in any of the samples. The most common pesticide residues found are DDT, malathion, chlorpyrifos-methyl, endosulfan, and dieldrin (Table 4.4). In the 1996 to 1999 surveys, all residues were well below regulatory tolerances. DDT and dieldrin are particularly persistent in the environment and bioaccumulate; they are likely to be found as food contaminants for many years, even though they are no longer used in agricultural production. Because this is a surveillance program and not a regulatory program, the analytical methods are modified to permit measurement at levels five to ten times lower than those normally used, making it possible to detect residues at or above one part per billion (1 microgram/kilogram) (14–17).

PESTICIDE DATA PROGRAM (PDP)

USDA's Agricultural Marketing Service coordinates a national survey of pesticide residues on raw agricultural produce, processed grain products, and fluid milk in the Pesticide Data Program (PDP; 21–25). Since its implementation in 1991, PDP has tested twenty-eight fresh commodities and twenty processed commodities for over one hundred insecticides, herbicides, fungicides, and growth regulators. Most commodities have been tested for multiple years. Both domestic

TABLE 4.4   Frequency of Occurrence of Pesticide Residues Found in Greater than 2 Percent of Total Diet Study Foods

Pesticide[a]	1996[b]		1997[c]		1998[d]		1999[e]	
	# samples	%	# samples	%	# samples	%	# samples	%
DDT	140	18	244	24	217	21	225	22
Malathion[h]	136	17	161	16	156	15	175	17
Chlorpyrifos-methyl[h]	122	16	165	16	185	18	188	18
Endosulfan	87	11	147	14	129	12	151	15
Dieldrin	76	10	127	12	107	10	145	14
Chlorpyrifos[h]	72	9	79	8	89	9	93	9
Chlorpropham	45	6	85	8	49	5	70	7
Iprodione	36	5	62	6	53	5	48	5
Carbaryl[f]	33	4	30	2.9	41	4	31	3
Methamidophos[h]	32	4	31	3	33	3	29	3
Dicloran	27	3	35	3	26	3	28	3
Thiabendazole[g]	27	3	36	3	37	4	33	3
Permethrin	23	3.0	45	4	49	5	54	5
Dimethoate[h]	22	2.8	29	2.8	23	2	24	2
Acephate[h]	21	2.7	21	2.0	29	3	—	—
Dicofol	21	2.7	—	—	—	—	—	—
Lindane	21	2.7	23	2.2	—	—	33	2
Diazinon[h]	19	2.4	—	—	—	—	—	—
BHC	18	2.3	24	2.3	24	2	32	3
Toxaphene	18	2.3	21	2.0	21	2	—	—
Hexachlorobenzene	—	—	27	2.6	—	—	32	3
Methoxychlor	—	—	26	2.5	—	—	29	3
Pirimiphos-methyl[h]	—	—	24	2.3	21	2	—	—
Azinphos-methyl[h]	—	—	21	2.0	—	—	—	—
Omethoate	—	—	21	2.0	—	—	—	—
Chlordane	—	—	—	—	—	—	36	3
Heptachlor	—	—	—	—	—	—	36	3

Source: Compiled from References 14–17, 20, 28

[a]Isomers, metabolites, and related compounds are not listed separately; they are covered under the "parent" pesticide from which they arise.

[b]Based on 3 market baskets analyzed in 1996 consisting of 778 items.

[c]Based on 4 market baskets analyzed in 1997 consisting of 1036 items.

[d]Based on 4 market baskets analyzed in FY 1998 consisting of 1,035 items.

[e]Based on 4 market baskets analyzed in 1999 consisting of 1,040 items.

[f]Reflects overall incidence; however, only 283 items were analyzed for N-methylcarbamates in 1996, 376 items in 1997, 378 items in 1998, and 384 items in 1999.

[g]Reflects overall incidence; however, only 199 items were analyzed for thiabendazole and benomyl in 1996, 264 items in 1997, 263 items in 1998, and 268 items in 1999.

[h]Organophosphate pesticide being reevaluated by the U.S. Environmental Protection Agency under the Food Quality Protection Act and targeted for reduction in Objective 10-7 of *Healthy People 2010.*

and imported products are sampled. Samples are collected as close to the point of consumption as possible and reflect foods available to consumers. However, for many commodities the samples do not directly reflect consumer exposure because they are not prepared, that is, washed, peeled, or cooked. PDP data are used to refine EPA estimates of dietary exposures for surveillance programs and for re-**registration** of chemicals for agricultural uses; to focus FDA surveillance activities; to evaluate pesticide alternatives; and to address specific food safety concerns, such as childhood exposures and potential acute versus chronic responses to foodborne pesticides. Data from PDP will also be used to assess Objective 10-7 in *Healthy People 2010* (Reduce human exposure to organophosphate pesticides from food; 20).

Of the 31,573 samples (composite and individual) examined from 1996 to 1999, fewer than 5 percent contained violative residues (22–25). Fewer than 0.2 percent of the violative residues were for contaminates that exceeded allowable tolerances. The remainder (4.4 percent) were for contaminates for which there were no established tolerances, that is, the chemical was not registered for the commodity on which it was found. These residue levels were very low and may have resulted from spray draft or from residues remaining after crop rotation. In general, there were more residues on fresh than processed products. PDP reports contain extensive data on individual commodities (21–25).

CUMULATIVE EXPOSURE PROJECT (CEP)

The Cumulative Exposure Project, conducted by EPA, examines the total exposure of Americans to toxic substances in air, food, and drinking water (26). The goal of the project is to estimate total exposure levels for different communities and demographic groups nationwide. The food component of the study estimates exposures to thirty-seven contaminants (pesticide residues and industrial pollutants) in thirty-four foods. Once exposure estimates are made, they are compared to benchmark data that describe lifetime risk of cancer and other deleterious effects. Risks that exceed the standard of one in one million will be high priorities for risk reduction.

Exposure estimates are based on contaminant data from TDS, PDP, and other surveillance systems combined with food consumption data from the USDA's nationwide food consumption survey (27; see Box 4.1). Exposure estimates are

BOX 4.1   Calculating Exposure Estimates for a Contaminant

Step 1: Calculate average daily exposure for the contaminant from each commodity.

Step 2: Add up the average daily exposures for the contaminant from all commodities.

Example:

  Step 1:

  If: Average daily consumption of apple is 25 g

       Average contamination of apples with azinphos methyl is 0.04 ppm

       Average mass of population (depends upon population being considered); for this example, standard adult mass is 70 kg

  Then: Consumption   = 25 g raw apple/70 kg

           Contamination   = [0.04 ppm azinphos methyl][25 g apple]

                              1 µg azinphos methyl/25 g apple

       Average Daily Exposure = [Consumption][Contamination]

                              [25 g apple/70 kg][1 µg azinphos methyl/25 g apple]

                              1 µg azinphos methyl/70 kg

                              0.014 µg azinphos methyl/kg

This step must be completed for every commodity.

Step 2: Add the dietary amounts of azinphos methyl across all commodities.

Steps 1 and 2 must be completed for each contaminant examined.

---

compared to benchmark data by calculating hazard ratios. These ratios are average daily exposures divided by benchmark concentrations. In cases where hazard ratios are greater than 1, the lifetime risk is greater than one in one million.

Using the most conservative estimation process, early reports (27) show six contaminants have cancer hazard ratios greater than 1 for average national exposure and for exposure of children under the age of twelve. These contaminants are arsenic, chlordane, DDT, dieldrin, dioxins, and polychlorinated biphenyls (PCBs). Using the same conservative estimation process only one contaminant, PCBs, had a noncancer hazard ratio greater than 1. For all six of the contaminants estimated to have hazard ratios greater than 1 for the U.S. diet, 70 percent or more of the exposure comes from fish (freshwater and saltwater) or shellfish. Rice was responsible for almost 11 percent of average national exposure to arsenic (higher for children); beef contributed 6 percent to 9 percent of the exposures to DDT, dieldrin, and dioxins; and milk contributed over 10 percent of the exposure to DDT for young children. No other dietary component accounted for more than 5 percent of the exposure to any of these hazardous contaminants.

Estimates in the CEP will improve as more relevant data become available. Current estimates are based on data from the early 1990s. Some foods, notably sugars, some oils, and soybeans, could not be included in the study because relevant data were not available. Other limitations to the study include the relatively small number of samples in some categories, the limited demographic data for assessment of populations risk groups, and the types of contaminant data available, that is, raw versus prepared or cooked samples. Additionally, estimates in the CEP will change over time. For example, as dietary patterns change, the food exposure data will change. Also, several of the contaminants are environmental contaminants that bioaccumulate in fish. Over time their levels will decrease, although this decrease will not be rapid. These early data are important in assessing and characterizing current risks to help target data needed for future decision making.

REFERENCES

1. Olsen SJ, MacKinnon LC, Goulding JS, et al. Surveillance for foodborne-disease outbreaks—United States, 1993–1997. *MMWR.* 2000;49(SS-01):1–51. Available at: ftp:// ftp.cdc.gov/pub/Publications/mmwr/SS/SS4901.pdf. Accessed May 25, 2001.
2. Mead PS, Slutsker L, Dietz V, et al. Food-related illness and death in the United States. *Emerg Infect Dis.* 1999;5(5):607–625. Available at: http://www.cdc.gov/ ncidod/eid/vol5no5/mead.htm. Accessed May 25, 2001.
3. Shallow S, Samuel M, McNees A, et al. Preliminary FoodNet data on the incidence of foodborne illnesses—selected sites, United States, 2000. *MMWR.* 2001;50(13):241–246. Available at: http://www.cdc.gov/mmwr/PDF/wk/mm5013.pdf. Accessed May 24, 2001.
4. Chambers J, Somerfeldt S, Mackey L, et al. Outbreaks of *Cyclospora cayetanensis* infection—United States, 1996. *MMWR.* 1996;45(25):549–551. Available at: ftp://ftp.cdc. gov/pub/Publications/mmwr/wk/mm4525.pdf. Accessed May 26, 2001.
5. Hofmann J, Liu Z, Genese C, et al. Update: outbreaks of *Cyclospora cayetanensis* infection—United States, 1996. *MMWR.* 1996;45(28):611–612. Available at: ftp://ftp.cdc. gov/pub/Publications/mmwr/wk/mm4528.pdf. Accessed May 26, 2001.

6. Jacquette G, Guido F, Jacobs J, et al. Outbreaks of *Cyclospora cayetanensis* infection—United States, 1997. *MMWR*. 1997;46(21):461–462. Available at: ftp://ftp.cdc.gov/pub/Publications/mmwr/wk/mm4621.pdf. Accessed May 26, 2001.

7. DeGraw E, Heber S, Rowan A. Update: Outbreaks of *Cyclospora cayetanensis* infection—United States and Canada, 1997. *MMWR*. 1997;46(23):521–523. Available at: ftp://ftp.cdc.gov/pub/Publications/mmwr/wk/mm4623.pdf. Accessed May 26, 2001.

8. Colley DG. Widespread foodborne cyclosporiasis outbreaks present major challenges. *Emerg Infect Dis* [serial online]. 1996;2(4):354–356. Available at: ftp://ftp.cdc.gov/pub/EID/vol2no4/adobe/letters.pdf. Accessed May 26, 2001.

9. Swaminathan B, Barrett TJ, Hunter SB, Tauxe RV, and the CDC PulseNet Task Force. PulseNet: the molecular subtyping network for foodborne bacterial disease surveillance, United States. *Emerg Infect Dis* [serial online]. 2001;7(3):382–389. Available at: http://www.cdc.gov/ncidod/eid/vol7no3/pdfs/swaminathan.pdf. Accessed May 24, 2001.

10. Centers for Disease Control and Prevention, National Center for Infectious Diseases, Division of Bacterial and Mycotic Diseases. National computer network in place to combat foodborne illness [CDC Web site]. February 1999. Available at: http://www.cdc.gov/ncidod/dbmd/pulsenet/pulsenet.htm. Accessed May 26, 2001.

11. Cody SH, Glynn MK, Farrar JA, et al. An outbreak of *Escherichia coli* O157:H7 infection from unpasteurized commercial apple juice. *Ann Intern Med*. 1999;130:202–209.

12. State and Local Health Departments, US Food and Drug Administration, Centers for Disease Control and Prevention. Multistate outbreak of *Salmonella* serotype *Agona* infections linked to toasted oats cereal—United States, April–May 1998. *MMWR*. 1998;47:462–464. Available at: http://www.cdc.gov/mmwr/PDF/wk/mm4722.pdf. Accessed May 24, 2001.

13. Local and State Health Departments and the Centers for Disease Control and Prevention. Multistate outbreak of listeriosis—United States, 1998. *MMWR*. 1998;47(50); 1085–1086. Available at: ftp://ftp.cdc.gov/pub/Publications/mmwr/wk/mm4750.pdf. Accessed May 24, 2001.

14. Food and Drug Administration Pesticide Program: Residue Monitoring [FDA Web site]. 1996. January 1998. Available at: http://www.cfsan.fda.gov/~dms/pes96rep.html. Accessed May 26, 2001.

15. Food and Drug Administration Pesticide Program: Residue Monitoring [FDA Web site].1997. August 1998. Available at: http://vm.cfsan.fda.gov/~acrobat/pes97rep.pdf. Accessed May 26, 2001.

16. Food and Drug Administration Pesticide Program: Residue Monitoring [FDA Web site]. 1998. March 1999. Available at: http://www.cfsan.fda.gov/~dms/pes98rep.html. Accessed May 26, 2001.

17. Food and Drug Administration Pesticide Program: Residue Monitoring [FDA Web site]. 1999. Center for Food Safety and Applied Nutrition, US Food and Drug Administration; April 2000. Available at: http://www.cfsan.fda.gov/~dms/pes99rep.html. Accessed May 24, 2001.

18. Food and Drug Administration, Center for Food Safety and Applied Nutrition, Office of Premarket Approval. Estimating exposure to direct food additives and chemical contaminants in the diet [FDA Web site]. September 1995. Available at: http://vm.cfsan.fda.gov/~dms/opa-cg8.html. Accessed May 25, 2001.

19. Pennington JAT, Young BE, Wilson DB. Nutritional elements in the U.S. diet: results from the Total Diet Study, 1982–1986. *J Am Diet Assoc*. 1989(89):659–664.

20. US Department of Health and Human Services. Food safety. In: *Healthy People 2010*. 2nd ed. With Understanding and Improving Health and Objectives for Improving Health. 2 vols. Washington, DC: US Government Printing Office; November 2000:10.3–10.19. Available at: http://www.health.gov/healthypeople/Document/pdf/Volume1/10Food.pdf. Accessed May 12, 2001.

21. US Department of Agriculture. Pesticide Data Program (PDP). On-line background paper. December 1998. Available at: http://www.ams.usda.gov:80/science/pdp/index.htm. Accessed May 25, 2001.

22. US Department of Agriculture, Agricultural Marketing Service. Pesticide Data Program: annual summary, calendar year 1999. Available at: http://www.ams.usda.gov:80/science/pdp/99summ.pdf. Accessed May 25, 2001.

23. US Department of Agriculture, Agricultural Marketing Service. Pesticide Data Program: annual summary, calendar year 1998. Available at: http://www.ams.usda.gov:80/science/pdp/98summ.pdf. Accessed May 25, 2001.

24. US Department of Agriculture, Agricultural Marketing Service. Pesticide Data Program: annual summary, calendar year 1997. Available at: http://www.ams.usda.gov:80/science/pdp/97summ.pdf. Accessed May 25, 2001.

25. US Department of Agriculture, Agricultural Marketing Service. Pesticide Data Program: annual summary, calendar year 1996. Available at: http://www.ams.usda.gov:80/science/pdp/96summ.pdf. Accessed May 25, 2001.

26. Environmental Protection Agency. Cumulative Exposure Project [EPA Web site]. April 19, 1999. Available at: http://www.epa.gov/cumulativeexposure/about/about2.htm. Accessed May 26, 2001.

27. Dougherty CP, Holtz SH, Reinert JC, Panyacosit L, Axelrad DA, Woodruff TJ. Dietary exposures to food contaminants across the United States. *Environ Res.* 2000;84:170–185.

28. US Environmental Protection Agency, Office of Pesticide Programs. Organophosphate pesticides in food: a primer on reassessment of residue limits. May 1999. EPA:735-F-99-014. Available at: http://www.epa.gov/pesticides/op/primer.htm. Accessed May 24, 2001.

CHAPTER 5

LAWS, REGULATIONS, AND REGULATORY BODIES

Each of the three branches of the federal government—legislative, executive (president and cabinet departments), and judicial—plays a role in maintaining the safety of the U.S. food supply. The legislative branch passes laws to establish food safety goals. Agencies within the executive branch develop **regulations** to implement the laws. They also establish monitoring systems to check compliance with the regulations. The judicial branch protects the rights of food producers, food processors, and the public by reviewing the policies and procedures of the regulatory process.

Laws and regulations governing food safety exist at the federal, state, and some local levels. The commerce clause of the U.S. Constitution empowers the federal government to regulate the production and marketing of food for interstate commerce. States have jurisdiction over foods produced, marketed, and consumed exclusively within their borders. State and local governments also develop and enforce laws related to retail food establishments.

Additionally, the Joint Commission on Accreditation of Healthcare Organizations (JCAHO) works with its constituent organizations to improve food quality in healthcare institutions, and the *Codex Alimentarius* establishes food safety regulations for international trade. JCAHO establishes standards and monitoring systems to meet the quality goals of its constituent organizations and to meet standards for federal reimbursement, although participation in the JCAHO program is not mandatory (1). The United States is one of over 160 member nations participating under the *Codex Alimentarius* to facilitate world trade in foods and promote consumer protection by establishing testing and inspection procedures, reviewing safety data, and determining international trade standards for food safety (2).

FOOD SAFETY LAWS AND REGULATIONS

At the federal level, the legislative branch of government is the U.S. Congress, which includes the House of Representatives and the Senate. Congress passes laws that establish food safety goals and authorize specific agencies to develop regulations to implement those goals. The laws specifically cover only foods involved in interstate commerce. However, as a condition of participation in some federal programs, states may be required to have laws as strict as the federal laws. State legislatures must pass such laws or forfeit participation in the relevant federal program. Box 5.1 lists major laws that govern food safety at the federal level. The laws are organized by topic (codified) in the *United States Code*

BOX 5.1   Major Food Safety Laws in the United States, in Chronological Order

- Tea Importation Act of 1897, ch 358, 29 Stat 604.
- Federal Meat Inspection Act of 1907, ch 2907, 34 Stat 1258.
- Filled Milk Act of 1923, ch 262, 42 Stat 1486.
- Federal Food, Drug, and Cosmetic Act of 1938, ch 675, 52 Stat 1040.
- Public Health Service Act of 1944, ch 373, 58 Stat 682.[a]
- Federal Insecticide, Fungicide, and Rodenticide Act of 1947, ch 125, 61 Stat 163.
- Food Additives Amendment of 1958 (includes the Delaney Clause), Pub L No. 85-929, 72 Stat 1784.
- Pesticide Amendment Act of 1960, Pub L No. 86-537, 74 Stat 251.
- Color Additive Amendments of 1960, Pub L No. 86-618, 74 Stat 397.
- Fair Packaging and Labeling Act of 1966, Pub L No. 89-755, 80 Stat 1296.
- Wholesome Meat Act of 1967, Pub L No. 90-201, 81 Stat 584.
- Wholesome Poultry Products Act of 1968, Pub L No. 90-492, 82 Stat 791.
- Egg Products Inspection Act of 1970, Pub L No. 91-597, 84 Stat 1620.
- Saccharin Study and Labeling Act of 1977, Pub L No. 95-203, Title XII, Subtitle A, §1205(c), 95 Stat 716.
- Infant Formula Act of 1980, Pub L No. 96-359, 94 Stat 1190.
- Swine Health Protection Act of 1980, Pub L No. 96-468, 94 Stat 2229.
- Dietary Supplement Health and Education Act of 1994, Pub L No. 103-417, 108 Stat 4325.
- Act of April 1, 1996, Pub L No. 104-124, 110 Stat 882 (repeals saccharin notice requirement on products "not for immediate consumption").
- Federal Tea Tasters Repeal Act of 1996, Pub L No. 104-128, 110 Stat 1198 (repeals the Tea Importation Act of 1897)
- Food Quality Protection Act of 1996, Pub L No. 104-170, 110 Stat 1489.
- Food and Drug Administration Modernization Act of 1997, Pub L No. 105-115, 111 Stat 2296.

[a]The Public Health Service Act of 1944 repealed and/or superseded the earlier Public Health Service Act, which had created and made provisions for the Public Health & Marine Hospital Service. The earlier acts dated back to July 1, 1902. Thus, 1944 represented a major reorganization of the Public Health Service, not its creation.

(USC). A 1999 FDA backgrounder outlines the history of food law in the United States (3). Since 1956, when a law is passed by Congress it is given a unique number. The law is designated PL (Public Law) XX and reported in Statutes at Large (Stat). Then most are organized (codified) in the *United States Code*. The agency with authority to implement the law will then report in the *Federal Register* the schedule for public hearings on the regulations to implement the law. After hearings the agency will draft and publish the resulting regulations in the *Federal Register* and the *Code of Federal Regulations* (CFR). The CFR is divided into topic areas. Most food safety regulations are found in section 21 (21 CFR).

Because laws passed by Congress state broad objectives, regulations that embody the will of Congress are necessary to implement the laws. Before developing regulations, the authorized department holds public hearings that allow all interested parties to express their views and offer their research for consideration (4). Public hearings typically last for at least sixty days and allow for both in-person oral comments and written comments. Comment periods are listed in the *Federal Register* (5). Once developed, regulations guide the day-to-day implementation of laws. A single law will generate many specific regulations. For example, regulations describe the amount and type of oil that can be used in canned tuna and the acidity required for canned fruit products. The regulations are recorded by category in the *Code of Federal Regulations*.

If a law is challenged in court, the resulting opinion becomes a part of case law. Thus, a decision made in one case helps to clarify the law for others. For a more comprehensive discussion of food laws and regulations see *A Practical Guide to Food and Drug Law and Regulation* from the Food and Drug Law Institute (6).

MAJOR FOOD REGULATORS

Several administrative units of the executive branch are responsible for maintaining the safety of the U.S. food supply. Those units include the:

- U.S. Food and Drug Administration (FDA) and the Centers for Disease Control and Prevention (CDC), both units of the U.S. Department of Health and Human Services
- Food Safety and Inspection Service (FSIS), a unit of the U.S. Department of Agriculture (USDA)
- Environmental Protection Agency (EPA)
- National Marine Fisheries Service (NMFS), a unit under the Department of Commerce

At the state level, food safety units are typically under the state department of agriculture or the state department of health. County health departments are usually the local contacts for food safety issues or problems.

The Federal Food, Drug, and Cosmetic Act and the Public Health Service Act establish the FDA as the **regulatory agency** with primary responsibility for food safety in the U.S. Amendments to the Federal Food, Drug, and Cosmetic Act, such as the Pesticide Amendment Act of 1960, the 1958 Food Additives Amendment **(Delaney Clause)**, the Color Additives Amendment of 1960, and the Food Quality Protection Act of 1996, have redefined the FDA's jurisdiction as new concerns have arisen. The FDA also administers the Fair Packaging and Labeling Act, the Infant Formula Act of 1980, and the Dietary Supplement Health and Education Act of 1994. FDA is responsible for the *Food Code* (7), a model food safety guide for retail establishments that contains recommended regulations for regulatory jurisdictions, and is the co-lead agency (with the Food Safety and Inspection Service of the U.S. Department of Agriculture) for the food safety focus in the *Healthy People 2010* plan (8).

The CDC investigates and records reports of foodborne illness. These reports are used to guide food safety regulations, areas for research, and industry and consumer education programs.

The FSIS is responsible for ensuring the safety of meat and poultry products in the United States. This unit of USDA administers the Wholesome Poultry Products Act of 1968, the Egg Product Inspection Act of 1970, the Federal Meat Inspection Act, the Wholesome Meat Act of 1967, the Swine Health Protection Act of 1980, and the Filled Milk Act. FSIS is co-lead agency (with FDA) for the food safety focus in the *Healthy People 2010* plan (8).

The EPA regulates the manufacture, use, and labeling of pesticides; monitors their presence in the environment; and registers approved pesticides under the Federal Insecticide, Fungicide, and Rodenticide Act and the Food Quality Protection Act. The registered products also include sanitizing and disinfecting agents used in food production and foodservice (see Box 5.2). The agency sets tolerances

BOX 5.2   Hazardous Product Labels

Products used in cleaning, sanitizing, and disinfecting need to be used correctly to achieve their intended purpose. The labels of products for home use carry the information consumers need to use the products correctly. Products for use in institutions make such information available on product labels or on material safety data sheet (MSDS) statements. Institutions are required to have MSDS statements accessible to employees. Products registered as **sanitizers** or **disinfectants** meet EPA standards that ensure their efficacy when they are used correctly. Labels for EPA-registered sanitizing and disinfection agents carry the following information (18):

- Product name (brand name and chemical name).
- Directions for use.
- Precautionary statements, such as hazards to humans, domestic animals, and the environment, and physical or chemical hazards.
- Storage and disposal instructions.
- Signal words that indicate potential hazard levels to humans. "Caution," "warning," "danger," and "danger—poison" are the primary signal words, with "danger—poison" being the most harmful. There is no federal definition for "nontoxic."
- First-aid instructions, when necessary or appropriate. If a product has been consumed, it is prudent to call a poison control center for advice.
- Active ingredients.
- Other (inert) ingredients.
- Manufacturer's address.
- Net weight/net contents statement.
- EPA registration number.
- EPA establishment number.

for pesticide residues in foods under the Federal Food, Drug, and Cosmetic Act, and the FDA and USDA enforce the tolerances. The Food Quality Protection Act of 1996 amends the Food, Drug, and Cosmetic Act to eliminate the application of the Delaney Clause to pesticides. It also amends several provisions in the Federal Insecticide, Fungicide, and Rodenticide Act to increase research and oversight on pesticide products and reduce existing tolerances to protect pregnant women, infants, and children. EPA is also responsible for setting specifications for community water standards and for bottled water (9). EPA is the lead agency for the environmental health focus in the *Healthy People 2010* plan (10).

NMFS participates in the development and implementation of food safety policies governing seafoods. The establishment of such policies is important because seafoods are growing in popularity and present a greater proportion of foodborne illness relative to consumption than most other food products in the United States (11–12). Food safety challenges presented by seafoods are closely linked to environmental quality of harvesting waters, making it important for NMFS and EPA to collaborate.

INSPECTION PROGRAMS

Inspection programs monitor food industries to ensure that they follow food safety regulations. Inspection of all foods produced or sold commercially within the United States is mandatory. This does not mean that each food unit is inspected. It means that food production and processing plants, storage and distribution units, and retail establishments are always open to inspection by federal, state, and local regulatory agencies. Legal action can be taken by those agencies against companies that are out of compliance.

Traditional inspection systems relied on external inspectors as their primary monitors. Today most inspection programs focus on development and implementation of Hazard Analysis Critical Control Point (HACCP) systems that emphasize the establishment's commitment to continuous problem solving and prevention of food safety problems rather than relying solely on periodic facility inspections by regulatory agencies (7). Because HACCP programs require establishment and maintenance of records that document internal monitoring procedures, inspectors have an ongoing record of manufacturing practices, not just a snapshot view afforded by traditional on-site visits. More detailed information on HACCP is presented in Chapter 7.

INTEGRATING REGULATORY RESPONSIBILITIES

Jurisdiction may appear easy to assign. However, in many instances agencies share jurisdiction. For example, under the Egg Products Inspection Act of 1970, the USDA has jurisdiction over fresh eggs. During a salmonellosis outbreak involving egg products, however, the FDA would share regulatory authority with the USDA because the Public Health Service Act gives the FDA the responsibility for preventing foodborne communicable diseases. In addition, epidemiologists at the CDC would help to determine the actual source of the outbreak and to monitor it. State and local agencies become involved when the outbreak occurs within their borders or is traced to industry housed within their borders.

Each citizen also has regulatory responsibilities. The original source of information on suspected outbreaks of foodborne illness is the consumer. Such information comes to light when an individual suspects that she or he has become ill as a result of eating a certain food and is examined by a physician or the local health department. Consumers can also report a suspect food product or practice. If you have a suspect food, government agencies recommend that you securely package it and refrigerate it. Then notify the local health department, the regional office of the FDA, the USDA's Cooperative Extension Service, or the state agriculture office. (See Appendix A for contact information.) They will tell you what to do with the suspect food. In some cases they will examine the food; otherwise, they will tell you how to dispose of it safely.

RECALLS

Recalls are actions taken by a firm to remove a product from the market (13–14). Most recalls are undertaken voluntarily, but FDA can order a product recall (or seize goods in the field). Although recalls that make headlines are for hazardous situations, most recalls are for less serious violations, such as minor mislabeling. Some mislabeling may be critical to special populations. An example would be a product label that does not list nuts as an ingredient even though the product does contain nuts. Recall categories are based on the likelihood that a product will cause harm to consumers (13; see Box 5.3).

BOX 5.3   Classes of Recalls

Class I. A Class I recall is a situation in which there is a reasonable probability that the use of or exposure to a violative product will cause serious adverse health consequences or death. Contamination of a product with *Salmonella* or *Listeria* would likely result in a Class I recall. This recall will typically target wholesale units, retail units, and consumers. Notice of Class I recalls will typically involve press releases and result in media coverage.

Class II. A Class II recall is a situation in which use of or exposure to a violative product may cause temporary or medically reversible adverse health consequences or in which the probability of serious adverse health consequences is remote. Having glass fragments in some units of a production run might trigger a Class II recall. Such a recall will typically target wholesale and retail units.

Class III. A Class III recall is a situation in which use of or exposure to a violative product is not likely to cause adverse health consequences. An example of a Class III recall would be the mislabeling of a product as lemon-flavored when it is actually lime-flavored. This recall will typically target wholesale purchasers.

Source: Compiled from References 13 and 14

Recalls are conducted by the firm involved with notice to the regulating agency, either FDA (most foods) or USDA (meat and poultry products). For retail foodservice establishments recalls will typically be facilitated by vendors, which is an important reason to use reputable food suppliers. For consumers reputable markets facilitate recalls by removing recalled product from shelves and by replacing or refunding recalled product. Current recall information is available from agency Web sites (13, 15). There are about one hundred food recalls each year in the United States (13, 15).

RISK/BENEFIT DECISIONS BY REGULATORS

Having jurisdiction means that an agency has the authority to establish regulations to implement laws. Usually this implies that a regulatory agency will have some flexibility in balancing the risks of using an ingredient or process against its benefits. For example, processors use sodium nitrite in bacon to control growth of bacteria that can cause foodborne illness—a benefit. However, carcinogenic nitrosamines form in bacon grilled at high temperatures—a risk.

The Delaney Clause absolutely prohibits the approval of additives that are carcinogens:

> [N]o additive shall be deemed to be safe if it is found to induce cancer when ingested by man or animal, or if it is found, after tests which are appropriate for the evaluation of the safety of food additives, to induce cancer in man or animal, except that this proviso shall not apply with respect to the use of a substance as an ingredient of feed for animals which are raised for food production, if the Secretary finds (i) that, under the conditions of use and feeding specified in proposed labeling and reasonably certain to be followed in practice, such additive will not adversely affect the animals for which such feed is intended, and (ii) that no residue of the additive will be found . . . in any edible portion of such animal after slaughter or in any food yielded by or derived from the living animal (16).

Many toxicologists find this clause too restrictive. There may be a threshold below which a chemical will not cause cancer, and carcinogenicity is the only detrimental effect singled out for this treatment. Thresholds for carcinogenicity have not been determined for most additives or for naturally occurring food chemicals. However, this law remains in effect for all additives except pesticide residues, which are held to the standard of "reasonable certainty of no harm." For example, if a pesticide residue has caused a rare cancer when administered at very high levels to rats but has shown no effect at lower levels in animals, then it can be considered for use on food crops and potential food contact surfaces.(17). This change from an absolute restriction to a risk assessment represents a significant philosophical change that applies a similar standard to food additives and naturally occurring foods. Another recent example of this philosophical change is the Saccharine Notice Repeal Act. As a food additive, saccharine would be treated under the Delaney Clause and could not be used in food. The Saccharine Notice Repeal Act removes saccharine from this proscription, since several decades of study have not shown saccharine to increase tumor production in humans who consume it in food. Again, in this case, saccharine can be used because there is reasonable certainty of no harm.

It is difficult to balance risk and benefit for a population. Risk alone is difficult to quantify, as is benefit alone. Additionally, the benefits and risks may not balance for individuals within a population. Government agencies make needed risk/benefit assessments and form public policy for food safety within the limits of laws passed by Congress and after public hearings to determine the public voice. Government food safety policy and supporting programs are the interface between industry and consumers. In the example of sodium nitrite, the clear benefit to both consumers and the industry is sodium nitrite's unique ability to retard growth and toxin production by *Clostridium botulinum*. While sodium nitrite also helps to produce desirable color changes in some products (an industry benefit), its use is restricted to the minimum amount necessary to protect the safety of the product (industry and consumer benefit, consumer risk).

It is important for dietetics professionals to represent their clients by testifying at public hearings that establish food regulations. Information on how consumers use products and interpret label information and package instructions helps agencies write regulations that will be effective both at maintaining food safety in the marketplace and at helping consumers understand the information provided. This information comes most reliably from a professional who works directly with the public and who can recognize food-use problems—the dietetics professional.

REFERENCES

1. Joint Commission on Accreditation of Healthcare Organizations Web site. Available at: http://www.jcaho.org/index.html. Accessed May 26, 2001.
2. *Codex Alimentarius* Web site. Available at: http://www.codexalimentarius.net. Accessed May 26, 2001.
3. US Food and Drug Administration. Milestones in U.S. food and drug law history. [FDA Web site] May 3, 1999. Available at: http://www.fda.gov/opacom/backgrounders/miles.html. Accessed May 26, 2001.
4. US Food and Drug Administration. Making your voice heard at FDA: how to comment on proposed regulations and submit petitions. [FDA Web site] October 27, 2000. Available at: http://www.fda.gov/opacom/backgrounders/voice.html. Accessed May 26, 2001.

5. *Federal Register* Web site. Available at: http://www.access.gpo.gov/su_docs/aces/aces140.html. Accessed May 26, 2001.

6. Pina KR, Pines WL. *A Practical Guide to Food and Drug Law and Regulation.* Washington, DC: Food and Drug Law Institute; 1998.

7. US Food and Drug Administration; *1999 Food Code.* Washington, DC: US Department of Commerce, Technology Administration, National Technical Information Service; 1999. PB99-115925. Available at: http://vm.cfsan.fda.gov/~dms/fc99-toc.html. Accessed May 12, 2001.

8. US Department of Health and Human Services. Food safety. In: *Healthy People 2010.* 2nd ed. With Understanding and Improving Health and Objectives for Improving Health. 2 vols. Washington, DC: US Government Printing Office; November 2000:10.3–10.19. Available at: http://www.health.gov/healthypeople/Document/pdf/Volume1/10Food.pdf. Accessed May 12, 2001.

9. US Environmental Protection Agency, Office of Ground Water and Drinking Water. Current drinking water standards. [FDA Web site] September 1998. Available at: http://www.epa.gov/safewater/mcl.html. Accessed May 26, 2001.

10. US Department of Health and Human Services. Environmental health. In: *Healthy People 2010.* 2nd ed. With Understanding and Improving Health and Objectives for Improving Health. 2 vols. Washington, DC: US Government Printing Office; November 2000:10.3–10.19. Available at: http://www.health.gov/healthypeople/Document/pdf/Volume1/08Environmental.pdf. Accessed May 12, 2001.

11. Olsen SJ, MacKinnon LC, Goulding JS, et al. Surveillance for foodborne-disease outbreaks—United States, 1993–1997. *MMWR.* 2000;49(SS-01):1–51. Available at: ftp://ftp.cdc.gov/pub/Publications/mmwr/SS/SS4901.pdf. Accessed May 25, 2001.

12. Dougherty CP, Holtz SH, Reinert JC, Panyacosit L, Axelrad DA, Woodruff TJ. Dietary exposures to food contaminants across the United States. *Environ Res.* 2000;84:170–185.

13. US Food and Drug Administration. Recalls and safety alerts. [FDA Web site] May 25, 2001. Available at: http://www.fda.gov/opacom/7alerts.html. Accessed May 26, 2001.

14. Nordenberg T. Recalls: FDA, industry cooperate to protect consumers. *FDA Consumer.* 1995;29(8). Available at: http://www.fda.gov/fdac/features/895_recalls.html. Accessed May 26, 2001.

15. US Department of Agriculture, Food Safety and Inspection Service. Meat and poultry product recalls: news releases and information for consumer. [FDA Web site] May 23, 2001. Available at: http://www.fsis.usda.gov/OA/news/xrecalls.htm. Accessed May 26, 2001.

16. *Federal Food, Drug, and Cosmetic Act, as Amended, and Related Laws.* Washington, DC: US Department of Health and Human Services, Public Health Service, Food and Drug Administration; 1986.

17. US Environmental Protection Agency, Office of Pesticide Programs. Food Quality Protection Act (FQPA) of 1996. [FDA Web site] March 7, 2001. Available at: http://www.epa.gov/oppfead1/fqpa. Accessed May 26, 2001.

18. US Environmental Protection Agency, Office of Pesticide Programs. Read the label first. [FDA Web site] December 6, 1999. Available at: http://www.epa.gov/pesticides/label. Accessed May 26, 2001.

CHAPTER 6

PEOPLE AND THEIR FOOD SAFETY BEHAVIORS

People are the focus for food safety in dietetic practice. Just as individuals are assessed for their body composition, eating behaviors, and nutritional status, they can be assessed for their food safety behaviors and their susceptibility to foodborne illness. National surveillance data document five major behaviors that contribute to foodborne illness—improper holding temperatures, inadequate cooking, contaminated equipment, food from an unsafe source, and poor personal hygiene (1). These behaviors are important for everybody, but they are especially important to individuals who are more susceptible to contracting foodborne illness and for whom the illness may be serious, chronic, and life-threatening. Integrating food safety into dietary practice may be as simple as including questions about food safety in health histories. For example, when obtaining a dietary recall, dietetic professionals can also ask about hand washing and about consumption of high-risk foods. Food safety education can be included in care plans, too. For highly susceptible individuals, food safety recommendations are an important part of medical therapy (2–4).

WHO IS MOST SUSCEPTIBLE TO FOODBORNE ILLNESS?

Highly susceptible (vulnerable) individuals include the very young, the elderly, and individuals who have weakened immune systems (2–6). Immune systems may be weakened by disease or by medical treatment. Individuals with weakened immune systems include those who have AIDS, are receiving chemotherapy, are receiving long-term therapy with glucocorticoids or other immunosuppressive agents, or have received an organ transplant. Other individuals who may be at increased risk of foodborne illness include

1. those who are receiving radiation therapy or antimicrobial treatment
2. those with autoimmune disorders such as Crohn's disease and lupus
3. those with cirrhosis or alcoholism
4. those with diabetes
5. those who have hypochlorhydria, either as a primary condition or secondary to use of medications that decrease gastric acid production
6. those who are undernourished

Additionally, pregnant women and their fetuses are a highly susceptible population for contracting listeriosis and toxoplasmosis. While all people are susceptible to foodborne illness, in populations that have weakened immune systems the infective dose is smaller and the course of the disease and the potential sequelae may be more serious.

Individuals in some settings are also considered "highly susceptible populations" (5–6). These include older adults in a facility that provides health care or assisted living services, such as a hospital or nursing home, and preschool-age children in a facility that provides custodial care, such as a day-care center. The greater risk of institutionalized elderly reflects their overall compromised health as well as the fact that any food contamination has the potential to infect many more people than would food prepared at home for a family. Some child and elder day-care facilities have rapid turnover of personnel, which makes training more difficult. They may also have foodservice facilities, such as serving areas, that are not dedicated to foodservice, making it difficult to ensure that food safety guidelines are followed. In some of the more informal settings that do not focus on health care, play areas, pets, and other factors may negatively affect food safety, if they are not controlled adequately.

EFFECTS OF CONSUMER DEMANDS ON THE FOOD SUPPLY AND FOOD SAFETY

Consumer demands affect the safety of the food supply. The food supply itself is shaped by consumer demands for foods that are appetizing and convenient (7). Convenience and time pressures, both perceived barriers to safe food-handling practices (8–9), result in less time being spent on meal preparation in the home and more food being purchased ready for consumption. Most Americans devote less than thirty minutes to preparing a meal, and 20 percent spend less than fifteen minutes on meal preparation (10). This short time for meal preparation typically means that many meals are assembled from prepared or partially prepared components. Indeed, 20 percent of shoppers visit supermarkets most often to purchase prepared foods that will be eaten at home (11). Americans consume 27 percent of their meals and snacks away from home (12) and frequently take home leftover food from outside meals. These trends show that Americans are dependent on many different food handlers and that consumers and other food handlers need food safety information beyond the traditional "how to cook" instructions. In particular, information on food holding, sanitation, and personal hygiene are critical to food safety in today's world.

Until the 1900s, most food was produced either locally or regionally, and outbreaks of foodborne illness typically affected a single family or a few people. Today food preparation at home and in retail foodservice establishments has evolved from a cook-serve system using locally produced agricultural ingredients to a meal assembly system using ingredients that may include fully and partially prepared foods in addition to raw agricultural ingredients. It is sometimes difficult to categorize foods strictly as home-prepared foods or purchased foods because many are fully or partially prepared at retail outlets for home consumption. In fact, much of our food is produced and processed in centralized facilities and shipped throughout the country to meet demands for convenience and access. Thus, contaminated product has the possibility of causing foodborne illness in people throughout the country before the cause can be identified and contained. For example, contaminated milk and infant formula (13–15), hotdogs and deli meats (16,17), dips (18), fresh parsley (19), raw shellfish (20,21), canned mushrooms (22), undercooked ground beef (23), alfalfa sprouts (24), unpasteurized apple cider (25), cereal (26), ice cream (27), berries (28,29), and foods served at large convention meals (30) have caused recent multistate outbreaks of foodborne illness.

Changing taste preferences and the desire for convenience have also led to an increased availability of fresh and minimally processed foods. One example is fresh precut produce. Fresh produce may be contaminated during growth, harvest, or distribution. Some farming practices and inadequate sanitation standards in many parts of the world that export fruits and vegetables, as well as lapses in sanitation practices in the United States, increase the likelihood of fresh fruits and vegetables being contaminated. Between 1990 and 2000, sliced cantaloupe (31), green onions (31), unpasteurized cider (25), freshly squeezed orange juice (31), lettuce (31), raspberries (28,29), alfalfa sprouts (24), sliced tomatoes (31), and fresh parsley (19) were among the fresh produce items associated with outbreaks of foodborne illness. Examples of minimally processed foods are those prepared using processing technologies such as MAP/CAP and *sous vide*, which result in foods that appear fresh but have extended shelf lives. (See Chapter 3 for a discussion of these technologies.) Such foods must be processed and packaged under stringent conditions to minimize growth of pathogens and then handled carefully in the retail and home settings to maintain their safety (32).

CONSUMER FOOD SAFETY KNOWLEDGE AND BEHAVIORS

Traditionally, transfer of knowledge about food handling and preparation has been through conditioning, observation, and reinforcement from mothers and grandmothers (8). As less food is prepared in the home, there are fewer opportunities for such knowledge transfer to occur. The lack of basic knowledge affects not only safety of food prepared at home, but also safety of foods prepared in foodservice settings because entry-level employees enter foodservice without basic sanitation and preparation knowledge and skills. As a result, food safety educators have begun stressing the need for basic food safety education through the schools and for basic food safety to be included in the employment orientation provided all foodservice workers. The need for food safety education is illustrated by recent surveys, which reveal that a significant percentage of consumers report engaging in such high-risk behaviors as:

- Eating undercooked eggs (50 percent), home-canned vegetables (24 percent), pink hamburgers (20 percent), raw oysters (8 percent), and unpasteurized milk (1 percent; 33)
- Failing to use thermometers to check doneness of meats and poultry (76 percent) and egg dishes (97 percent; 34)
- Inadequately washing hands before and during food preparation (50 percent to 79 percent; 33,34)
- Using the same plates for both raw and grilled foods (23 percent; 34)
- Inadequately cleaning cutting boards after contact with raw meat or chicken (11 percent to 19 percent; 33–35)

These risky behaviors were more common for men than for women and for younger adults (33,34), which is supported by epidemiologic observations that young men have higher rates of infection with *Campylobacter* than all other adults (36). Disturbingly, unlike many health-promoting behaviors, the risky behaviors were more common for better educated individuals and for individuals with higher incomes (33). Barriers to safe food-handing practices perceived by consumers include lack of knowledge, historical and cultural practices, feelings of invulnerability, taste preferences, timing and planning, and space and convenience (8,9).

CONTRIBUTING FACTORS

Practices that contribute to foodborne illness are behaviors that contaminate food, permit magnification of a toxic agent in food, or reduce the effectiveness of a step designed to eliminate the toxic agent in a food. The current foodborne-disease outbreak reports document five major **contributing factors** (practices): improper holding temperatures, inadequate cooking, contaminated equipment, food from an unsafe source, and poor personal hygiene (1; see Table 4.1 and Box 6.1).

Use of Improper Holding Temperatures

Use of improper holding temperatures is the single most important factor contributing to foodborne illness in the United States (1). In the years 1993 to 1997, it contributed to foodborne disease for 60 percent of bacterial outbreaks, 8 percent of viral outbreaks, and 43 percent of chemical outbreaks for which contributing practices were reported (1; see Table 4.1). Use of improper holding temperatures was the contributing factor most often reported in outbreaks due to *Bacillus cereus* (92 percent), *Clostridium botulinum* (60 percent), *Clostridium perfringens* (100 percent), salmonellae (60 percent), *Staphylococcus aureus* (83 percent), streptococci (100 percent), and scombrotoxin (83 percent). Examples of practices that fall within this category are improper hot holding, improper cooling, and inadequate or improper thawing (Box 6.2).

BOX 6.1   Example of Potential Contributing Practices in Preparing Chicken Salad

Practices that contribute to foodborne illness are behaviors that:

1. Contaminate food, as when a food handler uses the same knife to cut raw chicken and celery
2. Permit magnification of a toxic agent in food, as when chicken salad is held at room temperature for four hours
3. Reduce the effectiveness of a step designed to eliminate the toxic agent in a food, as when chicken is undercooked

Usually more than one practice contributes to the development of a hazardous food. In the previous examples:

- Celery was contaminated by the knife used to cut the chicken.
- The chicken was undercooked, allowing survival of pathogens in the chicken.
- Any bacterial pathogens in the chicken and on the celery would continue to grow while the chicken salad is held at room temperature.

In this instance, three practices contributed to the development of hazardous chicken salad: contaminated equipment (cross-contamination), inadequate cooking, and improper holding temperature.

BOX 6.2 Common Food Holding Issues

- Some foods, such as large roasts and turkeys or viscous soups, are held at room temperature to complete cooking. Once they reach their desired internal temperatures, they should be cooled rapidly in ice baths or special equipment designed for rapid cooling and refrigerated.
- Once refrigerated, cooked foods should be cooled from 140°F (60°C) to 70°F (21°C) within 2 hours and then from 70°F (21°C) to 40°F (4°C) within 4 hours (5). This typically requires storage in shallow (3 inches deep or less) pans, especially for dense foods, such as meats, bread puddings, and bread dressings or stuffings. If the food is not cooled from 140°F (60°C) to 70°F (21°C) within 2 hours, it must be reheated to 165°F (73°C) before service.
- Foods held hot for service should be kept at 140°F (60°C) or above (5). These foods should be stirred to equalize temperatures and covered to hold temperatures, when possible. Containers should be changed and not "refreshed" by adding more food. Cooked foods on buffet tables are especially vulnerable to recontamination after cooking and should be discarded.
- Meals and cooked foods purchased at restaurants and other retail outlets should be held at room temperature no longer than 2 hours—and that includes the time in the shopping cart and the car on the way home (63).
- Foods taken home after restaurant meals ("doggy bags") are particularly vulnerable to pathogen growth because they have probably been contaminated during the meal and have been at room temperature throughout meal service and while they are transported. They should be discarded unless they are held safely and reheated appropriately.
- Bag lunches and other meals prepared at home for consumption away from home typically require refrigeration during storage in the office, at school, or at the park. In general, food should not be out of the refrigerator or oven and held at room temperature for longer than 2 hours (64).
- During warm weather (above 80°F or 27°C) picnic foods should be held at ambient temperatures no longer than an hour. Current surveys show about half of consumers follow this guideline (34).

Improper holding temperatures involve two major controllable factors—temperature and time. Potentially hazardous foods held in the danger zone (40°F to 140°F; 4°C to 60°C) for several hours can support rapid growth and toxin production by many different bacterial pathogens. While HACCP programs (see chapter 7) are examining the requirements for specific foods, general guidelines are available for both foodservice and consumer settings. The *Food Code* recommends that potentially hazardous foods be held in the danger zone for no longer than four hours, including preparation, serving, cooling, and thawing time in controlled food retail settings (5). In consumer settings general recommendations are that potentially hazardous foods be held in the danger zone for no longer than two hours (37). Additionally, USDA recommends storage limits for refrigerated foods (Table 6.1). Although this is an important control measure for food safety, over half of consumers do not have refrigerator thermometers, and of those who have refrigerator thermometers, fewer than half know how to monitor for the correct temperature (35).

TABLE 6.1 Storage Times for Home-Refrigerated Foods

Food	Time
Eggs	
Fresh in shell	3–5 weeks
Raw yolks, whites	2–4 days
Hard cooked	1 week
Liquid pasteurized eggs, unopened	10 days
Liquid pasteurized eggs, opened	3 days
Cooked egg dishes	3–4 days

TABLE 6.1   Storage Times for Home-Refrigerated Foods *(continued)*

Fresh Poultry	
Chicken or turkey, whole	1–2 days
Chicken or turkey, parts	1–2 days
Giblets	1–2 days
Raw Meats (beef, veal, lamb, and pork)	
Ground meats	1–2 days
Steaks, chops, roasts	3–5 days
Stew meats	1–2 days
Variety meats (tongue, kidneys, liver, heart, chitterlings)	1–2 days
Fresh Fish and Shellfish	1–2 days
Ham	
Canned, labeled "Keep Refrigerated," unopened	6–9 months
Canned, labeled "Keep Refrigerated," opened	3–5 days
Fully cooked, whole	7 days
Fully cooked, half	3–5 days
Fully cooked, slices	3–4 days
Luncheon meat package, unopened	2 weeks
Luncheon meat package, opened	3–5 days
Corned Beef	
In pouch with pickling juices	5–7 days
Luncheon meat package, unopened	2 weeks
Luncheon meat package, opened	3–5 days
Deli and Vacuum-packed Products	
Store- or home-prepared salads (egg, chicken, tuna, etc.)	3–5 days
Prestuffed pork chops, lamb chops, and chicken breasts	1 day
Store-cooked convenience meals	3–4 days
Vacuum-packed dinners with USDA seal, unopened	2 weeks
Hotdogs and Luncheon Meats	
Hotdogs, unopened package	2 weeks
Hotdogs, opened package	1 week
Luncheon meats, unopened package	2 weeks
Luncheon meats, opened package	3–5 days
Bacon and Sausage	
Bacon	7 days
Sausage, raw from meat or poultry	1–2 days
Smoked breakfast links, patties	7 days
Summer sausage labeled "Keep Refrigerated," unopened	3 months
Summer sausage labeled "Keep Refrigerated," opened	3 weeks
Pepperoni, sliced	2–3 weeks
Soups and Stews	3–4 days
Leftover Cooked Meat, Poultry, and Fish	
Pieces	3–4 days
Casseroles	3–4 days
Patties and nuggets	1–2 days
Gravy and broth	1–2 days

Source: US Department of Agriculture, Food Safety and Inspection Service. Food safety focus: Refrigeration and food safety [USDA Web site]. January 1999. Available at: http://www.fsis.usda.gov/OA/pubs/focus_ref.htm. Accessed May 26, 2001.

Improper cooling is often a factor in staphylococcal and group A streptococcal food poisoning, salmonellosis, *Clostridium perfringens* enteritis, *Bacillus cereus* gastroenteritis, and *Vibrio parahaemolyticus* gastroenteritis. Improper holding temperature is always associated with scombroid intoxication; implicated fish may be mishandled shipboard, in marketing channels, or at the preparation site. This factor is particularly important for potentially hazardous foods (5).

USDA recommends thawing foods in the refrigerator, under cool running water, or in a microwave oven to reduce potential for rapid microbial growth (38). Improper thawing contributes to outbreaks of foodborne illness when subsequent cooking is insufficient to destroy pathogens or their toxins. This is more likely to happen when the exterior of a thawed food cooks normally, the interior thaws during the cooking process, and a thermometer is not used to verify doneness of the interior.

Inadequate Cooking

Inadequate cooking contributed to foodborne illness in 36 percent of bacterial, 12 percent of parasitic, 16 percent of viral, and 2 percent of chemical outbreaks from 1993 to 1997 for which contributing factors were reported (1; see Table 4.1). For inadequate cooking to contribute to foodborne illness, the problem food has to be contaminated with pathogens before it is cooked. Because mishandling can contaminate food, poor personal hygiene and inadequate cooking often combine to contribute to foodborne illness. Inadequate cooking was the contributing factor most often reported in outbreaks due to *Escherichia coli* (49 percent) and *Trichinella spiralis* (100 percent).

Inadequate cooking includes the controllable factors of temperature and time. The **time-temperature relationship** is described by specifying both the time and the temperature together. All foods must be heated to the time-temperature values required to kill pathogens. Cooking to appropriate internal temperatures using conventional methods usually kills pathogens that contaminate foods (Table 6.2). Those internal temperatures must be monitored by thermometer to ensure pathogen destruction (39). However, fewer than 25 percent of consumers report using thermometers to monitor temperatures of meat, and only 3 percent report measuring the temperature of cooked egg dishes (34–35). Because heating may not be uniform and may not provide the same total cooking energy, rapid microwave cooking does not always kill pathogens in large, dense pieces of meat and poultry or destroy bacterial toxins that may be present in foods (40–44).

Vegetative cells, the cells that can grow and produce toxin, are killed during normal cooking. However, the spores are resistant to heat destruction and can outgrow during holding or storage. For that reason, *C. perfringens* is a problem for foods held warm for long service periods, especially moist foods with sauces or gravies. Similarly, *B. cereus* is a problem for rice and similar foods held warm for long service periods. Temperatures of 240°F to 250°F (116°C to 121°C) for experimentally determined times are required to inactivate *C. botulinum* spores in low-acid, anaerobic foods. The temperatures are above the boiling point of water and can be reached only under pressure, as in a pressure canner.

TABLE 6.2   Minimum Internal Temperatures Foods Must Reach to Be Considered Safe and Done, No Matter How You Prepare Them

Products	Safe Internal Temperatures
Fresh ground beef, veal, lamb, pork	160°F (71°C)
Beef, veal, lamb (roasts, steaks, chops)	Medium rare: 145°F (63°C) Medium: 160°F (71°C) Well done: 170°F (77°C)
Fresh pork (roasts, steaks, chops)	Medium: 160°F (71°C) Well done: 170°F (77°C)
Ham	
Cook before eating	160°F (71°C)
Reheat fully cooked	140°F (60°C)
Poultry	
Ground chicken, turkey	165°F (73°C)
Whole chicken, turkey	180°F (82°C)
Breasts, roasts	170°F (77°C)
Stuffing, alone or in bird	165°F (73°C)
Egg dishes, casseroles	160°F (71°C)

Source: Reference 39

Reheating leftovers is riskier than thorough cooking. Recommendations for primary cooking are based on time-temperature combinations that kill pathogens. However, foods contaminated after cooking are seldom recooked; instead, they are reheated until warm. Warming is not sufficient to kill large numbers of contaminating bacteria. For example, leftover foods have frequently been handled and contaminated with toxin-producing *Staphylococcus aureus*. Temperature abuse—standing at room temperature too long, cooling slowly in a refrigerator, or transporting in a hot car—will allow *S. aureus* to produce heat-stable toxin that cannot be destroyed by reheating. In mixed dishes, if botulinum toxin is present, microwave reheating will not reliably destroy it (44). For these reasons, leftovers are not reused in foodservice settings. Home-stored leftovers should be kept refrigerated or frozen during storage. Refrigerated leftovers should be consumed within one to four days, depending on the food item (45; Table 6.1).

Contaminated Equipment

Contaminated equipment contributed to 26 percent of bacterial, 12 percent of parasitic, 5 percent of viral, and 4 percent of chemical outbreaks of foodborne illness from 1993 to 1997 for which contributing factors were reported (1). Cross-contamination, inadequately cleaned equipment, and use of inappropriate containers or equipment are all contributors.

Cross-contamination and inadequate cleaning of equipment frequently occur together. In cross-contamination, pathogens from one source are transferred to another. Some viruses can survive for several days on nonporous surfaces (46). One study examining cross-contamination during food preparation with *Campylobacter jejuni* and *Salmonella* species from raw chicken products showed recoveries of *C. jejuni* from 50 percent of tested cutting boards and 46 percent of tested plates, as well as salmonellae recoveries from 6 percent of tested cutting boards and 5 percent of tested plates (47). The same study showed recoveries of *C. jejuni* from 9 percent and salmonellae from 6 percent of raw vegetables that contacted the contaminated plates. Although chicken probably will be cooked thoroughly, other foods that come in contact with contaminated cutting boards or other contaminated surfaces may not be cooked thoroughly and will become potential vehicles of foodborne illness.

Preparation, service, and cleaning areas should be separated both by area and by food handler in foodservice settings to reduce the risk for cross-contamination. Both at home or in retail foodservice settings, equipment and surfaces should be cleaned and sanitized between tasks. Currently 77 percent of adults surveyed report using separate plates for raw and grilled foods (34).

Personal Hygiene

Personal hygiene is an important factor in foodborne illness, especially since many host-adapted viruses are carried to food only by human contact or contact with sewage. Contamination of food caused by poor personal hygiene was a factor in 30 percent of bacterial, 68 percent of viral, 25 percent of parasitic, and 1 percent of chemical outbreaks of foodborne illness during 1993 to 1997 for which contributing factors were reported (1). It is the most common mode of transmission for viruses (1,48). The *Food Code* (5) and most state sanitation codes have extensive references to personal hygiene, emphasizing that food handlers should wash their hands thoroughly between tasks and before entering any food preparation or service area.

Effective hand washing, especially after handling raw foods and after toileting, is essential in reducing contamination of food by this route. De Boer and Hahne (47) recovered *C. jejuni* from hands that held raw chicken 73 percent of the sampling times and salmonellae 18 percent of the sampling times. In recent surveys about 79 percent of adult consumers responded that they wash their hands after handling raw meat and poultry (33), and about half of adult consumers report washing hands during outside food preparation (34). To further reduce this route of contamination, food handlers should thoroughly wash their hands before they put on protective gloves to handle foods (49). Disposable gloves should be put on in ways that minimize contamination to their surfaces, removed carefully to avoid contamination to hands and surrounding environments, and changed between tasks. Disposable gloves should not be reused.

Smoking, eating, or chewing in areas of food production increases risk of food contamination by handlers, because bacteria or viruses from the mouth could contaminate food. Likewise, people diapering babies or working intimately with patients should not prepare or serve food without double-washing their hands. Pathogens can be transferred from feces to hands to food or from food to people.

Two foodborne outbreaks emphasize this point. In the first, a woman who had recently diapered her child prepared a salmon salad for teachers, mixing it with her bare hands. The asymptomatic child was infected with *Giardia lamblia*, and giardiasis developed in several teachers who ate the salad (50). In the second, child caregivers preparing chitterlings (pork intestines, a traditional holiday food in some African American families) at home transferred *Yersinia enterocolitica* from the raw intestines to the children (51). Yersiniosis developed in fifteen of the children. These examples illustrate the importance of training day-care workers to wash their own hands vigorously with soap and water and to observe client hand washing as an important step in reducing disease transmission in such settings.

Food from Unsafe Source(s)

Obtaining food from unsafe sources was a factor in 13 percent of bacterial, 24 percent of viral, 50 percent of parasitic, and 45 percent of chemical outbreaks of foodborne disease during 1993 to 1997 for which contributing factors were reported (1). Those outbreaks were due largely to consumption of raw (including certified) milk products, toxic mushrooms, and shellfish (1). Shellfish risks are high when shellfish are harvested from waters contaminated by sewage or industrial wastes, but they are low when shellfish are harvested from uncontaminated water. Government regulatory agencies prohibit seafood harvesting from contaminated areas. Such areas are posted in shallow waters near contaminated oyster beds and are described on maps for commercial fishing operators. The harvest areas are specified on containers of shellfish sold by licensed brokers to permit regulators to monitor outbreaks when they occur.

PROGRAMS FOCUSED ON IMPROVING FOOD SAFETY BEHAVIORS

Contributing factors may occur at any stage between the farm/ship and consumption of food. Practices at the farm/ship, processing, distribution, and marketing steps are continually being refined to improve the safety of the U.S. food supply. As improved practices are developed and validated, they are included in regulations and monitored by government regulatory agencies. While government regulatory agencies do not inspect home kitchens, they have produced many materials to help consumers make better food safety decisions and develop good food-handling skills. One of the newest U.S. dietary guidelines is "Keep food safe to eat" (52). Also, the American Dietetic Association Foundation–ConAgra Foundation program "Home Food Safety . . . It's in Your Hands" (53) and the Partnership for Food Safety Education's "Fight BAC!" campaign (54) focus on improving consumer food-handling behaviors. *Healthy People 2010* is the national guide for improvements in public health, which is well integrated with commercial food service safety programs and consumer-focused food safety programs.

Healthy People 2000 and Healthy People 2010

The *Healthy People 2000* plan emphasized the role of food safety in maintaining the health of the nation by including four food safety objectives under the Food and Drug Safety goal (goal 12; 55). Those objectives were to:

12.1 Reduce foodborne infections by Salmonella spp, *Listeria monocytogenes*, *Campylobacter jejuni*, and *Escherichia coli* O157:H7
12.2 Reduce *Salmonella enteritidis* infection outbreaks
12.3 Improve food handling techniques in homes
12.4 Adopt model food codes

According to reviews of the *Healthy People 2000* plan (6, 56–57) and extrapolation of the 1999 FoodNet reports (58), one of the *Healthy People 2000* objectives has been met, and progress has been made toward the other objectives. All targets for reducing foodborne infections (objective 12.1) have been met or exceeded, and *Salmonella enteritidis* outbreaks decreased from the baseline of seventy-seven per year in 1989 to forty-four per year in 1997 (objective 12.2). Household data are incomplete for assessment of objective 12.3, although some progress has been made. By 1999, sixteen state agencies, two federal agencies, and several local jurisdictions had adopted the FDA *Food Code*, and most other states have been reviewing the standards for possible adoption.

For the *Healthy People 2010* plan, food safety is a focus area with the overall goal of reducing the number of foodborne illnesses (6). The seven objectives under the food safety goal emphasize reduction in incidence of morbidity/mortality from ingestion of food, improvement in food handling practices, reassessment of pesticide residue tolerances, and implementation of risk reduction programs (6). In addition to the food safety objectives, several objectives from the environmental health goal relate directly to food and water safety. The specific relevant objectives are in Table 6.3. Some of the objectives in *Healthy People 2010* are measurable and others are developmental. While the measurable objectives have baseline data and focus on actions, the developmental objectives identify important areas for development of assessment systems to support future actions.

Those objectives with the most direct relationship for dietetics professionals are the ones related to reduction in food-induced anaphylaxis and to improvement in food-handling practices in the home and in retail food establishments. Because of their close contact with clients across all geographic, socioeconomic, healthcare, and foodservice settings, dietetics professionals can strongly contribute to the achievement those objectives.

National Consumer-Focused Food Safety Programs

While the National Food Safety Initiative has focused largely on safe food production and handling through the food marketing system (59), two major programs are focusing on the last link in the food safety chain—consumers. Both "Home Food Safety . . . It's in Your Hands" (American Dietetic Association Foundation–ConAgra Foundation) and "Fight BAC!" (the Partnership for Food Safety Education) focus on changing consumer behaviors that have been linked to foodborne disease (Table 6.4). Both "Home Food Safety . . . It's in Your Hands" (Figure 6.1) and "Fight BAC!" (Figure 6.2) are integrated with the *Healthy People 2010* goals and have information that is easy to access and use (53,54).

TABLE 6.3   *Healthy People 2010* Objectives for Food Safety and Selected Related Objectives from Environmental Health

Number	Objective			
Food Safety 10-1	Reduce infections caused by key foodborne pathogens.			
	Reduction in Infections Caused by Microorganisms		1997 Cases per 100,000	2010 Target Cases per 100,000
	10-1a	*Campylobacter* species	24.6	12.3
	10-1b	*Escherichia coli* O157:H7	2.1	1.0
	10-1c	*Listeria monocytogenes*	0.5	0.25
	10-1d	*Salmonella* species	13.7	6.8
	10-1e	*Cyclospora cayetanensis*		Developmental
	10-1f	Postdiarrheal hemolytic uremic syndrome		Developmental
	10-1g	Congenital *Toxoplasma gondii*		Developmental
Food Safety 10-2	Reduce outbreaks of infections caused by key foodborne bacteria.			
	Reduction in Infections Caused by Foodborne Bacteria		1997 Baseline	2010 Target
			Number of Outbreaks per Year	
	10-2a	*Escherichia coli* O157: H7	22	11
	10-2b	*Salmonella* serotype Enteritidis	44	22
Food Safety 10-3	Prevent an increase in the proportion of isolates of *Salmonella* species from humans and from animals at slaughter that are resistant to antimicrobial drugs.			
Food Safety 10-4*	Reduce deaths from anaphylaxis caused by food allergies.			
Food Safety 10-5	Increase the proportion of consumers who follow key food safety practices.			
Food Safety 10-6*	Improve food employee behaviors and food preparation practices that directly relate to foodborne illnesses in retail food establishments.			
Food Safety 10-7*	Reduce human exposure to organophosphate pesticides from food.			
Environmental Health 8-5	Increase the proportion of persons served by community water systems who receive a supply of drinking water that meets the regulations of the Safe Drinking Water Act.			
Environmental Health 8-6	Reduce waterborne disease outbreaks arising from water intended for drinking among persons served by community water systems.			
Environmental Health 8-8*	Increase the proportion of assessed rivers, lakes, and estuaries that are safe for fishing and recreational purposes.			
Environmental Health 8-10*	Reduce the potential human exposure to persistent chemicals by decreasing fish contaminant levels.			
Environmental Health 8-24	Reduce exposure to pesticides as measured by blood and urine concentrations of metabolites.			
Environmental Health 8-25*	Reduce exposure of the population to pesticides, heavy metals, and other toxic chemicals as measured by blood and urine concentrations of the substances or their metabolites.			
Environmental Health 8-29	Reduce the global burden of disease due to poor water quality, sanitation, and personal and domestic hygiene.			
Environmental Health 8-30	Increase the proportion of the population in the United States–Mexico border region that have adequate drinking water and sanitation facilities.			

* Developmental

Source: Compiled from References 6 and 67

Figure 6.1

Figure 6.2

TABLE 6.4   Links between Surveillance Programs and Consumer Programs

Foodborne-Disease Reports	Healthy People 2010 Objective 10.5	Fight BAC!	Home Food Safety . . . It's In Your Hands
Improper holding temperatures	Chill: Refrigerate promptly.	Chill	Refrigerate promptly below 40°F.
Inadequate cooking	Cook hamburgers thoroughly.	Cook	Cook to proper temperatures.
Contaminated equipment	Separate: Wash cutting board or use a different board after cutting raw meat or poultry.	Separate Clean	Keep raw meats and ready-to-eat foods separate.
Poor personal hygiene	Clean: Wash hands after touching raw meat or poultry.	Clean	Wash hands often.
Food from an unsafe source			

Source: Compiled from References 1, 6, 53, and 54

The American Dietetic Association (ADA) Commitment to Food Safety

ADA is providing leadership in professional food safety efforts through its national consumer research (34–35), its outreach to consumers (53, 60), and its education of dietetics professionals. ADA's position statement on food and water safety charges qualified dietetics professionals in all areas of practice to "accept their role as highly credible educators on issues related to food and water safety" (61). After educating themselves, dietetics professionals are charged with selecting appropriate food safety information for their clientele and adapting for clinical populations, where necessary (Table 6.5). Facilities that group people

TABLE 6.5 Food Safety Information for Clientele, with Program Aids

Guidelines for Everyone		Program Aids
Cook	• Cook potentially hazardous foods to appropriate internal temperatures, and heat leftovers thoroughly (Table 6.2). • Use a clean thermometer to monitor internal temperatures of cooked foods. • Cook eggs until the yolks are gelled and the whites are firm. • Use pasteurized eggs in recipes where eggs are likely to be undercooked. Avoid foods that might contain raw or undercooked eggs, such as hollandaise sauce, Caesar salad dressing, homemade mayonnaise, homemade eggnog, french toast, and bread pudding.	Home Food Safety . . . It's in Your Hands (53) Fight BAC! (54) Safe Eating: A Guide to Preventing Foodborne Illness (60) *1999 Food Code* (5) Basics for Handling Food Safely (70) Use a Meat Thermometer (39) How Temperatures Affect Foods (37) Doneness versus Safety (68) Kitchen Thermometers (69) An Ounce of Prevention Keeps the Germs Away: Handle and Prepare Food Safely (71)
Clean	• Wash hands often, especially before preparing food. • Double wash hands after handling potentially hazardous foods. • Wash all utensils and food contact surfaces with hot, soapy water after preparing each food item. • Rinse produce in water. Scrub with a vegetable brush to remove dirt, when possible.	Home Food Safety . . . It's in Your Hands (53) Fight BAC! (54) Safe Eating: A Guide to Preventing Foodborne Illness (60) *1999 Food Code* (5) Basics for Handling Food Safely (70) An Ounce of Prevention Keeps the Germs Away: Handle and Prepare Food Safely (71) An Ounce of Prevention Keeps the Germs Away: Routinely Clean and Disinfect Surfaces (73)

TABLE 6.5 Food Safety Information for Clientele, with Program Aids *(continued)*

Chill	• Keep refrigerator temperature between 33°F and 40°F (1°C and 4°C). • Monitor refrigerator temperatures with a thermometer. • Allow space between foods for cold air to circulate. • Chill foods quickly—store in shallow containers and chill in ice baths before storing, if necessary. • Refrigerate foods within two hours at room temperature or within an hour outside in hot weather. • Use foods within recommended storage times. • Buy only refrigerated eggs, and keep them refrigerated until use. • Thaw food in the refrigerator, under cold running water, or in the microwave.	Home Food Safety . . . It's in Your Hands (53) Fight BAC! (54) Safe Eating: A Guide to Preventing Foodborne Illness (60) *1999 Food Code* (5) Basics for Handling Food Safely (70) Refrigeration and Food Safety (45) Safe Storage of Meat and Poultry: The Science behind It (74) Fighting BAC!TM by Chilling Out (75) Appliance Thermometers (76) Kitchen Thermometers (69)
Separate	• Use utensils, plates, cutting boards, and food preparation equipment for one food/one task. Clean in hot, soapy water before reusing. • Keep ready-to-eat and ready-to-cook foods separated from each other in your grocery cart, in your refrigerator, and in food preparation areas. • In the refrigerator store cooked foods above raw foods to keep "drip" from contaminating cooked foods. • Use separate plates and utensils for ready-to-eat and ready-to-cook foods. • Package foods securely before storing them. • Use gloves after washing if you have a cut or sore on your hands.	Home Food Safety . . . It's in Your Hands (53) Fight BAC! (54) Safe Eating: A Guide to Preventing Foodborne Illness (60) *1999 Food Code* (5) Basics for Handling Food Safely (70) Be Smart, Keep Foods Apart—Don't Cross-Contaminate (77)

To further reduce risk for individuals with weakened immune systems:

	• Cook poultry to an internal temperature of 180°F (82.2°C) and meats to an internal temperature of 165°F (73.8°C) or higher. • Do not eat raw shellfish, products that contain raw seafoods, or shellfish that do not open during cooking. Boil shellfish until shells open and continue boiling 5 more minutes or steam until shells open and continue steaming 9 more minutes. Boil shucked oysters at least 3 minutes, or fry them in oil at least 3 minutes at 375°F. • Reheat all hotdogs and cold cuts (deli meats) until steaming hot, whether prepared from leftovers, purchased "fresh" from a deli counter, or purchased in vacuum packaging. • Order meat well-done in situations where you cannot monitor temperatures (such as in a restaurant). If you are served undercooked meat or poultry in a restaurant, send it back. • Clean inside surfaces of your refrigerator often. • Select only pasteurized milk and other dairy products, treated water, and pasteurized juices. • Avoid sprouts.	Diagnosis and Management of Foodborne Illnesses: A Primer for Physicians (2) Guidelines for Preventing Opportunistic Infections among Hematopoietic Stem Cell Transplant Recipients (3) 1999 USPHS/IDSA Guidelines for the Prevention of Opportunistic Infections in Persons Infected with Human Immunodeficiency Virus (4) Food Safety for Persons with AIDS (78) Eating Defensively: Food Safety Advice for Persons with AIDS (79) Guidance for People with Severely Weakened Immune Systems (80) Cryptosporidiosis: A Guide for Persons with HIV/AIDS (81) Seniors Need Wisdom on Food Safety (82) Seniors and Food Safety: Preventing Foodborne Illness (83) Keep Your Baby Safe: Eat Hard Cheeses instead of Soft Cheeses during Pregnancy (84)

according to their special needs, such as acute care, long-term care, and day care, also have special food safety needs. In addition to the food safety needs considered in the foodservice departments of those settings, the food safety behaviors of their clients are important. Dietetics professionals in foodservice settings are charged with providing safe food to their clients and with providing food safety education for their staffs, other healthcare professionals, their clients, and family members and others who provide care for clients.

Food Safety in Dietetic Practice

Concern for food safety issues has traditionally been attributed only to dietetics professionals practicing in foodservice settings. However, with the expanded roles of dietetics professionals and the increasing numbers of vulnerable populations, every dietetics professional needs expertise in specific areas of food safety. Table 6.6 identifies special problems related to food safety that affect different areas of dietetic practice and provides some resources that may be used to address those challenges.

TABLE 6.6   Food Safety Problems in Dietetic Practice Settings with Targeted Resources

Practice Setting	Special Problems	Resources
Acute Care	• Vulnerable populations • Increased exposure to pathogens • Early release of patients • Food from home • Food handler and client hygiene • Foodservice sanitation • Food preparation, holding, storage, and delivery • Use of food in enteral feedings • Integrating foodservice with care delivery and testing	*1999 Food Code* (5) ADA and state diet manuals Materials from the American Society for Healthcare Food Service Administrators (85)
Subacute Care	• Vulnerable populations • Food from home • Food handler and client hygiene • Foodservice sanitation • Food preparation, holding, storage, and delivery	*1999 Food Code* (5) ADA and state diet manuals Materials from the American Society for Healthcare Food Service Administrators (85)
Long-Term Care	• Vulnerable populations • Food from home • Pet and plant therapies • Food handler and client hygiene • Foodservice sanitation • Food preparation, holding, storage, and delivery • Cross-contamination during client feeding	*1999 Food Code* (5) ADA and state diet manuals Consultant Dietitians in Health Care Facilities dietetic practice group of the ADA Materials from the American Society for Healthcare Food Service Administrators (85)
Home Health Care	• Vulnerable populations • Food storage, preparation, and service • Pets • Environmental contamination • Knowledge and behaviors of caregivers	ADA and state diet manuals Consultant Dietitians in Health Care Facilities dietetic practice group of the ADA Materials used in client counseling will also be useful.

TABLE 6.6   Food Safety Problems in Dietetic Practice Settings with Targeted Resources *(continued)*

Schools	• Food from home	USDA
	• Food handler and client hygiene	*1999 Food Code* (5)
	• Foodservice sanitation	American School Food Service Association (86)
	• Food holding, storage, and delivery	State Departments of Education
	• Food preparation in class settings	*Healthy People 2010* (6, 67)
	• Class pets	*The Dietary Guidelines for Americans 2000* (52)
Day-Care Programs	• Participation experiences with food	*Making Food Healthy and Safe for Children: How to*
	• Class pets	*Meet the National Health and Safety Performance*
	• Food handler and client hygiene	*Standards—Guidelines for Out-of-Home Child Care*
	• Foodservice sanitation	*Programs* (87)
	• Food holding, storage, and delivery	*ABCs of Safe and Healthy Child Care: A Handbook for*
	• Medicine storage	*Child Care Providers* (88)
	• Lack of dedicated foodservice resources	*1999 Food Code* (5)
	• Food from home	*Healthy People 2010* (6, 67)
Public Health Programs and Private Counseling	• Home sanitation and client hygiene	ADA client education materials and professional
	• Food selection, storage, preparation, and service	materials
		Healthy People 2010 (6, 67)
		The Dietary Guidelines for Americans 2000 (52)
		CDC, FDA, USDA consumer and professional
		publications
		State and local foodservice inspection reports
		1999 Food Code (5)
Shelters and Soup Kitchens	• Vulnerable populations	Safe Food for the Hungry (89)
	• Food handler and client hygiene	*1999 Food Code* (5)
	• Foodservice sanitation	
	• Food preparation, holding, storage, and delivery	
	• Use of donated foods	
	• Environmental contamination	
	• Lack of dedicated foodservice resources	

Dietetics professionals working in acute care, subacute care, long-term care, home care, and day care are most likely to deal with populations that are particularly vulnerable to foodborne illness and with food safety issues from all aspects of foodservice and delivery. All workers in all settings who may come into contact with food should be instructed in safe food-handling practices, and plans to monitor adherence to those practices should be developed and implemented. Examples of appropriate food safety programs are outlined in Chapter 7. (Also see Boxes 6.3 and 6.4.)

Assuring safety of food brought from home or other settings may also be a challenge for dietetics professionals. This may include foods for individual clients in healthcare settings, lunches for students in schools or day care, or party foods.

In acute-care settings, long-term-care settings, or for clients with weakened immune systems, it may be appropriate to control or prohibit foods from home. It is especially important that potentially hazardous foods, such as casseroles, sandwiches, pizza, and home-preserved foods, be controlled in healthcare settings. This control may take several forms. It may limit the consumption to certain individuals, require appropriate storage prior to consumption, and limit holding time for foods.

BOX 6.3   Food Safety for Travelers and for Outdoor Eating

Traveling is a lifestyle factor that has implications for food safety. Both the Centers for Disease Control and Prevention (CDC; 4,65) and the World Health Organization (WHO; 66) make food safety recommendations for travelers, which apply to all eating situations, from street vendors to hotel restaurants. These recommendations include:

- Make sure that food has been thoroughly cooked and is still steaming hot when served.
- Avoid all uncooked foods, except for fruits and vegetables that can be peeled or shelled by the traveler. Avoid fruits with damaged skin. Remember the dictum "Cook it, peel it, or leave it."
- Avoid dishes containing raw or undercooked eggs.
- Avoid ice cream from unreliable sources.
- Ask local people for advice about safe species of fish and shellfish. The most common type of fish poisoning is ciguatera fish poisoning. The potential for this poisoning is present in all subtropical and tropical insular areas of the West Indies and the Pacific and Indian Oceans. Barracuda is the most toxic fish and should be avoided. Red snapper, grouper, amberjack, sea bass, and a wide range of tropical reef fish may contain the toxin.
- Avoid unpasteurized milk and other unpasteurized dairy products.
- Boil or disinfect drinking water.
- Avoid ice unless you are sure it is made from safe water. If questionable ice has been in contact with containers used for drinking, the containers should be thoroughly cleaned, preferably with soap and hot water, after the ice has been discarded.
- Limit beverages to steaming hot tea or coffee, wine, beer, bottled or canned carbonated soft drinks and bottled or canned fruit juices.
- Feed infants either breast milk or commercial formula prepared with boiled water and placed in sanitized bottles.

Food safety is also an issue for short-duration travel, such as picnics, barbecues, and tail-gate parties. A recent survey focusing on these outdoor eating experiences showed that few consumers follow basic food safety precautions, such as washing hands during food preparation (44%) and using thermometers to check doneness of grilled meats (fewer than 20%; 34). The Food Safety and Inspection Service of USDA has prepared fact sheets on food safety for foods prepared for consumption outside the home that stress the importance of starting with safe foods, maintaining temperatures outside the zone for microbial growth, and storing leftovers appropriately (63,64).

BOX 6.4   Treatment of Water to Ensure Safety

Boiling is the most reliable method to ensure safety of water (65). Boiling can inactivate bacteria, viruses, and parasites. To prepare water in a boil-water advisory, bring water to a vigorous rolling boil for 1 minute, covered, and allow it to cool to room temperature. At altitudes above 6,562 feet (2 km), boil water for 3 minutes. Once water has been prepared, keep it covered and refrigerate it, if possible. To make ice, prepare the boiled water and freeze it in sanitized ice trays.

Alternatively, water can be disinfected with iodine by using either tincture of iodine or tetraglycine hydroperiodide tablets. However, this method is not as reliable against *Cryptosporidium,* a parasite that can cause severe diarrhea, especially in individuals with weakened immune systems. If the water is clear, add 5 drops of tincture of iodine per liter of water. If the water is cloudy, strain it through a clean cloth and add 10 drops of tincture of iodine per liter. Follow manufacturers' directions for use of tetraglycine hydroperiodide tablets, except that if the water is cloudy, strain it and use twice the number of tablets recommended for clear water. Allow water purified with iodine to stand for at least 30 minutes. To be effective against *Cryptosporidium,* it must stand for at least 15 hours. Treated water is intended for use over a couple of weeks, not over the long term.

Cryptosporidium can be removed from water using filters, but filters will not remove bacteria or viruses. If you want to know which filters in your market area can remove *Cryptosporidium,* call NSF at 800-673-8010 and ask for their "Standard 53 Cyst Filters" list. NSF International is an independent testing group. CDC does not recommend use of chlorine or portable filters for purifying water at this time because of insufficient data to confirm their effectiveness against bacteria and viruses (65).

Food safety needs of individuals who have documented idiosyncratic reactions (such as allergies) may affect practices relating to outside food. The three practices that have the most potential for reducing exposure to allergens are eliminating cross-contamination of service ware, eliminating service of foods containing known allergens to the affected individual, and eliminating food swaps. For commercially prepared and served foods, standard procedures would address these practices. However, for foods brought in from home such controls may not be in place. For example, a platter of homemade cookies may include brownies with black walnuts and lemon squares. An individual with tree nut allergies may have a reaction even to the lemon squares, if they have been cross-contaminated. A familiar food may also contain an unusual ingredient, such as apple crisp that contains small nut pieces. While affected individuals need to inspect the food they are served and be aware of unfamiliar flavors and textures, caregivers and others must recognize the importance of removing the food instead of instructing clients to eat around it.

For school and day-care settings, it is appropriate to provide caregivers and parents information on packing lunches that are safe as well as nutritious and to train clients in hand washing.

Additionally, in long-term-care, home-care, day-care, and school settings, appropriate hand washing after handling plants, pets, and pet litter should be stressed. Pets can be a serious issue even in settings involving healthy children and adults, since many reptiles, amphibians, and birds are carriers for salmonella; rodents may be carriers for several pathogens; and cat feces may carry bacterial and parasitic pathogens. Similarly, appropriate hand washing following exposure to soils and plant materials should be stressed when plants are being used for therapeutic or educational purposes. Allowing children to assist with growing and preparing foods is a valuable learning experience to increase their understanding of agriculture and their acceptance of different foods; it can also be an opportunity to teach, model, and stress appropriate food safety practices.

Dietetics professionals in public health programs and in private counseling may also teach food safety to their clients by stressing appropriate home food handling and personal hygiene practices, providing guidance on precautions to be taken when eating outside the home, and assisting clients in identifying specific food practices that may increase their risk of foodborne illness. Techniques used to teach these messages are similar to those used in teaching clients to reduce risk of developing chronic diseases. Governmental agencies that have food safety responsibilities have many consumer food safety publications available. Appendix A provides a listing of those agencies as well as types of information available from them.

IDENTIFYING PROFESSIONAL NEEDS FOR FOOD SAFETY INFORMATION

Dietetics professionals are meeting consumer, regulatory, and industry demands for competency assurance and upskilling by implementing the Commission on Dietetic Registration (CDR) portfolio-based professional development system. This five-step program allows for development of an individualized learning plan for a five-year period (62). The first phase of the professional development system is professional self-reflection. That self-reflection includes assessing current practice areas, roles and responsibilities, professional strengths, and leadership positions, as well as external factors affecting professional practice and future practice areas. One of the external factors affecting all areas of dietetic practice is the increasing numbers of individuals who are at risk for foodborne illness. In the second step, assessing learning needs, specific areas of food safety relevant to current and future practice may be identified. These needs will then be reflected in the learning plan (step 3) and addressed through the implementation (step 4) and evaluation (step 5) phases of the professional development plan. For example:

- A clinician in a transplant unit identifies a need to know more about food safety for immunocompromised clients, accesses information from CDC on food safety for immunocompromised clients, and develops a brochure explaining to family members why outside food is not permitted.
- An educator in the Special Supplemental Nutrition Program for Women, Infants, and Children (WIC Program) identifies a need to address the role of listeriosis in spontaneous abortions among Hispanic farm workers. She accesses, evaluates, and uses an existing brochure on listeriosis for pregnant Hispanic farm workers.
- A dietitian in an acute-care setting identifies a need to know more about food safety for clients receiving enteral feedings. She takes a continuing education course on food safety with enteral and parenteral feedings and teaches that information to other members of the nutrition support team.
- A dietetics professional in a foodservice facility identifies HACCP as the preferred method for assuring food safety in that facility, completes training in HACCP, and helps to implement HACCP principles in the facility.
- A dietetics professional identifies the need to educate foodservice employees throughout the community in food safety, completes training to become a facilitator for courses in food safety, and teaches a series of courses for employees in a variety of foodservice settings.

Additionally, dietetics professionals may seek food safety certifications within their practice settings, such as the Certified Food Safety Professional (CFSP) credential offered through the American School Food Service Association.

REFERENCES

1. Olsen SJ, MacKinnon LC, Goulding JS, et al. Surveillance for foodborne-disease outbreaks—United States, 1993–1997. *MMWR*. 2000;49(SS-01):1–51. Available at: ftp://ftp.cdc.gov/pub/Publications/mmwr/SS/SS4901.pdf. Accessed May 25, 2001.
2. Centers for Disease Control and Prevention. Diagnosis and management of foodborne illnesses: a primer for physicians. *MMWR*. 2001;50(RR-2):1–67. Available at: http://www.cdc.gov/mmwr/PDF/RR/RR5002.pdf. Accessed May 26, 2001.
3. Centers for Disease Control and Prevention. Guidelines for preventing opportunistic infections among hematopoietic stem cell transplant recipients: recommendations of

CDC, the Infectious Disease Society of America, and the American Society of Blood and Marrow Transplantation. *MMWR*. 2000;49(RR-10):48–52. Available at: http://www.cdc.gov/mmwr/PDF/RR/RR4910.pdf. Accessed May 26, 2001.

4. Centers for Disease Control and Prevention. 1999 USPHS/IDSA guidelines for the prevention of opportunistic infections in persons infected with human immunodeficiency virus: US Public Health Service (USPHS) and Infectious Diseases Society of America (IDSA). *MMWR*. 1999;48(RR-10):1–82. Available at: http://www.cdc.gov/mmwr/PDF/RR/RR4810.pdf. Accessed May 26, 2001.

5. US Food and Drug Administration. *1999 Food Code*. Washington, DC: US Department of Commerce, Technology Administration, National Technical Information Service; 1999. PB99-115925. Available at: http://vm.cfsan.fda.gov/~dms/fc99-toc.html. Accessed May 12, 2001.

6. US Department of Health and Human Services. Food safety. In: *Healthy People 2010*. 2nd ed. With Understanding and Improving Health and Objectives for Improving Health. 2 vols. Washington, DC: US Government Printing Office; November 2000:10.3–10.19. Available at: http://www.health.gov/healthypeople/Document/pdf/Volume1/10Food.pdf. Accessed May 12, 2001.

7. Zink DL. The impact of consumer demands and trends on food processing. *Emerg Infect Dis*. 1997;3(4):467–469. Available at: http://www.cdc.gov/ncidod/eid/vol3no4/adobe/zink.pdf. Accessed May 26, 2001.

8. Food Marketing Institute. Food safety: a qualitative analysis. Washington DC: Food Marketing Institute; 1996.

9. The American Dietetic Association Foundation–ConAgra Foundation. Summertime food safety survey. Chicago, IL: The American Dietetic Association Foundation; 1999.

10. American Meat Institute. Putting the food handling issue on the table: the pressing need for food safety education. Washington, DC: American Meat Institute and Food Marketing Institute; 1996.

11. TRENDS in the United States: consumer attitudes and the supermarket 1997. Washington, DC: Research Department of the Food Marketing Institute; 1997.

12. Lin B-H, Frazao E, Guthrie J. Away-from-home foods increasingly important to quality of American diet. Washington, DC: US Department of Agriculture, Agricultural Marketing Service; 1999. Agriculture Information Bulletin No. 749.

13. Lecos C. Of microbes and milk: probing America's worst *Salmonella* outbreak. *Dairy Food Sanit*. 1986;6:136–140.

14. Ryan CA, Nickels MK, Hargrett-Bean NT, et al. Massive outbreak of antimicrobial-resistant salmonellosis traced to pasteurized milk. *JAMA*. 1987;258:3269–3274.

15. Louie KK, Paccagnella AM, Osei WD, et al. *Salmonella* serotype *Tennessee* in powdered milk products and infant formula—Canada and United States, 1993. *MMWR*. 1993;42(26);516–517. Available at: ftp://ftp.cdc.gov/pub/Publications/mmwr/wk/mm4226.pdf. Accessed May 23, 2001.

16. Centers for Disease Control and Prevention. Update: multistate outbreak of listeriosis—United States, 1998–1999. *MMWR*. 1999;47(51):1117–1118. Available at: ftp://ftp.cdc.gov/pub/Publications/mmwr/wk/mm4751.pdf. Accessed May 26, 2001.

17. Hurd S, Phan Q, Hadler J, et al. Multistate outbreak of listeriosis—United States, 2000. *MMWR*. 2000;49(50):1129–1130. Available at: http://www.cdc.gov/mmwr/PDF/wk/mm4950.pdf. Accessed May 27, 2001.

18. Centers for Disease Control and Prevention. Outbreak of *Shigella sonnei* associated with eating a nationally distributed dip—California, Oregon, and Washington, January 2000. *MMWR*. 2000;49(3):60–61. Available at: http://www.cdc.gov/mmwr/PDF/wk/mm4903.pdf. Accessed May 27, 2001.

19. Crowe L, Lau W, McLeod L, et al. Outbreaks of *Shigella sonnei* infection associated with eating fresh parsley—United States and Canada, July–August 1998. *MMWR*. 1999;48(14):285–9. Available at: http://www.cdc.gov/mmwr/PDF/wk/mm4814.pdf. Accessed May 27, 2001.

20. Wechsler E, D'Aleo C, Hill VA, et al. Outbreak of *Vibrio parahaemolyticus* infection associated with eating raw oysters and clams harvested from Long Island Sound—Connecticut, New Jersey, and New York, 1998. *MMWR*. 1999;48(03):48–51. Available at: http://www.cdc.gov/mmwr/PDF/wk/mm4803.pdf. Accessed May 27, 2001.

21. Conrad C, Hemphill K, Wilson S, et al. Multistate outbreak of viral gastroenteritis related to consumption of oysters—Louisiana, Maryland, Mississippi, and North Carolina. *MMWR*. 1993;42(49):945–948.

22. Collins RK, Henderson MN, Conwill DE, et al. Epidemiologic notes and reports: multiple outbreaks of staphylococcal food poisoning caused by canned mushrooms. *MMWR*. 1989;38(24):417–418.

23. Davis M, Osaki C, Gordon D, et al. Update: Multistate outbreak of *Escherichia coli* O157:H7 infections from hamburgers—Western United States, 1992–1993. *MMWR*. 1993;42(14):258–263. Available at: ftp://ftp.cdc.gov/pub/Publications/mmwr/wk/mm4214.pdf. Accessed May 23, 2001.

24. Como-Sabetti K, Reagan S, Allaire S, et al. Outbreaks of *Escherichia coli* O157:H7 infection associated with eating alfalfa sprouts—Michigan and Virginia, June–July 1997. *MMWR*. 1997;46(32):741–744. Available at: ftp://ftp.cdc.gov/pub/Publications/mmwr/wk/mm4632.pdf. Accessed May 23, 2001.

25. Mshar PA, Dembek ZF, Cartter ML, et al. Outbreaks of *Escherichia coli* O157:H7 infection and cryptosporidiosis associated with drinking unpasteurized apple cider—Connecticut and New York, October 1996. *MMWR*. 1997;46(01):4–8. Available at: ftp://ftp.cdc.gov/pub/Publications/mmwr/wk/mm4601.pdf. Accessed May 23, 2001.

26. Centers for Disease Control and Prevention. Multistate outbreak of *Salmonella* serotype *Agona* infections linked to toasted oats cereal—United States, April–May, 1998. *MMWR*. 1998;47(22);462–464. Available at: ftp://ftp.cdc.gov/pub/Publications/mmwr/wk/mm4722.pdf. Accessed May 23, 2001.

27. Centers for Disease Control and Prevention. Emerging infectious diseases outbreak of *Salmonella enteritidis* associated with nationally distributed ice cream products—Minnesota, South Dakota, and Wisconsin, 1994. *MMWR*. 1994;43(40);740–741. Available at: ftp://ftp.cdc.gov/pub/Publications/mmwr/wk/mm4340.pdf. May 23, 2001.

28. Chambers J, Somerfeldt S, Mackey L, et al. Outbreaks of *Cyclospora cayetanensis* infection—United States, 1996. *MMWR*. 1996;45(25):549–551. Available at: ftp://ftp.cdc.gov/pub/Publications/mmwr/wk/mm4525.pdf. Accessed May 23, 2001.

29. Jacquette G, Guido F, Jacobs J, et al. Outbreaks of *Cyclospora cayetanensis* infection—United States, 1997. *MMWR*. 1997;46(21):461–462. Available at: ftp://ftp.cdc.gov/pub/Publications/mmwr/wk/mm4621.pdf. Accessed May 23, 2001.

30. Mahon BE, Rohn DD, Pack SR, Tauxe RV. Electronic communication facilitates investigation of a highly dispersed foodborne outbreak: *Salmonella* on the superhighway. *Emerg Infect Dis*. 1995;1(3):94–95. Available at: ftp://ftp.cdc.gov/pub/EID/vol1no3/adobe/mahon.pdf. Accessed May 26, 2001.

31. Altekruse SF, Cohen ML, and Swerdlow DL. Emerging foodborne diseases. *Emerg Infect Dis*. 1997;3(3):285–293. Available at: ftp://ftp.cdc.gov/pub/EID/vol3no3/adobe/cohen.pdf. Accessed May 26, 2001.

32. Marth EH. Institute of Food Technologists' scientific status summary: extended shelf life refrigerated foods: microbiological quality and safety. *Food Tech*. 1998;52(2):57–62.

33. Yang S, Leff MG, McTague D, et al. Multistate surveillance for food-handling, preparation, and consumption behaviors associated with foodborne diseases: 1995 and 1996 BRFSS food-safety questions. In CDC Surveillance Summaries, September 11, 1998. *MMWR*. 1998;47(SS-4):33–57. Accessed May 25, 2001.

34. Home Food Safety . . . It's in Your Hands. Home food safety summer survey key findings [press release]. The American Dietetic Association; June 24, 1999. Available at: http://www.homefoodsafety.org. Accessed May 28, 2001.

35. Home Food Safety . . . It's in Your Hands. Home food safety benchmark survey key findings [press release]. The American Dietetic Association; October 19, 1999. Available at: http://www.homefoodsafety.org. Accessed May 28, 2001.

36. Altekruse SF, Stern NJ, Fields PI, Swerdlow DL. *Campylobacter jejuni*— an emerging foodborne pathogen. *Emerg Infect Dis.* 1999;5(1):28–35. Available at: http://www. cdc.gov/ncidod/EID/vol5no1/pdf/altekruse.pdf. Accessed May 26, 2001.

37. US Department of Agriculture, Food Safety and Inspection Service. How temperatures affect food [USDA Web site]. May 1998. Available at: http://www.fsis.usda. gov/OA/pubs/tempfood.htm. Accessed May 26, 2001.

38. US Department of Agriculture, Food Safety and Inspection Service. The big thaw— safe defrosting methods for consumers [USDA Web site]. January 1999. Available at: http://www.fsis.usda.gov/OA/pubs/bigthaw.htm. Accessed May 26, 2001.

39. US Department of Agriculture, Food Safety and Inspection Service. Use a meat thermometer [USDA Web site]. June 1997. Available at: http://www.fsis.usda.gov/OA/ pubs/cithermo.htm. Accessed May 26, 2001.

40. Lindsay RE, Krissinger WA, Fields BF. Microwave versus conventional oven cooking of chicken: relationship of internal temperature to surface contamination by *Salmonella typhimurium. J Am Diet Assoc.* 1986;86:373–374.

41. Zimmerman WJ. Power and cooking time relationship for devitalization of trichinae in pork roast cooked in microwave ovens. *J Food Sci.* 1984;49:824–826.

42. Zimmerman WJ. Microwave recooking of pork roasts to attain 76.7°C throughout. *J Food Sci.* 1984;49:969–970.

43. Fruin JT, Gutheritz LS. Survival of bacteria in food cooked by microwave oven, conventional oven, and slow cookers. *J Food Protect.* 1982;45:695–702.

44. Notermans SJ, Dufrenne J, Lund BM. Botulism risk of refrigerated, processed foods of extended durability. *J Food Protect.* 1990;86:373–374.

45. US Department of Agriculture, Food Safety and Inspection Service. Food safety focus: refrigeration and food safety [USDA Web site]. January 1999. Available at: http://www.fsis.usda.gov/OA/pubs/focus_ref.htm. Accessed May 26, 2001.

46. LeBaron CW, Furutan NP, Lew JF, et al. Viral agents of gastroenteritis. *MMWR.* 1990;37(RR-5):1–24.

47. De Boer D, Hahne M. Cross-contamination with *Campylobacter jejuni* and *Salmonella* spp. from raw chicken products during food preparation. *J Food Protect.* 1990;53: 1067–1068.

48. Jones ME, Jenkerson SA, Middaugh JP, et al. Epidemiologic notes and reports foodborne hepatitis A—Alaska, Florida, North Carolina, Washington. *MMWR.* 1990; 39(14):228–232.

49. Restaino L, Wind CE. Antimicrobial effectiveness of hand washing for food establishments. *Dairy Food Environ Sanitation.* 1990;10:136–141.

50. Osterholm MT, Forfang JC, Ristenen TL. An outbreak of foodborne giardiasis. *N Engl J Med.* 1981;304:24–28.

51. Centers for Disease Control. *Yersinia enterocolitica* infections during the holidays in Black families—Georgia. *MMWR.* 1990;39:819–821.

52. US Departments of Agriculture and Health and Human Services. *The Dietary Guidelines for Americans 2000.* 5th ed. Washington, DC: US Departments of Agriculture and Health and Human Services; 2000. Home and Garden Bulletin No. 232. Available at: http://www.usda.gov/cnpp/DietGd.pdf. Accessed May 25, 2001.

53. The American Dietetic Association Foundation–ConAgra Foundation. Home Food Safety . . . It's in Your Hands Web site. Available at: http://www.homefoodsafety.org. Accessed May 26, 2001.

54. Partnership for Food Safety Education Web site. Available at: http://www.fightbac. org. Accessed May 26, 2001.

55. US Department of Health and Human Services. *Healthy People 2000: National Health Promotion and Disease Prevention Objectives.* Washington, DC: US Department of

Health and Human Services; 1991. GPO 017-001-00474-0. Available at: http://odphp.
osophs.dhhs.gov/pubs/hp2000. Accessed May 25, 2001.

56. US Department of Health and Human Services. *Healthy People 2000: Midcourse Review and 1995 Revisions.* Washington, DC: US Department of Health and Human Services; 1995. GPO 017-001-00-526-6. Available at: http://odphp.osophs.dhhs.gov/pubs/hp2000/pdf/midcours/ch2-12.pdf. Accessed May 25, 2001.

57. US Department of Health and Human Services. *Healthy People 2000: Progress Review for Food and Drug Safety.* Washington, DC: US Department of Health and Human Services, ODPHP Communication Support Center; 1995. ODPHP R0139. Available at: http://odphp.osophs.dhhs.gov/pubs/hp2000/progrvw/FOOD.HTM. Accessed May 26, 2001.

58. Shallow S, Samuel M, McNees A, et al. Preliminary FoodNet data on the incidence of foodborne illnesses—selected sites, United States, 2000. *MMWR.* 2001;50(13):241–246. Available at: http://www.cdc.gov/mmwr/PDF/wk/mm5013.pdf. Accessed May 24, 2001.

59. US Food and Drug Administration, US Department of Agriculture, US Environmental Protection Agency, and Centers for Disease Control and Prevention. National Food Safety Initiative background Web site; May 8, 2001. Available at: http://www.foodsafety.gov/~dms/fs-toc2.html. Accessed May 27, 2001.

60. The American Dietetic Association. Safe eating: a guide to preventing foodborne illness. Chicago, IL: The American Dietetic Association; 1997.

61. Ingham S, Thies ML. Food and water safety—position of ADA. *J Am Diet Assoc.* 1997;97: 184–189. Available at: http://www.eatright.com/adap0297.html. Accessed May 27, 2001.

62. Commission on Dietetic Registration. *Professional Development Portfolio Guide.* Chicago, IL: American Dietetic Association; 2001.

63. US Department of Agriculture, Food Safety and Inspection Service. Safe handling of complete meals to go [USDA Web site]. September 1998. Available at: http://www.fsis.usda.gov/OA/pubs/mealtogo.htm. Accessed May 26, 2001.

64. US Department of Agriculture, Food Safety and Inspection Service. Safe food to go [USDA Web site]. May 1998. Available at: http://www.fsis.usda.gov/OA/pubs/foodtogo.htm. Accessed May 26, 2001.

65. Centers for Disease Control and Prevention. Travelers' health: safe food and water [CDC Web site]. Available at: http://www.cdc.gov/travel/foodwater.htm. Accessed May 26, 2001.

66. World Health Organization. International travel and health [WHO Web site]. Available at: http://www.who.int/ith/english/index.htm. Accessed May 26, 2001.

67. US Department of Health and Human Services. Environmental health. In: *Healthy People 2010.* 2nd ed. With Understanding and Improving Health and Objectives for Improving Health. 2 vols. Washington, DC: US Government Printing Office; November 2000:10.3–10.19. Available at: http://www.health.gov/healthypeople/Document/pdf/Volume1/08Environmental.pdf. Accessed May 12, 2001.

68. US Department of Agriculture, Food Safety and Inspection Service. Doneness versus safety [USDA Web site]. October 1998. Available at: http://www.fsis.usda.gov/OA/pubs/doneness.htm.

69. US Department of Agriculture, Food Safety and Inspection Service. Kitchen thermometers [USDA Web site]. April 2000. Available at: http://www.fsis.usda.gov/OA/pubs/thermy/kitchen.pdf. Accessed May 26, 2001.

70. US Department of Agriculture, Food Safety and Inspection Service. Basics for handling food safely [USDA Web site]. September 1997. Available at: http://www.fsis.usda.gov/OA/pubs/basics.pdf. Accessed May 26, 2001.

71. Centers for Disease Prevention and Control, National Center for Infectious Diseases. An ounce of prevention keeps the germs away: handle and prepare food safely [CDC Web site]. April 5, 2000. Available at: http://www.cdc.gov/ncidod/op/food.htm. Accessed May 27, 2001.

72. Centers for Disease Prevention and Control, National Center for Infectious Diseases. An ounce of prevention: keeps the germs away: wash hands often [CDC Web site]. April 5, 2000. Available at: http://www.cdc.gov/ncidod/op/handwashing.htm. Accessed May 27, 2001.

73. Centers for Disease Prevention and Control, National Center for Infectious Diseases. An ounce of prevention: keeps the germs away: routinely clean and disinfect surfaces [CDC Web site]. April 5, 2000. Available at: http://www.cdc.gov/ncidod/op/cleaning.htm. Accessed May 27, 2001.

74. US Department of Agriculture, Food Safety and Inspection Service. Safe storage of meat and poultry: the science behind it [USDA Web site]. May 1998. Available at: http://www.fsis.usda.gov/oa/pubs/storage.htm. Accessed May 26, 2001.

75. US Department of Agriculture, Food Safety and Inspection Service. Fighting BAC! by chilling out [USDA Web site]. January 1999. Available at: http://www.fsis.usda.gov/OA/pubs/chillout.htm. Accessed May 26, 2001.

76. US Department of Agriculture, Food Safety and Inspection Service. Appliance thermometers [USDA Web site]. January 1999. Available at: http://www.fsis.usda.gov/OA/pubs/aptherm.htm. Accessed May 26, 2001.

77. US Department of Agriculture, Food Safety and Inspection Service. Be smart, keep foods apart—don't cross-contaminate [USDA Web site]. August 2000. Available at: http://www.fsis.usda.gov/OA/pubs/keep_apart.htm. Accessed May 26, 2001.

78. US Department of Agriculture, Food Safety and Inspection Service. Food safety for persons with AIDS [USDA Web site]. May 2000. Available at: http://www.fsis.usda.gov:80/oa/pubs/aids.htm. Accessed May 26, 2001.

79. US Food and Drug Administration. Eating defensively: food safety advice for persons with AIDS [FDA Web site]. Available at: http://www.cfsan.fda.gov/~dms/aidseat.html. Accessed May 26, 2001.

80. US Environmental Protection Agency and Centers for Disease Control and Prevention. Guidance for people with severely weakened immune systems [EPA Web site]. Available at: http://www.epa.gov/ogwdw000/crypto.html. Accessed May 26, 2001.

81. Centers for Disease Control and Prevention, National Center for Infectious Diseases. Cryptosporidiosis: a guide for persons with HIV/AIDS [CDC Web site]. May 26, 2001. Available at: http://www.cdc.gov/ncidod/diseases/crypto/hivaids.htm. Accessed May 26, 2001.

82. US Department of Agriculture, Food Safety and Inspection Service. Seniors need wisdom on food safety [USDA Web site]. February 1997. Available at: http://www.fsis.usda.gov/OA/pubs/seniors.htm. Accessed May 26, 2001.

83. US Food and Drug Administration. Seniors and food safety: preventing foodborne illness [FDA Web site]. May 1999. Available at: http://vm.cfsan.fda.gov/~dms/seniors.html. Accessed May 27, 2001.

84. US Food and Drug Administration. Keep your baby safe: eat hard cheeses instead of soft cheeses during pregnancy [FDA Web site]. July 1997. Available at: http://vm.cfsan.fda.gov/~dms/listeren.html. Accessed May 27, 2001.

85. American Society for Healthcare Food Service Administrators Web site. Available at: http://www.ashfsa.org/default.htm. Accessed May 26, 2001.

86. American School Food Service Association Web site. Available at: http://www.asfsa.org. Accessed May 26, 2001.

87. National Center for Education in Maternal and Child Health. *Making Food Healthy and Safe for Children: How to Meet the National Health and Safety Performance Standards—Guidelines for Out-of-Home Child Care Programs.* Washington, DC: National Center for Education in Maternal and Child Health; 1997. Available to order free of charge at: http://www.nmchc.org/html/cf/fullrec.cfm?ID=3619. Accessed May 26, 2001.

88. Hale CM, Polder JA. The ABCs of safe and healthy child care: a handbook for child care providers. US Department of Health and Human Services [CDC Web site]. 1996

(updated December 11, 1998). Available at: http://www.cdc.gov/ncidod/hip/abc/abc1.pdf. Accessed May 25, 2001.

89. Purdue University Cooperative Extension Service. Safe food for the hungry [site materials for videoconference]. October 1996. Available at: http://www.aes.purdue.edu/ACS/safe/sfh96.html. Accessed May 25, 2001.

CHAPTER 7

FOODSERVICE PROGRAMS THAT REDUCE FOODBORNE ILLNESS

Preparation and service of wholesome foods for clientele is a primary focus of strong foodservice programs. Achieving this focus requires development, implementation, and verification of food safety programs. The primary types of food safety programs in foodservice settings are standard operating procedures (SOPs), sanitation standard operating procedures (SSOPs), and Hazard Analysis Critical Control Point (HACCP) programs. When integrated well, these programs constitute a highly effective food safety system. While understanding the importance and the basic concepts of food safety programs for foodservice is a part of dietetic practice, designing and supervising such programs requires extensive training and experience beyond entry-level competencies. There are many excellent materials to help practitioners review or develop effective food safety programs for foodservice (1–16). These efforts are supported in *Healthy People 2010* by the developmental objective 10-6: Improve food employee behaviors and food preparation practices that directly relate to foodborne illnesses in retail food establishments (17).

STANDARD OPERATING PROCEDURES AND STANDARD SANITATION OPERATING PROCEDURES

Establishing the basic food safety program SOPs and SSOPs facilitates employee education and adherence, development of HACCP plans, and compliance with accreditation and regulatory requirements. Box 7.1 contains examples of items

BOX 7.1 Sample Standard Operating Procedures and Standard Sanitation Operating Procedures for a Food Safety Program

---

Personnel Hygiene and Other Practices
Requirements for preemployment health examinations
Exclusion of employees with diarrhea, hepatitis, foodborne illness, infected cuts and abrasions, persistent coughing and sneezing
Use of bandages and gloves with minor cuts and abrasions
Use of hair restraints and gloves
Exclusion of jewelry, fingernail polish, artificial fingernails
Guidelines for single and double hand washing
Restriction of food consumption and tobacco use in food preparation areas
Buildings and Facilities
Schedule for cleaning storage areas, floors, walls and ceilings
Regular use and maintenance of ventilation hoods
Implementation of regular pest control program
Cleaning and appropriate use of refuse and garbage containers

---

BOX 7.1   Sample Standard Operating Procedures and Standard Sanitation Operating Procedures for a Food Safety Program *(continued)*

Equipment and Utensils
  Cleaning of food contact surfaces
  Monitoring of refrigerator and freezer temperatures
  Calibration of thermometer/temperature sensors
  Ware washing (manual and machine)
Production and Process Controls
  Purchasing and receiving
    Using approved vendors
    Purchasing only pasteurized dairy products and inspected meats, poultry and seafood products
    Refusing delivery of products that have been damaged by insects, rodents, filth, water, or thawing/refreezing, and cans that are bulging or dented
    Checking temperature of refrigerated or frozen products upon receipt
    Properly storing and dating all products upon receipt
  Storage
    Use and maintenance of dry, refrigerated, and frozen storage areas
    Monitoring refrigerator and freezer temperatures
    System of stock rotation
    System for separation of raw foods from cooked foods
    System for rapid cooling and storage of prepared foods
    System for thawing frozen foods
  Preparation
    Cleaning fresh fruits and vegetables
    Cleaning and sanitizing food contact surfaces
    Monitoring time foods are held at room temperature
    Monitoring holding times for foods on tables
    Monitoring temperatures of foods

---

that could be included in SOPs and SSOPs. Checklists such as those used for internal or external facility audits and Joint Commission on Accreditation of Healthcare Organizations' surveys can be used as guides for individualizing SOPs and SSOPS for foodservice facilities. These SOPs and SSOPs are foundations for food safety plans for individual food products, such as HACCP plans (7).

HAZARD ANALYSIS CRITICAL CONTROL POINT (HACCP) SYSTEMS

HACCP systems are designed to assess, monitor, and improve food safety. HACCP was developed for the U.S. National Aeronautics and Space Administration (NASA) to ensure the safety of the food prepared for the astronauts in space. Currently, HACCP plans are mandated for seafood, poultry, and meat processing plants in the United States. Many other facets of the food industry, including food distributors and the companies that supply them, are also implementing HACCP plans. FDA recommends the implementation of HACCP in retail food establishments as well (3).

HACCP systems focus on proactive assurance of food safety by emphasizing the establishment's role in continuous problem solving and prevention rather than relying solely on periodic facility inspections by regulatory agencies (3). Additional benefits of HACCP over conventional inspection techniques include clearly identifying the food establishment as the final party responsible for ensuring the safety of the food it produces and allowing for comprehensive regulatory determination of compliance.

HACCP can be applied to foodservice settings. However, it can be more difficult to develop a comprehensive HACCP program in a foodservice setting than in food processing units, where the concept was originally conceived and applied. Differences in the two systems include differences in inputs (types of foods), numbers of different products produced, and use of specialized equipment and processes. A typical foodservice unit may prepare one hundred or more different food items in a single day, while a food processing plant is likely to produce a single food in a session. Equipment in foodservice settings is multi-functional, and staff are seldom dedicated to preparation of a single food item. However, food processing equipment is designed for a single product type, and modern computerized equipment even monitors product output. Similarly, food processing industry production staff are dedicated to completing a limited number of tasks.

The HACCP concept has been adapted to foodservice settings. Examples of this adaptation include purchasing foods from vendors who certify the HACCP programs of their suppliers, including critical control points in standardized recipes and grouping similar foods with various process mapping systems (12–16). While monitoring the large number of foods produced in a typical foodservice setting is difficult, tracking aids are being developed to monitor critical control points, such as internal temperatures/times.

As in all HACCP programs, foodservice HACCP teams include both internal and external members. These teams are responsible for the development, implementation, and audit of the plans. Members of the HACCP team include administrators, supervisors, and foodservice workers, as well as outside consultants and auditors. For a HACCP program to be effective, it is important that all levels of foodservice employees be involved to increase buy-in and identify areas where training is needed. Very often, outside consultants help to develop the HACCP plan, train employees, and perform audits, while in-house employees maintain the monitoring and record-keeping requirements. Since the HACCP plan will include personnel responsibilities and remediations, including crisis management, it is important to review the plan frequently to account for menu and personnel changes.

Seven Steps in HACCP

The seven steps in developing HACCP plans are listed in Box 7.2, with some distinctions made between the food processing industry and the foodservice industry. These distinctions are largely based on the differences in inputs—most foodservice units depend on their suppliers having strong HACCP programs. This allows foodservice professionals to purchase foods that meet critical limits for pathogens, chemical residues, and other hazards without performing the analyses themselves.

The more complex the preparation and delivery systems in foodservice settings, the more safety issues to consider. Delivery systems in foodservice may be as simple as a cafeteria line or as complex as delivery of plated meals to satellite facilities. Preparation systems may be as simple as an assembly-serve system or as complicated as a cook-freeze system. For example, an assembly-serve facility would have a single CCP for the reheating step, but a cook-freeze facility would have CCPs for the initial cooking step, the chilling step, the thawing step, and the reheating step. Examples of safety issues to consider are in Box 7.3.

BOX 7.2   The Seven Steps of Developing a Hazard Analysis Critical Control Point (HACCP) Plan

---

1. **Assess hazards in ingredients and processes.**
   Hazards are biological, chemical, or physical properties that can cause a food to be unsafe. Issues considered during hazard analysis relate to ingredients, processing, distribution, and the intended use of the product. Examples of those issues are provided in box 7.3. Hazard analysis includes risk assessment. The potential significance or risk of each hazard should be assessed by considering its likelihood of occurrence and severity.

Food Processing Industry	*Foodservice Industry*
Pathogens	Pathogens
Pesticide/herbicide residues in excess of allowable limits	Microbial toxicants
	Pieces of metal, glass, plastic, rocks, etc.
Chemical sanitizers in excess of allowable limits	Large particle sizes in modified texture diets
Naturally occurring toxicants	
Microbial toxicants	
Pieces of metal, glass, plastic, rocks, etc.	

2. **Identify critical control points for controlling hazards.**
   Critical control points (CCPs) are factors that can be controlled to reduce the risks from hazards to an acceptable level. CCPs must be specific to product safety, not quality. CCPs might vary for different types of foodservice operations.

3. **Establish critical limits for each control point.**
   A critical limit is the maximum or minimum value to which a hazard must be controlled at a critical control point to prevent, eliminate, or reduce the hazard to an acceptable level. Many of the critical limits are defined by the FDA *Food Code* (1).

Food Processing Industry	*Foodservice Industry*
Time and temperature	Time and temperature
Water activity	Viscosity (for modified texture diets)
pH and titratable acidity	
Concentrations of chemicals	
Viscosity	
Levels of microorganisms	

4. **Establish procedures to monitor the control points.**
   Monitoring is observing or measuring specific indicators to determine if the critical limits are being met or whether there has been a loss of control. What is monitored will depend on the critical limits set for the CCP. The monitoring documentation should identify the person responsible for monitoring. Examples of monitoring procedures are measurements of internal temperatures during cooking, chilling, and holding times. Equipment used for monitoring must be accurate and routinely calibrated.

5. **Establish corrective actions.**
   Corrective actions are the steps to be taken if the critical limits are not met. The plan for corrective action should also identify the individual who is authorized to take and document the action. It is probably the person who performs that activity. If a corrective action is taken, the food safety system should be reassessed and modified, if necessary.

6. **Establish record keeping procedures.**
   It pays to remember the axiom "If you didn't document it, you didn't do it." Examples of forms are in the *Food Code* (1).

7. **Establish procedures for verifying HACCP system.**
   Verification is usually performed by someone other than the person responsible for performing the activities specified in the plan. Ongoing verification can be conducted by designated employees, while regulatory authorities may conduct long-term verification. Procedures used for verification may include observing, checking monitoring records, checking corrective action records, reviewing the total plan, testing product in process, and reviewing calibration records.

BOX 7.3   Questions for Hazard Analysis

Ingredients

• Does the food contain any sensitive ingredients that are likely to present microbiological hazards (e.g., *Salmonella*, *Staphylococcus aureus*), chemical hazards (e.g., aflatoxin, antibiotic, or pesticide residues), or physical hazards (stones, glass, bone, metal)?

Intrinsic Factors of Food

• Which intrinsic factors of the food must be controlled to ensure food safety?

• Does the food permit survival or multiplication of pathogens and/or toxin formation before or during preparation?

• Will the food permit survival or multiplication of pathogens and/or toxin formation during subsequent steps of preparation, storage, or consumer possession?

• Are there other similar products in the marketplace? What has been the safety record for such products?

Procedures Used for Preparation/Processing

• Does the preparation procedure or process include a controllable step that destroys pathogens or their toxins? Consider both vegetative cells and spores.

• Is the product subject to recontamination between the preparation step (e.g., cooking) and service?

Microbial Content of the Food

• Is the food commercially sterile, i.e., a low-acid canned food?

• Is it likely that the food will contain viable pathogens?

• What is the normal microbial content of the food stored under proper conditions?

• Does the microbial population change during the time the food is stored before consumption?

• Does that change in microbial population alter the safety of the food?

Facility Design

• Does the layout of the facility provide an adequate separation of raw materials from ready-to-eat foods?

• Is the traffic pattern for people and moving equipment a potentially significant source of contamination?

• Is it possible to provide sanitary conditions consistently and adequately to ensure production of safe foods?

Equipment Design

• Will the equipment provide the time/temperature control that is necessary for safe food?

• Is the equipment properly sized for the volume of food that will be prepared?

• Can the equipment be sufficiently controlled so that the variation in performance will be within the tolerances required to produce a safe food?

• Is the equipment reliable or is it prone to frequent breakdowns?

• Is the equipment designed so that it can be cleaned and sanitized?

• Is there a chance for product contamination with hazardous substances, such as glass or sanitizer residue in excess of allowable limits?

• What product safety devices, such as time/temperature integrators, are used to enhance consumer safety?

Packaging

• Does the method of packaging affect the multiplication of microbial pathogens and/or the formation of toxins?

• Is the packaging material resistant to damage, thereby preventing the entrance of microbial contamination?

• Is the package clearly labeled "Keep Refrigerated" if refrigeration is required for safety?

• Does the package include instructions for the safe handling and preparation of the food?

• Are tamper-evident packaging features used?

Employee Health, Hygiene, and Education

• Do the employees understand the food preparation process and the factors they must control to ensure safe foods? Are effective employee training and retraining available?

• Will the employees inform management of a problem that could affect food safety?

BOX 7.3   Questions for Hazard Analysis *(continued)*

Conditions of Storage
- What is the likelihood that the food will be improperly stored at the wrong temperature?
- Would storage at improper temperatures lead to a microbiologically unsafe food?

Intended Use
- Will the food be heated by the consumer?
- Will there probably be leftovers?

Intended Consumer
- Is the food intended for the general public, that is, a population that does not have an increased risk of becoming ill?
- Is the food intended for consumption by a population with increased susceptibility to illness, such as infants, the elderly, the infirm, and immunocompromised individuals?

Successful HACCP programs in foodservice facilities integrate food safety into recipes and employee training. For example, in all settings a recipe for chili would include a temperature check as a CCP. This temperature check can easily be written into the recipe and highlighted as a CCP to remind the preparer of its importance. Having this CCP in the recipe makes it easier to provide continuous food safety training to the preparer.

DEVELOPMENT OF AN INTEGRATED FOOD SAFETY PLAN

The more food preparation that takes place in a foodservice setting, the greater the food safety documentation required. For example, preparing meatloaf from raw ingredients requires more ingredient specifications, more food handling, and greater temperature control than reheating a purchased frozen meatloaf. Facilities where extensive food preparation occurs can make efficient use of SOPs and SSOPs to increase the effectiveness of their HACCP plans. Many food safeguards are similar. For example, development of an SOP specifying that all frozen foods with drip at receiving be rejected would eliminate the need to include such a CCP in the HACCP plans for affected foods.

SOPs, SSOPs, and HACCP plans are complementary, with the common goal of serving safe food to clients and customers. Developing these plans with employee input can produce simple, easy-to-use plans that meet the needs of the facility. The resulting records provide evidence of the ways in which the foods have been handled and produced and can demonstrate a commitment by management to food safety (18).

REFERENCES

1. US Food and Drug Administration. *1999 Food Code.* Washington, DC: US Department of Commerce, Technology Administration, National Technical Information Service; 1999. PB99-115925. Available at: http://vm.cfsan.fda.gov/~dms/fc99-toc.html. Accessed May 12, 2001.
2. US Food and Drug Administration. HACCP: a state-of-the-art approach to food safety [FDA backgrounder]. August 1999. Available at: http://vm.cfsan.fda.gov/~lrd/bghaccp.html. Accessed May 12, 2001.

3. US Food and Drug Administration. Managing food safety: a HACCP principles guide for operators of food establishments at the retail level [draft]. April 1998. Available at: http://vm.cfsan.fda.gov/~dms/hret-toc.html. Accessed May 12, 2001.

4. US Department of Agriculture Food Safety Inspection Service. Pathogen reduction and HACCP systems . . . and beyond. May 1998 [backgrounder]. Available at: http://www.fsis.usda.gov/OA/background/bkbeyond.htm. Accessed May 12, 2001.

5. Lafferty L, Dowling RA. Management of health care food and nutrition services—position of ADA. *J Am Diet Assoc.* 1997;97:1427–1430. Available at: http://www.eatright.org/adap1297.html. Accessed May 12, 2001.

6. Marriott NG. *Principles of Food Sanitation.* 4th ed. Gaithersberg, MD: Aspen Publishers Inc; 1999.

7. Loken JK. *The HACCP Food Safety Manual.* New York: John Wiley & Sons Inc; 1995.

8. McSwane DZ, Rue N, Linton R. *Essentials of Food Safety and Sanitation.* 2nd ed. Englewood Cliffs, NJ: Prentice Hall Inc; 2000.

9. National Assessment Institute. *NAI Handbook for Safe Food Service Management.* 2nd ed. Englewood Cliffs, NJ: Prentice Hall Inc; 1998.

10. Longree K, Armbruster G. *Quantity Food Sanitation.* 5th ed. New York: John Wiley & Sons Inc; 1996.

11. Marriott NG, Robertson G, eds. *Essentials of Food Sanitation.* Gaithersburg, MD: Aspen Publishers Inc; 1997.

12. Mortimore S, Wallace C. *HACCP: A Practical Approach.* Gaithersburg, MD: Aspen Publishers Inc; 1998.

13. Lachney A. *The HACCP Cookbook and Manual.* Eatonville, WA: Nutrition Development Systems; 1999.

14. Corlett DA. *HACCP User's Manual.* Gaithersburg, MD: Aspen Publishers Inc; 1998.

15. Puckett R. *HACCP the Future Challenge—Practical Application for the Foodservice Administrator.* Missouri City, TX: Norton Group Inc; 1996.

16. LaVella BW, Bostic JL. *HACCP for Food Service—Recipe Manual & Guide.* St. Louis, MO: LaVella Food Specialists; 1997.

17. US Department of Health and Human Services. Food safety. In: *Healthy People 2010.* 2nd ed. With Understanding and Improving Health and Objectives for Improving Health. 2 vols. Washington, DC: US Government Printing Office; November 2000:10.3–10.19. Available at: http://www.health.gov/healthypeople/Document/pdf/Volume1/10Food.pdf. Accessed May 12, 2001.

18. Setiabuhdi M, Theis M, Norback J. Integrating Hazard Analysis and Critical Control Point (HACCP) and sanitation for verifiable food safety. *J Am Diet Assoc.* 1997;97:889–891.

FARM/SHIP TO FORK: RESOURCES FOR DIETETICS PROFESSIONALS

Food safety is everybody's responsibility. From the farm or ship to the fork, food passes through many hands. Because there are so many food safety interests, there are many different resources available to dietetics professionals—some suitable for professional development, some suited to client education, and some suited to answering specific food safety questions or otherwise addressing the food safety system. The resources below focus on helping dietetics professionals meet the broad scope of food safety demands within their varied practice settings.

GOVERNMENT AGENCIES WITH FOOD SAFETY RESPONSIBILITIES

General Information

General food safety information is available through the government gateway and through searchable sites that catalog training materials and consumer education materials available from government sources.

- Government gateway to food safety information
  http://www.foodsafety.gov

- National Food Safety Education Month
  http://www.foodsafety.gov/september.html

- USDA/FDA Foodborne Illness Educational Materials Database
  http://www.nal.usda.gov/fnic/foodborne

- USDA/FDA HACCP Training Programs and Resources Database
  http://www.nalusda.gov/fnic/foodborne/haccp/index.shtml

- Foodborne Illness Education Information Center Publications
  http://www.nalusda.gov/fnic/foodborne/pub.html

- USDA Food and Nutrition Information Center (FNIC)
  http://www.nal.usda.gov/fnic

- Healthy People 2010
  http://health.gov/healthypeople

- National Food Safety Initiative
  http://vm.cfsan.fda.gov/~dms/fs-toc.html

Specific Information

Centers for Disease Control and Prevention (CDC)
1600 Clifton Road
Atlanta, GA 30333
Voice: (800) 311-3435 or (404) 639-3534
http://www.cdc.gov

The food safety role for this agency is to investigate sources, rates, and trends in foodborne disease outbreaks; maintain a nationwide system of foodborne disease surveillance and monitoring; develop and advocate public health policies to prevent foodborne diseases; conduct research to help prevent foodborne illness; and train local and state food safety personnel. The CDC Web site contains consumer information, disease prevention guidelines, traveler information, the on-line journal *Emerging Infectious Diseases*, and the on-line version of *Morbidity and Mortality Weekly Report (MMWR)*.

- *Emerging Infectious Diseases* (free; searchable)
  http://www.cdc.gov/ncidod/eid

- Health Topic: Foodborne Diseases
  http://www.cdc.gov/health/foodill.htm

- *Morbidity Mortality Weekly Report* (free; searchable)
  http://www.cdc.gov/mmwr

- Travelers' Health
  http://www.cdc.gov/travel

Federal Trade Commission (FTC)
600 Pennsylvania Avenue, NW
Washington, DC 20580
Voice: (202) 326-2222
http://www.ftc.gov

The food safety role of this agency is to enforce a variety of laws that protect consumers from unfair, deceptive, or fraudulent practices, including deceptive and unsubstantiated advertising. The FTC Web site includes information on actions taken against companies accused of these practices.

- Consumer Help Line
  (877) 382-4357

U.S. Customs Service (USCS)
1300 Pennsylvania Avenue, NW
Washington, DC 20229
Voice: (202) 927-1000
http://www.customs.ustreas.gov

The food safety role of this agency is to work with federal regulatory agencies to ensure that all goods entering and exiting the United States do so according to U.S. laws and regulations. The agency's Web site includes information on regulations on importing and exporting materials and other aspects of customs.

U.S. Department of Agriculture Cooperative State Research, Education, and Extension Service (CSREES)
Washington, D.C. 20250-0900
Voice: (202) 720-3029
http://www.reeusda.gov

The food safety role for this agency is to develop research and education programs on food safety for farmers and consumers, which are conducted through U.S. colleges and universities. For more information, contact the local cooperative extension services, listed in the blue pages of the phone book under "County Government." Several food safety gateway sites are maintained by state extension offices; these sites will have publications from many different states on many different topics at various reading levels.

- Gateway to Food Safety Information (North Carolina State University)
  http://www.ces.ncsu.edu/depts/foodsci/agentinfo

- Iowa State University Food Safety Project
  http://www.exnet.iastate.edu/Pages/families/fs/homepage.html

- Michigan State University Extension Food Safety Education Database
  http://www.msue.msu.edu/msue/imp/modfs/masterfs.html

U.S. Department of Agriculture, Food Safety and Inspection Service (FSIS)
14th & Independence Avenue, SW
Washington, DC 20250-3700
Voice: (202) 720-2791
http://www.fsis.usda.gov/index.htm

USDA's Food Safety and Inspection Service enforces food safety laws governing domestic and imported meat and poultry products. Their Web site includes consumer advice and help for educators, guidelines for HACCP implementation, the *Food Safety Educator* newsletter and listserv, and the Food Safety Virtual University (FSVU). The FSVU is an effort to use distance education technologies to deliver training and education in the area of food safety to a widely dispersed and highly diverse audience.

- *Food Safety Educator* newsletter
  http://www.fsis.usda.gov/OA/educator/educator.htm

  Contact for free print subscription:
  FSIS Food Safety Education and Communications Staff
  Dianne Durant, Editor
  Voice: (202) 720-7943
  Fax: (202) 720-9063

- Food Safety Index
  http://www.nal.usda.gov/fnic/foodborne/fbindex/index.htm

- Food safety publications
  http://www.fsis.usda.gov/OA/pubs/consumerpubs.htm

- Meat and Poultry Hotline
  (800) 535-4555

- Meat and poultry product recalls: news releases and information
  for consumers
      http://www.fsis.usda.gov/OA/news/xrecalls.htm

U.S. Department of Commerce, National Marine Fisheries Service (NMFS)
1315 East-West Highway SSMC3
Silver Spring, MD 20910
Voice: (800) 422-2750
http://nmfs.noaa.gov

The food safety role of this agency is to inspect and certify fishing vessels, seafood processing plants, and retail facilities for federal sanitation standards. The agency's Web site includes information related to management of all aspects of the fisheries industry.

U.S. Environmental Protection Agency (EPA)
1200 Pennsylvania Avenue, NW
Washington, DC 20460
Voice: (202) 260-2090
http://www.epa.gov

The food safety role for this agency is to establish safe drinking water standards and monitor the quality of drinking water, to regulate toxic substances and wastes to prevent their entry into the environment and the food chain, and to determine safety and tolerance levels for pesticides. The agency's Web site includes information on the Food Quality Protection Act, safety of drinking water, and pesticide regulations.

- Food Quality Protection Act
      http://www.epa.gov/oppfead1/fqpa

- Office of Ground Water and Drinking Water
      http://www.epa.gov/ogwdw/

- Office of Pesticide Programs
      http://www.epa.gov/pesticides/

- Office of Pollution Prevention and Toxics
      http://www.epa.gov/opptintr/

- Safe Drinking Water Hotline
      (800) 426-4791

U.S. Food and Drug Administration (FDA) (HFE-88)
5600 Fishers Lane
Rockville, MD 20857
Voice: (888) 463-6332 or (301) 827-4422
Fax: (301) 443-9767
E-mail: execsec@oc.fda.gov
http://www.fda.gov

FDA's Center for Food Safety and Applied Nutrition (CFSAN) regulates domestic and imported foods (except for meat and poultry), bottled water, and cosmetics sold across state lines. This regulation takes place from the product's point of U.S. entry or processing to its point of sale. The center promotes and protects the public health and economic interest by ensuring that food is safe, nutritious, and wholesome; that cosmetics are safe; and that food and cosmetics are honestly, accurately, and informatively labeled. The FDA's Web site contains information on the National Food Safety Initiative and on FDA's program areas, such as food additives, dietary supplements, imports, exports, recalls, inspections, chemical residues, consumer advice, and industry assistance (including HACCP). This is the Web site that contains the *Bad Bug Book* and the FDA *Food Code.*

- *Bad Bug Book*
  http://vm.cfsan.fda.gov/~mow/intro.html
- Consumer advice
  http://vm.cfsan.fda.gov/~lrd/advice.html
- Dietary supplements
  http://vm.cfsan.fda.gov/~dms/supplmnt.html
- *FDA Consumer* (free; searchable)
  http://www.fda.gov/fdac/
- Food additives and premarket approval
  http://vm.cfsan.fda.gov/~lrd/foodadd.html
- *Food Code*
  http://vm.cfsan.fda.gov/~dms/fc99-toc.html
- Food Information and Seafood Hotline
  (888) 723-3366
- How to report adverse reactions and other problems with products regulated by FDA
  http://www.fda.gov/opacom/backgrounders/problem.html
- Information about food preparation and foodborne illness
  http://vm.cfsan.fda.gov/~dms/wh-food.html
- National Food Safety Initiative
  http://vm.cfsan.fda.gov/~dms/fs-toc.html
- Pesticides, metals, and chemical contaminants
  http://vm.cfsan.fda.gov/~lrd/pestadd.html
- Product alerts and warnings (includes recalls)
  http://www.fda.gov/opacom/7alerts.html

COOPERATIVE PARTNERSHIPS WITH FOOD SAFETY FOCUSES

"Home Food Safety . . . It's in Your Hands"
http://www.homefoodsafety.org

This campaign is designed to raise consumer awareness that home food safety is a serious problem and to provide simple solutions so that adults can easily engage in proper food handling in their own kitchens.

Partners:

- American Dietetic Association
  216 W. Jackson Boulevard, Suite 800
  Chicago, IL 60606-6995
  Voice: (800) 877-1600 or (312) 899-0040
  http://www.eatright.org

- The ConAgra Foundation
  One ConAgra Drive
  Omaha, NE 68102-5001
  Voice: (402) 595-4000
  http://www.conagra.com

The Partnership for Food Safety Education
http://www.fightbac.org

The Partnership for Food Safety Education is a public-private partnership created to reduce the incidence of foodborne illness by educating Americans about safe food handling practices. This coalition of seven food trade associations, two government agencies, three consumer/public health organizations, and the Association of Food and Drug Officials was formed in 1997. The current campaign of this partnership is "Fight BAC!"

Partners:

- American Dietetic Association Foundation
  216 W. Jackson Boulevard, Suite 800
  Chicago, IL 60606-6995
  Voice: (800) 877-1600 or (312) 899-0040
  http://www.eatright.org

- American Egg Board
  1460 Renaissance Drive
  Park Ridge, Illinois 60068
  Voice: (847) 296-7043
  Fax: (847) 296-7007
  E-mail: aeb@aeb
  http://www.aeb.org

- American Meat Institute
  1700 N. Moore Street, Suite 1600
  Arlington, VA 22209
  Voice: (703) 841-2400
  Fax: (703) 527-0938
  http://www.meatami.org

- The Canadian Partnership for Consumer Food Safety Education
  75 Albert Street, Suite 1101
  Ottawa, Ontario, K1P 5E7
  Voice: (613) 798-3042
  Fax: (613) 952-6400
  E-mail: fightbac@nin.ca
  http://www.canfightbac.org/english/index.shtml

- Food Marketing Institute
  655 15th Street, NW
  Washington, DC 20005
  Voice: (202) 452-8444
  Fax: (202) 429-4519
  E-mail: fmi@fmi.org
  http://www.fmi.org

- National Chicken Council
  http://www.eatchicken.com

- National Cattlemen's Beef Association
  1301 Pennsylvania Avenue, NW, Suite 300
  Washington, DC 20004
  Voice: (202) 347-0228
  Fax: (202) 638-0607
  E-mail: cows@beef.org
  http://www.beef.org

- National Pork Producers Council
  P.O. Box 10383
  Des Moines, IA 50306
  Voice: (515) 223-2600
  http://www.nppc.org/

- Produce Marketing Association
  1500 Casho Mill Road, P.O. Box 6036
  Newark, DE 19714-6036
  Voice: (302) 738-7100
  Fax: (302) 731-2409
  http://www.pma.com

- The Soap and Detergent Association
  1500 K Street, NW, Suite 300
  Washington, DC 20005
  Voice: (202) 347-2900
  Fax: (202) 347-4110
  http://www.sdahq.org

- U.S. Poultry and Egg Association
  1530 Cooledge Road
  Tucker, GA 30084-7303
  Voice: (770) 493-9401
  Fax: (770) 493-9257
  http://www.poultryegg.org

- U.S. Department of Agriculture (USDA)
  14th & Independence Avenue, SW
  Washington, DC 20250-3700
  Voice: (202) 720-2791
  www.usda.gov

- U.S. Department of Education (ED)
  400 Maryland Avenue, SW
  Washington, DC 20202
  Voice: (800) 872-5327
  Fax: (202) 401-0689
  E-mail: customerservice@inet.ed.gov
  http://www.ed.gov

- U.S. Department of Health and Human Services (HHS)
  200 Independence Avenue, SW
  Washington, DC 20201
  Voice: (877) 696-6775

OTHER SELECTED RESOURCES

- American Council for Science and Health (ACSH)
  1995 Broadway, Second Floor
  New York, NY 10023-5860
  Voice: (212) 362-7044
  Fax: (212) 362-4919
  http://www.acsh.org/

- American Public Health Association (APHA)
  800 I Street, NW
  Washington, DC 20001-3710
  Voice: (202) 777-2742
  http://www.apha.org

- Association of Food and Drug Officials (AFDO)
  P.O. Box 3425
  2550 Kingston, Suite 311
  York, PA 17402
  Voice: (717) 757-2888
  Fax: (717) 755-8089
  E-mail: afdo@blazenet.net
  www.afdo.org

- Consumer Federation of America (CFA)
  1424 16th Street, NW, Suite 604
  Washington, DC 20036
  Voice: (202) 387-6121
  http://www.consumerfed.org

- Council for Agricultural Science and Technology (CAST)
  4420 W. Lincoln Way
  Ames, IA 50014-3447
  Voice: (515) 292-2125
  Fax: (515) 292-4512
  E-mail: cast@cast-science.org
  http://www.cast-science.org

- European Food Information Council (EUFIC)
  1, place des Pyramides
  75001 Paris, France
  Voice: 33 1 40 20 44 40
  Fax: 33 1 40 20 44 41
  E-mail: eufic@eufic.org
  http://www.eufic.org/open/fopen.htm

- Institute of Food Technologists (IFT)
  221 N LaSalle Sreet, Suite 300
  Chicago, IL 60601
  Voice: (312) 782-8424
  Fax: (312) 782-8348
  E-mail: info@ift.org
  http://www.ift.org

- International Association for Food Protection (IAFP)
  6200 Aurora Avenue, Suite 200W
  Des Moines, IA 50322-2863
  Voice: (800) 369-6337
  Fax: (515) 276.8655
  http://www.foodprotection.org

- International Food Information Council (IFIC)
  1100 Connecticut Avenue, NW, Suite 430
  Washington, DC 20036
  Voice: (202) 296-6540
  Fax: (202) 296-6547
  E-mail: foodinfo@ific.org
  http://ific.org

- National Council Against Health Fraud (NCAHF)
  P.O. Box 1276
  Loma Linda, CA 92354-9983
  http://www.ncahf.org

- National Environmental Health Association (NEHA)
  720 S. Colorado Boulevard
  South Tower, Suite 970
  Denver, CO 80246-1925
  Voice: (303) 756-9090
  Fax: (303) 691-9490
  E-mail: staff@neha.org
  http://www.neha.org

- National Restaurant Association (International Food Safety Council)
  1200 17th Street, NW
  Washington, DC 20036
  Voice: (202) 331-5900
  E-mail: info@dineout.org
  http://www.restaurant.org
  http://www.foodsafetycouncil.org

- NSF International
  P.O. Box 130140
  789 N. Dixboro Road
  Ann Arbor, MI 48113-0140
  Voice: (800) 673-6275
  Fax: (734) 769-0109
  E-mail: info@nsf.org
  http://www.nsf.org

- World Health Organization Food Safety Programme
  http://www.who.int/fsf/

APPENDIX B

CONTINUING PROFESSIONAL EDUCATION

SELF-ASSESSMENT QUESTIONS

1. What is the position of the American Dietetic Association on food and water safety?
   A. The number of foodborne illnesses in the United States should be reduced by half.
   B. Regulation of food and water safety must be through a single government agency.
   C. The public has a right to a safe food and water supply.
   D. Food safety is the responsibility of food producers.

2. What is the best term to substitute for "toxic"?
   A. hazardous
   B. unsafe
   C. harmful
   D. life-threatening

3. Which is an individualistic response to food?
   A. bacterial infection
   B. seafood intoxication
   C. allergic reaction
   D. mushroom intoxication

4. Which is not a body defense against foodborne illness?
   A. acid conditions in the stomach
   B. phagocytes along the gastrointestinal tract
   C. antibodies along the gut
   D. production of insulin

5. Which is not an example of a chronic sequela from foodborne illness?
   A. hemolytic uremic syndrome (HUS)
   B. reactive arthritis
   C. Guillain-Barre syndrome
   D. diarrhea

6. Which response involves the immune system?
   A. allergic reaction
   B. lactose intolerance
   C. aflatoxicosis
   D. lead poisoning

7. Which foodborne disease has the shortest time to onset?
   A. staphylococcal intoxication
   B. botulism
   C. salmonellosis
   D. hemolytic uremic syndrome

8. Which term means "causes birth defects"?
   A. mutagen
   B. nephrotoxin
   C. teratogen
   D. carcinogen

9. Which component is not required in a toxicity statement?
   A. identity of toxic agent
   B. species tested
   C. dosage
   D number of animals tested

10. What is the proposed mechanism for involvement of prions in Creutzfeldt-Jacob disease (mad cow disease)?
    A. recruit proteins
    B. replicate proteins
    C. synthesize proteins
    D. deaminate proteins

11. Which symptom is atypical for foodborne parasitic diseases?
    A. severe diarrhea
    B. abortion or stillbirth
    C. tissue damage
    D. reduced nutrient absorption

12. Which seafood toxin is not a neurotoxin produced by dinoflagellates?
    A. ciguatoxin
    B. saxitoxin
    C. scombrotoxin
    D. All are neurotoxins produced by dinoflagellates.

13. Which grouping is inappropriate?

    A. lead, ceramic containers, anemia

    B. mercury, seafood, neurological damage

    C. cadmium, galvanized buckets, kidney damage

    D. copper, vended drinks, cancer

14. Which bacteria are typically in human nose and/or throat secretions?

    A. *Listeria monocytogenes* and *Staphylococcus aureus*

    B. *Clostridium botulinum* and *Clostridium perfringens*

    C. *Salmonella* and *Listeria monocytogenes*

    D. *Staphylococcus aureus* and *Salmonella*

15. Which foodborne bacterium can cause stillbirth and meningitis?

    A. *Listeria monocytogenes*

    B. *Clostridium botulinum*

    C. *Escherichia coli*

    D. *Bacillus cereus*

16. Which bacterium is particularly toxic to individuals who have liver disease?

    A. *Vibrio vulnificus*

    B. *Vibrio cholerae*

    C. *Vibrio parahaemolyticus*

    D. *Escherichia coli*

17. Which bacterium can cause foodborne illness that potentially results in secondary complications involving organs other than the gastrointestinal tract?

    A. *Staphylococcus aureus*

    B. *Clostridium perfringens*

    C. *Campylobacter jejuni*

    D. *Bacillus cereus*

18. Which is not required in a food additive petition?

    A. potential cost of the additive

    B. food in which the additive will be used

    C. purpose of additive

    D. amount of additive which can be used

19. When pesticides are approved, they can be used at:

    A. specified levels on any crop.

    B. specified levels on specified crops.

    C. specified levels on similar crops.

    D. any level that does not leave a residue.

20. Which foodborne pathogen would most likely contaminate cooked rice or pasta held in open containers at room temperature?

    A. *Bacillus cereus*

    B. *Clostridium perfringens*

    C. *Campylobacter jejuni*

    D. *Escherichia coli*

21. Home-canned beef stew with vegetables was determined to be the vehicle for an outbreak of botulism. Which ingredient in the stew was the *most likely* source of the contamination?

    A. beef cubes

    B. onions

    C. peas

    D. flour

22. Which foodborne pathogen most commonly contaminates food via infected food handlers?

    A. *Clostridium perfringens*

    B. *Bacillus cereus*

    C. *Shigella*

    D. *Clostridium botulinum*

23. What is the temperature zone at which optimal growth of most bacteria occurs?

    A. 40°F to 75°F

    B. 40°F to 140°F

    C. 70°F to 145°F

    D. 75°F to 165°F

24. Which of the following food pathogens can survive the cooking process and cause disease associated with temperature-abused cooked foods?

    A. *Salmonella*

    B. *Shigella*

    C. *Listeria monocytogenes*

    D. *Bacillus cereus*

25. Which food should not be fed to infants under the age of one year because of the danger of infant botulism?

    A. honey

    B. sugar

    C. orange juice

    D. nonfat dry milk

26. Which term describes bacteria that grow only in the absence of oxygen?

    A. obligate aerobe

    B. facultative aerobe

    C. facultative anaerobe

    D. obligate anaerobe

27. Which organism causes invasive bacterial infections in humans?

    A. *Staphylococcus aureus*

    B. *Salmonella*

    C. *Bacillus cereus*

    D. *Clostridium perfringens*

28. For which foodborne infection is the characteristic symptom appendicitis-like abdominal pain?

    A. campylobacteriosis

    B. salmonellosis

    C. shigellosis

    D. yersiniosis

29. Which organism can grow in refrigerated foods?

    A. *Clostridium perfringens*

    B. *Listeria monocytogenes*

    C. *Staphylococcus aureus*

    D. *Campylobacter jejuni*

30. Which is an example of bioamplification?

    A. alkylation of mercury

    B. binding of cadmium to protein in shellfish

    C. PCB cogeners

    D. ability of PCBs and mercury to cause birth defects

31. Which is the most typical symptom for acute heavy metal poisoning?

    A. diarrhea

    B. dizziness

    C. vomiting

    D. burning sensation

32. If an apple contains 50 ppm pesticide A, how much of the pesticide is in an apple weighing 0.25 pounds?

    A. 0.6 mg

    B. 6 mg

    C. 60 mg

    D. 6 g

33. SH weighs 110 pounds. If he consumes 10 mg of compound X, what dosage has he consumed?
    A. 0.01 mg/kg
    B. 0.1 mg/kg
    C. 0.2 mg/kg
    D. 2 mg/kg

34. Which toxic agents multiply rapidly in nutrient-rich foods?
    A. bacteria
    B. parasites
    C. viruses
    D. All multiply rapidly in nutrient-rich foods.

35. Which term describes the amount of a chemical that kills half of a population?
    A. ED
    B. ED_{50}
    C. LD
    D. LD_{50}

36. Which is not a mycotoxin?
    A. tetrodotoxin
    B. patulin
    C. aflatoxin
    D. fumonisin

37. For which type of foodborne illness is a toxin produced in the body instead of in food?
    A. fungal intoxication
    B. bacterial intoxication
    C. invasive bacterial infection
    D. noninvasive bacterial infection

38. Which symptom is typical of an invasive infection but not of an intoxication or a noninvasive infection?
    A. diarrhea
    B. vomiting
    C. meningitis
    D. fever

39. Which seafood toxin is an amine that causes headache and gastrointestinal distress?
    A. tetrodotoxin
    B. scombroid
    C. ASP
    D. saxitoxin

40. Which is the threshold for a chemical effect?

    A. NOAEL

    B. ED

    C. LD

    D. MTD

41. Mold growth and mycotoxin production are a potential problem in which food?

    A. meats

    B. seafoods

    C. raw vegetables

    D. nuts

42. Which preservation method inactivates bacterial spores in foods?

    A. freezing

    B. drying

    C. pasteurization

    D. canning

43. Which food is typically associated with outbreaks of *Salmonella enteritidis?*

    A. chicken

    B. protein salads

    C. milk

    D. eggs

44. What a_w value separates potentially hazardous foods from other foods?

    A. 0.25

    B. 0.85

    C. 4.6

    D. 7.0

45. Which is a potentially hazardous food?

    A. bearnaise sauce

    B. pickles

    C. cornflakes

    D. strawberry preserves

46. Which statement about potentially hazardous foods is true?

    A. Excluded are raw foods of animal origin.

    B. Included are foods with a pH of 4.6 or below.

    C. Included are foods with water activities below 0.85.

    D. Included are cooked foods of plant origin.

47. What kind of storage is required for potentially hazardous foods?
    A. clean and dry
    B. refrigerated
    C. freezer temperatures
    D. isolated from other foods

48. Which is a safety problem associated with fresh produce?
    A. anaphylaxis
    B. contamination with pesticide residues
    C. contamination with pathogens
    D. All of the above are safety problems associated with fresh produce.

49. Many products reformulated to dietary guidelines are of greater concern to manufacturers than their original counterparts from the standpoint of spoilage and/or safety. Which reformulated product would be of least concern from a food safety standpoint?
    A. low-salt ham
    B. cholesterol-free mayonnaise
    C. reduced-sugar jam
    D. tomatoes bred for lower acidity

50. Which factor is most likely to contribute to foodborne illness caused by chemicals?
    A. improper holding temperatures
    B. inadequate cooking
    C. contaminated equipment
    D. obtaining food from unsafe sources

51. The majority of confirmed foodborne-disease outbreaks are attributed to:
    A. chemical toxins
    B. bacteria
    C. parasites
    D. viruses

52. Based on FoodNet data, which bacteria are the top three causes of food-borne infections?
    A. *Escherichia coli, Listeria monocytogenes,* and *Salmonella*
    B. *Campylobacter jejuni, Escherichia coli,* and *Salmonella*
    C. *Campylobacter jejuni, Salmonella,* and *Clostridium perfringens*
    D. *Campylobacter jejuni, Salmonella,* and *Shigella*

53. For which type of foodborne illness is poor personal hygiene the most common contributing factor?

    A. bacterial intoxication

    B. chemical intoxication

    C. viral infection

    D. bacterial infection

54. Which factor is not reported in CDC's foodborne-disease outbreak reports?

    A. number of cases

    B. food vehicles

    C. contributing practices

    D. secondary complications

55. Which factor contributes to the most foodborne illness outbreaks in the United States?

    A. improper holding temperatures

    B. inadequate cooking

    C. contaminated equipment

    D. poor personal hygiene

56. Which food safety surveillance program is a joint effort by FDA, USDA, and CDC?

    A. FoodNet

    B. PDP

    C. Market Basket Survey

    D. CEP

57. Which program focuses specifically on *Escherichia coli?*

    A. FoodNet

    B. PulseNet

    C. CEP

    D. Total Diet Survey

58. Which causes the most foodborne chemical intoxications?

    A. heavy metals

    B. mushrooms

    C. seafood toxins

    D. food additives

59. Which term describes a small amount of an undesirable chemical left on food?

    A. tolerance

    B. residue

    C. GRAS

    D. allowable limit

60. Which best describes the *1999 Food Code?*

    A. compilation of mandatory regulations

    B. compilation of recommended regulations

    C. interpretation of federal laws

    D. description of federal inspection programs

61. Which law is not administered by the U.S. Department of Agriculture?

    A. Federal Meat Inspection Act of 1907

    B. Infant Formula Act of 1980

    C. Wholesome Meat Act of 1967

    D. Egg Products Inspection Act of 1970

62. Which law empowers the federal government to regulate foods that cross state lines?

    A. Delaney Clause

    B. Commerce Clause

    C. Transport Clause

    D. Federation Clause

63. Which law is administered by EPA?

    A. Food Quality Protection Act of 1996

    B. Public Health Service Act of 1944

    C. Fair Packaging and Labeling Act of 1966

    D. Delaney Clause

64. Which agency registers sanitizers used in home and foodservice settings?

    A. EPA

    B. FDA

    C. FSIS

    D. NMFS

65. To which recall category would *Listeria monocytogenes* contamination of packaged deli meats belong?

    A. Class I

    B. Class II

    C. Class III

    D. Class IV

66. Which foodborne chemical is not covered by the Delaney Clause?

    A. preservatives

    B. pesticides

    C. thickeners

    D. flavor enhancers

67. Which group is not a highly susceptible population as defined by the *1999 Food Code?*

    A. individuals with AIDS

    B. elderly in long-term-care facilities

    C. children in day-care centers

    D. teenagers

68. What would be the safest food choice from a salad bar for an individual with AIDS?

    A. tossed salad

    B. coleslaw

    C. fresh fruit salad

    D. canned pickled beets

69. Which pathogen is not targeted for reduction in *Healthy People 2010* objectives?

    A. *Clostridium botulinum*

    B. *Escherichia coli*

    C. *Listeria monocytogenes*

    D. *Salmonella*

70. What is the overall food safety goal of *Healthy People 2010?*

    A. reduce deaths from foodborne illness

    B. reduce chronic sequelae from foodborne illness

    C. reduce outbreaks of foodborne illness

    D. reduce the number of foodborne illnesses

71. Which is not an emphasis of HP 2010?

    A. elimination of naturally occurring toxins in foods

    B. reduction in morbidity/mortality from ingestion of food

    C. improvement in food handling practices

    D. reassessment of pesticide residue tolerances

72. In an outbreak of shigellosis attributed to stir-fried chicken with vegetables, which two practices were the most likely contributing factors?

    A. poor personal hygiene and improper hot holding

    B. inadequate cooking and improper hot holding

    C. cross-contamination and inadequate cooking

    D. poor personal hygiene and inadequate cooking

73. Which instruction is not included in current consumer food safety education campaigns?

    A. cook

    B. clean

    C. chill

    D. select

74. Which behaviors in current consumer food safety campaign are targeted at reducing contamination of foods?

    A. clean and cook

    B. clean and separate

    C. cook and separate

    D. clean and chill

75. Which contributing factor to foodborne illness is not included in current food safety consumer education campaigns?

    A. improper holding temperatures

    B. inadequate cooking

    C. poor personal hygiene

    D. food from an unsafe source

76. Which time:internal temperature relationship is appropriate for roast chicken?

    A. 3 hours:75°F (serving)

    B. 1 minute:140°F (reheating)

    C. 1 minute:180°F (cooking)

    D. All of the above are appropriate.

77. Which statement about HACCP is false?
    A. The HACCP system requires monitoring steps.
    B. Measurement of holding temperature is an example of an HACCP control.
    C. HACCP is a continuous system.
    D. HACCP systems are applied only to production of preserved products.

78. Which step is not a part of HACCP systems?
    A. determining critical control points
    B. monitoring critical control points and recording data
    C. correcting immediate problems, where possible
    D. analyzing end products for microbial and chemical contamination

79. Which statement about HACCP is true?
    A. HACCP ensures consistent quality.
    B. HACCP programs always include microbiological surveillance.
    C. HACCP programs require external inspectors.
    D. HACCP programs always include record keeping.

80. Which is not a critical control point?
    A. internal temperature of beef stew during serving
    B. internal temperature of meatloaf at end of cooking
    C. temperature of the pantry in which shelf goods are stored
    D. All of the above are critical control points.

81. Which is an acceptable hazard, based on the HACCP system?
    A. presence of *Salmonella* in raw chicken
    B. presence of *Salmonella* in chicken salad
    C. production of botulin toxin in grilled onions
    D. contamination of sandwiches with hepatitis A virus by a food handler

82. Which term does not describe HACCP?
    A. surveilling
    B. preventative
    C. corrective
    D. generalized

83. Which step is the primary critical control point in preparing a turkey for a meal?
    A. determining that the turkey is contaminated with *Salmonella*
    B. thawing the turkey in the refrigerator
    C. roasting the turkey to an internal temperature of 180°F
    D. monitoring the temperature of the oven used to roast the turkey

Answers are in Table B.1 at the end of this appendix.

THE PROFESSIONAL DEVELOPMENT PORTFOLIO: FOOD SAFETY

The Professional Development Portfolio is based on several steps that have been documented by the Commission on Dietetic Registration (CDR). They include:

- Professional self-reflection
- Learning needs assessment
- Learning plan development
- Implementation of learning plan
- Evaluation of learning plan

The following examples may help you to establish your own plan for including acquisition of food safety knowledge and application of that knowledge to dietetic practice.

Professional Self-Reflection

Food safety is an integral component of *Healthy People 2010* and *Dietary Guidelines for Americans*. It can be integrated into your goals, whatever your practice setting.

Learning Needs Assessment

What do you currently know about food safety, and what do you need to know to accomplish your goals? For other knowledge and practice areas in dietetics, the range of expertise needed in food safety is broad. For some dietetics practitioners, maintaining general expertise may be appropriate. For others, food safety is a primary competency, and expert knowledge is critical. The ADA Commission on Dietetic Registration (CDR) has developed a Personal Learning Needs Assessment form to help practitioners assess their own learning needs. To use this form, you would select a learning needs area (several potential areas from food safety are listed on the sample form in Figure B.1 at the end of this appendix). Each area you select should be numbered (1, 2, etc.). Then you would mark your current (X) and desired (*) levels of proficiency along the continuum, from novice to expert. At this time, there is no specific proficiency test in food safety; you would need to mark your perceived proficiency.

Learning Plan Development

The learning plan is the map for meeting your personal learning needs. It may include conventional professional development activities, such as attending lectures, workshops, or seminars. It may also include self-study programs, such as completion of the self-assessment questions in *Food Safety for Professionals*, or experiential skill development, such as learning how to access and evaluate information for inclusion in your practice.

Implementation of the Learning Plan

Implementation is participation in the professional development activities mapped out in the learning plan. This step includes maintenance of a log as part of the portfolio documentation. A sample log is presented in Figure B.2 at the end of this appendix.

Evaluation of the Learning Plan

The portfolio is a vehicle for evaluating the learning plan. The portfolio includes the learning plan (map), the learning activities log of completed activities, documentation for activities, and a self-evaluation of progress toward meeting your goal(s). This self-evaluation is the first step (professional self-reflection) for your next recertification period.

EXAMPLES OF FOOD SAFETY ISSUES IN DIETETIC PRACTICE AND IMPLEMENTATION OF THE PROFESSIONAL DEVELOPMENT PORTFOLIO

The Professional Development Portfolio begins with self-reflection. The impetus for the plan may come from opportunities in day-to-day practice, from a desire to become expert in an area, or from the need to maintain expertise. The examples in Figures B.3 and B.4 at the end of this appendix are from dietetics practitioners who, on self-reflection, decided to incorporate food safety learning needs in their professional development goals. They show how food safety goals can be incorporated into professional development to strengthen dietetic practice.

TABLE B.1　Answers to Self-Assessment Questions

Q	A	Q	A	Q	A	Q	A
1	C	22	A	43	A	64	A
2	C	23	D	44	B	65	D
3	C	24	D	45	D	66	C
4	D	25	B	46	B	67	B
5	D	26	C	47	D	68	B
6	A	27	B	48	B	69	C
7	A	28	C	49	D	70	B
8	C	29	D	50	C	71	D
9	D	30	D	51	A	72	B
10	A	31	B	52	D	73	D
11	B	32	B	53	D	74	C
12	D	33	D	54	D	75	A
13	A	34	D	55	B	76	B
14	A	35	A	56	B	77	D
15	A	36	B	57	A	78	A
16	C	37	A	58	C	79	D
17	A	38	D	59	B	80	D
18	A	39	D	60	B	81	A
19	C	40	C	61	D	82	D
20	B	41	B	62	A	83	D
21	D	42	B	63	A		

FIGURE B.1   Personal Learning Needs Assessment for Food Safety

Food Safety Learning Need (Examples)	Novice ————————➤ Expert
1. Laws and regulations related to food supply and food safety	N ————————➤ E
2. Causative organisms for foodborne illness	N ————————➤ E
3. *1999 Food Code*	N ————————➤ E
4. HACCP systems	N ————————➤ E
5. Implementation of HACCP systems	N ————————➤ E
6. Counseling at-risk clients about risk of foodborne illness	N ————————➤ E
7. Consumer food safety programs	N ————————➤ E
8. Use of technology to find food safety information	N ————————➤ E
9. Roles of food processing in minimizing risk of foodborne illness; novel foods and technologies	N ————————➤ E
10. Allergic reactions and ways to minimize likelihood of allergic individuals having a reaction	N ————————➤ E

Numbered items: Needs that apply

X: Current level of proficiency

★: Desired level of proficiency

FIGURE B.2   Learning Activities Log

Learning Need Number	Activity	Documentation

FIGURE B.3 Example 1

A clinical dietitian for a hospital in a rural area was asked to speak to a local civic organization about incorporating soy into the diet. Members of the audience asked questions about the safety of soy sprouts (they had heard that alfalfa sprouts are not safe to eat), whether tofu should be refrigerated, and how long soybeans can be left at room temperature to soak after they have been brought to a boil. The dietitian said that he did not have the answers to those questions and would get back to them.

Self-Reflection

I need to know how to find reliable answers to questions about the safety of foods and about safe handling of foods by consumers.

Learning Needs Assessment

1. Use of technology to find food safety information   Novice  Expert

Learning Plan Development

1. Read *Food Safety for Professionals* and complete the self-assessment questions.
2. Access on-line references in *Food Safety for Professionals* to become familiar with professional on-line resources.
3. Learn how to use search tools efficiently.
4. Evaluate resources before use.

Implementation of Learning Plan

Learning Activities Log		
Learning Need Number	**Activity**	**Documentation**
1	Read	*Completed self-assessment questions*
1	Access	*Annotated log of resources with URLs*
1	Search	*Log of questions with referenced answers*
1	Evaluate	*Justification for reference sources and answers*

Evaluation of Learning Plan

- Learning plan
- Learning activities log (including actual documentation)
- Self-evaluation, leading to development of further goals

FIGURE B.4   Example 2

A dietitian has been retained as a consultant by a parochial school to develop and implement an HMR program. The school advisory board recognizes that many children were not getting nutritious meals in the evening and wants parents to be able to buy a nutritious meal when they pick up their children in the afternoon. This program would be available to parents of children in the school, employees of the school and the parish, and members of the parish at large. In addition to planning for nutritionally adequate meals, the dietitian is expected to design a plan that minimizes food safety concerns.

Self-Reflection

I need to know how to develop and implement a HACCP system for preparation of food that will be sold for consumption off-site. I need to educate my clients about safe food handling practices.

Learning Needs Assessment

1. Development of HACCP programs   Novice ———— X ———— * ————➤ Expert

2. Implementation of HACCP programs   Novice ———— X ———— * ————➤ Expert

3. Implementation of "Home Food Safety . . .
   It's in Your Hands"   Novice —— X ———— * ————➤ Expert

Learning Plan Development

1. Complete HACCP certification program.
2. Seek review of activities by health department inspectors.
3. Access and review materials from ADA's "Home Food Safety . . . It's in Your Hands."

Implementation of Learning Plan

Learning Activities Log		
Learning Need Number	**Activity**	**Documentation**
1	HACCP certification	*Program description; program completion certificate*
2	Review	*Copy of HACCP program with approval*
3	Access and Review	*Copies of educational plan and materials used with clients*

Evaluation of Learning Plan

- Learning plan
- Learning activities log (including actual documentation)
- Self-evaluation, leading to development of further goals

GLOSSARY

acceptable daily intake (ADI).   Predicted dose that can be consumed by a population daily over a long period of time without causing harm. Also called *reference dose (RfD)*.

acidulated.   Acid has been added to reduce pH; typically done to retard bacterial growth.

acute.   Occurs in a short period of time or as the result of consuming a single dose.

ADI (acceptable daily intake).   Predicted dose that can be consumed by a population daily over a long period of time without causing harm. Also called *reference dose (RfD)*.

adulteration.   Dilution, contamination, or misbranding of a product.

aerobic.   Requires oxygen for metabolism.

aflatoxins.   A group of structurally related toxic compounds produced by certain strains of the fungi *Aspergillus flavus* and *A. parasiticus*. The major aflatoxins of concern are designated B1, B2, G1, and G2. These toxins are usually found together in various foods and feeds in various proportions; however, aflatoxin B1 is usually predominant and is the most toxic. Aflatoxins produce acute necrosis, cirrhosis, and carcinoma of the liver in a number of animal species; no animal species is resistant to the acute toxic effects of aflatoxins; hence it is logical to assume that humans may be similarly affected.

allergy.   An immunologically mediated response to a foreign substance.

amnesic shellfish poisoning (ASP).   A naturally occurring, dinoflagellate-caused foodborne illness having short-term memory loss as a characteristic symptom. Also called *domoic acid poisoning (DAP)*.

anaerobic.   Does not require oxygen for metabolism.

antigen.   A substance (usually a protein) that elicits an antibody response.

ASP (amnesic shellfish poisoning).   A naturally occurring, dinoflagellate-caused foodborne illness having short-term memory loss as a characteristic symptom. Also *called domoic acid poisoning (DAP)*.

assumption.   Condition taken for granted when making a decision.

autoimmune.   An immune response directed toward one's own tissues.

a_w (water activity).   Water available to support bacterial growth or participate in chemical reactions. The water activity of pure water is 1.0. Most bacteria will not grow in foods with an a_w less than 0.85 and most molds will not grow on foods with an a_w less than 0.80. For example, the a_w of most fresh fruits and vegetables is greater than 0.98, the a_w of jams ranges from 0.75 to 0.80, and that of dried fruits ranges from 0.60 to 0.65.

bacteria.   Extremely small, unicellular microorganisms which can multiply by cell division. Many foods support growth of bacteria and some foodborne bacteria have the ability to cause disease in humans.

bioamplification.   The magnification of a substance in the food chain. For example, binding of cadmium to protein in shellfish magnifies the amount of cadmium in shellfish, and predators often contain chemicals from the organisms they consume.

biochemical.   Description of chemical reactions taking place within a cell, tissue, organ, or organism.

biologically active.   Causes changes in functioning of cells, tissues, or organs.

boil-water advisory.   An advisory issued by a water utility in response to the potential presence of pathogens in the water, recommending that customers boil all water used for drinking and food preparation.

botulism.   A disease caused by potent protein neurotoxins produced by *Clostridium botulinum*. Symptoms include abdominal pain, vomiting, motor disturbances, and visual difficulties. The Centers for Disease Control and Prevention classify botulism into four types: (1) foodborne, (2) infant, (3) wound, and (4) indeterminate.

campylobacteriosis.   An invasive infection caused by *Campylobacteria jejuni*. Acute symptoms include fever, vomiting, and diarrhea. Guillain-Barre syndrome may be a sequela.

CAP (controlled atmosphere packaging).   Packaging that changes the gaseous environment of food, usually by restricting the level of oxygen in the package.

carcinogen.   Chemical that causes or promotes cancer.

case.   Single episode of illness.

CCP (critical control point).   Factor that can be controlled to reduce chemical, biological, or physical contamination of food or growth of pathogens in food.

ceviche.   Raw seafood dish prepared by marinating fish or shellfish in lemon or lime juice and spices until the flesh is opaque.

CFP (ciguatera fish poisoning).   Naturally occurring, dinoflagellate-caused seafood toxin that causes gastrointestinal distress and neurological symptoms; toxin largely contaminates fish from tropical and subtropical waters.

cholera.   An acute diarrheal disease whose causative agent is *Vibrio cholerae*. This condition can lead to severe dehydration in a matter of hours unless quickly treated.

chronic.   Occurs over a long span of time, usually as the result of multiple exposures.

ciguatera fish poisoning (CFP).   Naturally occurring, dinoflagellate-caused seafood toxin that causes gastrointestinal distress and neurological symptoms; toxin largely contaminates fish from tropical and subtropical waters.

colonize.   To grow in without causing disease.

color additive.   Chemical added to food to change its color, as defined by the Color Additives Amendment of 1960.

commercial sterility.   The level of sterility at which all pathogenic, toxin-forming, and spoilage organisms have been destroyed. Some heat-resistant bacterial spores may remain, but would not typically be able to multiply.

contributing factor.   Behavior that increases the level of the toxic agent in the food that causes an outbreak.

controlled atmosphere packaging (CAP).   Packaging that changes the gaseous environment of food, usually by restricting the level of oxygen in the package.

Creutzfeldt-Jacob disease (CJD).   An infectious disease caused by a prion designated nvCJD for *new variant* Creutzfeldt-Jacob disease. The disease course for nvCJD in humans includes behavioral changes, ataxia, progressive dementia, and death.

critical control point (CCP).   Factor that can be controlled to reduce chemical, biological, or physical contamination of food or growth of pathogens in food.

cross-contamination.   Contamination of food by the transfer of pathogens or chemicals from other foods, utensils, or hands.

cryptosporidiosis.   Disease caused by infection with the protozoan parasite *Cryptosporidium parvum*; typically presents with severe diarrhea.

cyst.   Survival form of parasites such as *Entamoeba histolytica* and *Giardia lamblia*.

danger zone.   Temperature range of fastest bacterial growth in food (40°F to 140°F; 4°C to 60°C).

DAP (domoic acid poisoning).   A naturally occurring, dinoflagellate-caused foodborne illness having short-term memory loss as a characteristic symptom. Also called *amnesic shellfish poisoning (ASP)*.

death-to-case ratio.   Number of deaths per 1,000 cases of known outcome.

Delaney Clause.   Section of the Federal Food, Drug, and Cosmetic Act that prohibits the addition to food (at any level) of any chemical found to cause cancer in any animal; the Food Quality Protection Act of 1996 removes the Delaney Clause from pesticide regulations.

depuration.   Technique in which shellfish are flushed with clean saline water treated with ultraviolet light to remove pathogens. Depuration is more effective for bacteria than for viruses.

dinoflagellates.   Protozoans of the class *Phytomastigophora*, found mainly in the oceans. They are characterized by flagella that propel them in a rotating manner through the water. Some dinoflagellates are toxic, and their concentrations are magnified by animals higher in the food chain. Proliferations of dinoflagellates cause bloom or red tide.

disinfect.   Remove or destroy all pathogens on a surface.

disinfectant.   Chemical that destroys all pathogens on a surface when EPA-approved directions are followed.

domoic acid poisoning (DAP).   A naturally occurring, dinoflagellate-caused foodborne illness having short-term memory loss as a characteristic symptom. Also called *amnesic shellfish poisoning (ASP)*.

dose.   Weight of a chemical or number of microorganisms consumed at a single time. A chemical dose is usually expressed relative to the weight of the person consuming it, for example, milligrams of chemical per kilogram of body weight. The number of microorganisms consumed is usually expressed relative to the weight of the food consumed, for example, number of microorganisms per gram of food. *See also* ADI, ED_{50}, LD_{50}, MTD, NOEL, RfD, ID_{50}, and threshold.

dysentery.   Severe, watery diarrhea.

ED (effective dose).   Dose that elicits a measurable response in the organism consuming it.

ED$_{50}$.   Dose that will produce an effect (may be beneficial or harmful) in 50 percent of a well-characterized population.

effective dose (ED).   Dose that elicits a measurable response in the organism consuming it.

emerging pathogens.   Microorganisms that were formerly unknown or considered nonpathogenic that are now causing disease. Some emerging pathogens have developed virulence factors that make it easier for them to cause disease, and some have been identified with newer methods.

emetic.   Causes nausea and vomiting.

encephalitis.   Inflammation of the brain.

endemic.   Widely prevalent in a population.

enteric.   Found in the intestine.

enterohemorrhagic.   Causing hemorrhaging in the intestinal tract.

enterotoxin.   Chemical that is toxic to the intestinal tract and causes vomiting, diarrhea, and other forms of gastrointestinal distress; most common enterotoxins are produced by bacteria.

epidemiological.   Relating diseases and their causes to populations.

essential.   Indispensable dietary nutrient.

etiology.   Cause.

facultative anaerobe.   An organism that can survive without oxygen but prefers an oxygen-containing environment.

food additive.   Any substance added intentionally to food or that becomes a part of food during its production, manufacture, packing, processing, preparing, treating, packaging, transporting, or holding. (GRAS and prior-sanctioned substances, pesticides and related substances, color additives, and new animal drugs are treated separately in legal contexts, although they are usually included in informal discussion of food additives.)

foodborne illness.   Any illness caused by consuming food contaminated with toxic chemicals or pathogenic organisms.

Food Code.   Document containing FDA recommendations for retail food handling. Also known as unicode.

FoodNet (Foodborne Disease Active Surveillance Network).   Active surveillance system for foodborne illness. CDC, FDA, and USDA all participate in FoodNet.

fungi.   Microscopic plants that cannot produce chlorophyll and that reproduce by means of spores. Many foods support growth of fungi; some fungi produce toxic chemicals when they grow on foods.

gastroenteritis.   Inflammation of the mucus membranes of the gastrointestinal system.

generally recognized as safe (GRAS).   Food additives that are "generally recognized as safe," based on a history of common usage in foods and expert review of available data.

giardiasis.   Disease caused by infection with the protozoan parasite *Giardia lamblia;* typically presents with a foul-smelling diarrhea.

GRAS (generally recognized as safe).   Food additives that are "generally recognized as safe," based on a history of common usage in foods and expert review of available data.

HACCP (Hazard Analysis Critical Control Point system).   System for monitoring processes and products used in food production to improve safety of food production.

Haff disease.   Disease caused by eating certain fish (buffalo fish in the United States) that results in an unexplained destruction of skeletal muscle cells.

halophilic.   Salt-loving; requires a high-salt environment for growth.

Hazard Analysis Critical Control Point system (HACCP).   System for monitoring processes and products used in food production to improve safety of food production.

hazardous.   Likely to cause harm under realistic or expected conditions

heavy metal.   Metals such as lead, zinc, copper, and iron.

helminth.   Parasitic worm.

hemolytic uremic syndrome (HUS).   Syndrome of hemolytic anemia, thrombocytopenia, and acute renal failure, with pathological finding of thrombotic microangiopathy in kidney and renal cortical necrosis.

hemorrhagic colitis.   Invasive infection caused by *E. coli* O157:H7. One typical manifestation is bloody stools.

hepatitis.   A viral infection that frequently causes liver disease, resulting in jaundice and debilitation; hepatitis A is the most frequent foodborne form of the disease.

host.   Organism invaded by parasite. Parasites have complicated life cycles that require specific, living hosts.

host cell.   Cell invaded by a virus. Viruses do not contain cellular organelles required to produce energy or replicate. They must enter a susceptible host cell to replicate. Foodborne viruses cause infections only when there are receptors for them on human gastrointestinal mucosal cell membranes.

HUS (hemolytic uremic syndrome).   Syndrome of hemolytic anemia, thrombocytopenia, and acute renal failure, with pathological finding of thrombotic microangiopathy in kidney and renal cortical necrosis.

ID$_{50}$ (infectious dose).   Number of microorganisms required to start an infection in 50 percent of a well-characterized population. After receiving this dose, half the population will exhibit disease symptoms. More susceptible individuals, such as those who are immunocompromised, will exhibit disease symptoms at lower doses.

immunocompromised.   Individuals whose immune mechanism is deficient; may be primary or secondary. Primary causes include immature or naturally weakened immune systems. Secondary causes include use of immunosuppressive agents and presence of immunodeficiency disorders.

infection, foodborne.   Illness caused by eating food that contains pathogenic bacteria or parasites.

infectious dose (ID$_{50}$).   Number of microorganisms required to start an infection in 50 percent of a well-characterized population. After receiving this dose, half the population will exhibit disease symptoms. More susceptible individuals, such as those who are immunocompromised, will exhibit disease symptoms at lower doses.

inspection.   Examination of food to ensure wholesomeness, minimum quality levels, and appropriate labeling.

intolerance.   Nonimmune-mediated, individualistic response to food.

intoxication, foodborne.   Illness caused by eating food that contains a toxic chemical.

invasive infection.   Illness caused by organisms that penetrate the gastric mucosa to invade a person who has eaten contaminated food.

in vitro test.   Laboratory test performed in cell or tissue culture with enzymes or other chemicals.

in vivo test.   Laboratory test performed in intact, usually vertebrate, animals.

irradiation.   Addition of radiant energy to food, usually for the purpose of pasteurization. Also called *cold pasteurization* or *radurization*.

LADD (lifetime average daily dose).   Estimated dose to an individual averaged over a lifetime of seventy years. The LADD is used primarily in assessments of carcinogenic risk.

law.   Requirement passed by a legislative body that may be clarified by judicial review or by development of regulations.

LD (lethal dose).   Dose that kills the organism that consumes it.

LD$_{50}$.   Dose that will kill 50 percent of a well-characterized population.

lethal dose (LD).   Dose that kills the organism that consumes it.

lifetime average daily dose (LADD).   Estimated dose to an individual averaged over a lifetime of seventy years. The LADD is used primarily in assessments of carcinogenic risk.

listeriosis.   An invasive infection caused by *Listeria monocytogenes*. While adults may experience only mild fever and diarrhea, severe pharyngitis, meningitis, and encephalitis may also occur. Listeriosis can cause stillbirth or abortion of fetuses carried by infected women.

MAP (modified atmosphere packaging).   Packaging that changes the gaseous environment of food, usually by restricting the level of oxygen in the package.

maximum tolerated dose (MTD).   The largest dose of a chemical that causes an adverse effect without causing a severe health problem.

mesophilic microorganism.   A bacterium, yeast, or mold that grows at temperatures between 68°F and 123°F (20°C and 45°C), moderate environmental temperatures.

microaerophilic.   Microorganism that requires only small amounts of air.

modified atmosphere packaging (MAP).   Packaging that changes the gaseous environment of food, usually by restricting the level of oxygen in the package.

morbidity.   Injury.

MTD (maximum tolerated dose).   The largest dose of a chemical that causes an adverse effect without causing a severe health problem.

mutagen.   Chemical that changes DNA or RNA in a cell without killing the cell. Mutagens may be carcinogens or teratogens.

mycotoxin.   Toxic chemical produced by mold growing on food.

neurotoxic shellfish poisoning (NSP).   Naturally occurring, dinoflagellate-derived seafood toxin that causes paresthesia, reversal of hot and cold temperature sensations, myalgia, and vertigo.

NOAEL (no observable adverse effect level).   Highest dose that does not adversely affect the measured (observed) activities of cells, tissues, or organs.

noninvasive infection.   Illness caused by foodborne organisms that produce toxins as they grow inside the gastrointestinal tract. Also called *toxicoinfection*.

no observable adverse effect level (NOAEL).   Highest dose that does not adversely affect measured (observed) activities of cells, tissues, or organs.

Norwalk-like.   A small, round, structured virus; like the Norwalk virus.

NSP (neurotoxic shellfish poisoning).   Naturally occurring, dinoflagellate-derived seafood toxin that causes paresthesia, reversal of hot and cold temperature sensations, myalgia, and vertigo.

occult.   Hidden, not easy to observe without using appropriate laboratory tests.

oocyst.   Survival form of the parasite *Cryptosporidium.*

organophosphates.   Phosphate-containing compounds that have carbon bases.

outbreak.   Incident involving two or more cases of illness caused by eating food from the same source.

paralytic shellfish poisoning (PSP).   A naturally occurring, dinoflagellate-caused seafood intoxication caused by saxitoxin or related neurotoxins.

parasite.   Organism that must live in or on a specific host to survive.

pasteurization.   Process (usually heat) that is designed to inactivate (kill) bacterial pathogens.

pathogen, foodborne.   Microorganism in food that can cause disease if ingested.

pesticide.   Chemical designed to kill unwanted organisms.

pH.   A measure of the available acid (hydrogen ions) in a product. pH is reported on a scale of 0 to 14, with 7 being neutral. Values above 7 are basic. Values below 7 are acidic.

physiological. Affects body organs, tissues, or systems.

pneumonitis. Inflammation of the lungs.

potable. Safe for drinking.

potentially hazardous food. Generally a food that supports rapid growth of bacteria (see the complete *Food Code* definition in Chapter 3).

ppb. Parts per billion, for example, 1 g in 1,000,000,000 g.

ppm. Parts per million, for example, 1 g in 1,000,000 g.

prion. Variant of normal protein that may cause disease if ingested.

protozoa. Unicellular organisms, some of which are human parasites.

PSP (paralytic shellfish poisoning). A naturally occurring, dinoflagellate-caused seafood intoxication caused by saxitoxin or related neurotoxins.

psychrotrophic microorganism. Bacteria, yeasts, and molds that grow slowly at temperatures lower than 45°F (7°C; slightly above recommended refrigerator temperatures) and grow most rapidly at 77°F to 86°F (25°C to 30°C)

PulseNet (National Molecular Subtyping Network for Foodborne-Disease Surveillance). Surveillance program that traces DNA "fingerprints" of pathogens that have caused serious foodborne disease

reactive arthritis. Rheumatoid-type arthritis resulting from foodborne illness.

recruitment. Action of prions to reshape proteins into pathogenic forms.

reference dose (RfD). Predicted dose that can be consumed by a population daily over a long period of time without causing harm. Also called *acceptable daily intake (ADI)*.

registration. Approval of a pesticide; the specific chemical to be used, the concentration of the chemical, the product on which it will be used, and allowable residues are specified.

regulation. A procedure or standard established by a regulatory agency to implement a law.

regulatory agency. Government body, other than a court or legislature, that exercises control or authority, subject to the rule of law, over certain parties by establishing rules and/or making binding judgments that affect the rights of those parties.

RfD (reference dose).   Predicted dose that can be consumed by a population daily over a long period of time without causing harm. Also called *acceptable daily intake (ADI)*.

rice-water stool. Stool that contains a high water-to-solids ratio; typically, such stools also contain a higher concentration of gastrointestinal cells that have been sloughed due to infection or death of tissue.

risk.   Chance of undesired outcome resulting from exposure to a hazard.

safe.   Unlikely to cause harm under realistic or expected conditions.

salmonellosis.   An invasive infection caused by *Salmonella.* Acute symptoms include fever and diarrhea. Reactive arthritis may be a sequela.

sanitize.   Remove or destroy at least 99.999 percent of pathogens on a surface.

sanitizer (sanitizing agent).   Chemical that destroys at least 99.999 percent of pathogens on a surface when EPA-approved instructions are followed.

saxitoxin.   Naturally occurring neurotoxin that causes paralytic shellfish poisoning (PSP).

scombroid poisoning.   Illness caused by the ingestion of foods that contain high levels of histamine and possibly other vasoactive amines and compounds. Histamine and other amines are formed by the growth of certain bacteria and the subsequent action of their decarboxylase enzymes on histidine and other amino acids in food, either during the production of a product such as Swiss cheese or by spoilage of foods such as fishery products, particularly tuna or mahimahi.

septicemia.   Systemic disease caused by spread of microorganisms and toxins in the bloodstream.

sequela.   Chronic condition that occurs after acute infection; plural is *sequelae.*

serotype (serovar).   A subdivision of a species that can be distinguished from other subdivisions by antigenic reactivity.

serovar (serotype).   A subdivision of a species that can be distinguished from other subdivisions by antigenic reactivity.

shiga-like toxin.   Toxin that causes severe diarrhea, presumably transferred from *Shigella* to strains of *Escherichia coli.*

shigellosis.   An invasive infection caused by *Shigella.* Acute symptoms include fever and severe diarrhea, possibly even dysentery. Reactive arthritis may be a sequela.

SLTEC.   Shiga-like toxin-producing *E. coli.*

sous vide.   Process that includes vacuum-sealing fresh foods in impermeable plastic pouches, cooking them slowly at low temperatures in circulating water, and chilling them for up to three weeks.

spoilage.   Any change in food that makes it undesirable for its intended use.

spore.   Bacterial form that is more stable to heat and other environmental stresses than vegetative (growing) cells. *Clostridium botulinum, Clostridium perfringens,* and *Bacillus cereus* produce spores.

SSOP (Standard Sanitary Operating Procedure).   A procedure designed to minimize surface contamination by pathogens or toxic chemicals.

Standard Sanitary Operating Procedure (SSOP).   A procedure designed to minimize surface contamination by pathogens or toxic chemicals.

surveillance.   Monitoring and recording.

teratogen.   Chemical that causes birth defects by changing DNA or RNA in cells of rapidly developing fetal tissues or reproductive cells of parents.

tetrodotoxin.   A toxin found mainly in the liver and ovaries of fishes in the order Tetradontiformes (puffers or fugu, porcupinefish, sharp-nosed puffers, and ocean sunfish globefish) that causes paresthesia and paralysis through interference with neuromuscular conduction.

thrombotic thrombocytopenic purpura (TTP).   Hemolytic uremic syndrome plus fever and neurologic symptoms.

time-temperature relationship.   Length of time a process must continue at a specific temperature to cause the desired effect.

tolerance.   Legal allowance for a food contaminant.

toxic.   Capable of causing harm. A toxic agent is any organism or chemical that can cause harm when it is ingested.

toxicity.   Ability to cause harm.

toxicoinfection.   Illness caused by foodborne organisms that produce toxins as they grow inside the gastrointestinal tract. Also called *noninvasive infection.*

Transmissible Spongiform Encephalopathies (TSE).   Infectious disease that causes alteration in brain tissue.

trichinosis.   Disease caused by infection with the parasite *Trichinella spiralis;* typically presents early with gastrointestinal symptoms and later with eye swelling, aching joints and muscle pains, itchy skin, and diarrhea or constipation.

TSE (Transmissible Spongiform Encephalopathies).   Infectious disease that causes alteration in brain tissue

TTP (thrombotic thrombocytopenic purpura).   Hemolytic uremic syndrome plus fever and neurologic symptoms.

typhoid.   An acute enteric infection caused by *Salmonella typhi.*

vacuum-packaged.   Packaged to develop a severely oxygen-restricted environment.

vehicle.   Food or water that carries toxic chemical or microorganisms to people.

verotoxin.   A shiga-like toxin that causes severe diarrhea.

virulent.   Extremely toxic.

virus.   Noncellular parasite consisting of nucleic acids and protein that replicates only in host cells.

voluntary risk.   Risk taken with full knowledge of potential consequences.

vomitoxin (deoxynivalenol, DON).   Mycotoxin implicated in Scabby Grain Intoxication (GSI), which results in severe gastrointestinal distress.

water activity (a_w).   Water available to support bacterial growth or participate in chemical reactions. The water activity of pure water is 1.0. Most bacteria will not grow in foods with an a_w less than 0.85 and most molds will not grow on foods with an a_w less than 0.80. For example, the a_w of most fresh fruits and vegetables is greater than 0.98, the a_w of jams ranges from 0.75 to 0.80, and that of dried fruits ranges from 0.60 to 0.65.

yersiniosis.   An invasive infection caused by *Yersinia enterocolitica.* Acute symptoms include fever and severe diarrhea, possibly even dysentery. In severe cases acute appendicitis-like pain may occur in the abdominal area.

INDEX